# Metaheuristics for Machine Learning

**Scrivener Publishing**
100 Cummings Center, Suite 541J
Beverly, MA 01915-6106

## Artificial Intelligence and Soft Computing for Industrial Transformation

**Series Editor: Dr S. Balamurugan (sbnbala@gmail.com)**

The book series is aimed to provide comprehensive handbooks and reference books for the benefit of scientists, research scholars, students and industry professional working towards next generation industrial transformation.

*Publishers at Scrivener*
Martin Scrivener (martin@scrivenerpublishing.com)
Phillip Carmical (pcarmical@scrivenerpublishing.com)

# Metaheuristics for Machine Learning

## Algorithms and Applications

Edited by
### Kanak Kalita
*Vel Tech University, Avadi, India*
### Narayanan Ganesh
*Vellore Institute of Technology, Chennai, India*
and
### S. Balamurugan
*Intelligent Research Consultancy Services, Coimbatore, Tamilnadu, India*

Scrivener
Publishing

This edition first published 2024 by John Wiley & Sons, Inc., 111 River Street, Hoboken, NJ 07030, USA and Scrivener Publishing LLC, 100 Cummings Center, Suite 541J, Beverly, MA 01915, USA
© 2024 Scrivener Publishing LLC
For more information about Scrivener publications please visit www.scrivenerpublishing.com.

**Wiley Global Headquarters**
111 River Street, Hoboken, NJ 07030, USA

For details of our global editorial offices, customer services, and more information about Wiley products visit us at www.wiley.com.

**Limit of Liability/Disclaimer of Warranty**
While the publisher and authors have used their best efforts in preparing this work, they make no representations or warranties with respect to the accuracy or completeness of the contents of this work and specifically disclaim all warranties, including without limitation any implied warranties of merchantability or fitness for a particular purpose. No warranty may be created or extended by sales representatives, written sales materials, or promotional statements for this work. The fact that an organization, website, or product is referred to in this work as a citation and/or potential source of further information does not mean that the publisher and authors endorse the information or services the organization, website, or product may provide or recommendations it may make. This work is sold with the understanding that the publisher is not engaged in rendering professional services. The advice and strategies contained herein may not be suitable for your situation. You should consult with a specialist where appropriate. Neither the publisher nor authors shall be liable for any loss of profit or any other commercial damages, including but not limited to special, incidental, consequential, or other damages. Further, readers should be aware that websites listed in this work may have changed or disappeared between when this work was written and when it is read.

*Library of Congress Cataloging-in-Publication Data*

ISBN 978-1-394-23392-2

Cover image: Pixabay.Com
Cover design by Russell Richardson

Set in size of 11pt and Minion Pro by Manila Typesetting Company, Makati, Philippines

Printed in the USA

10  9  8  7  6  5  4  3  2  1

# Contents

# Foreword

In the dynamic landscape of today's technological revolution, machine learning and its applications span multiple domains, offering both opportunities and challenges. As we navigate this terrain, the significance of data has shifted; it has transformed from merely passive entities to active drivers influencing decisions, sculpting perceptions, and determining collective trajectories. This book serves a pivotal reference that sheds light upon complex computational arenas and provides clarity to those navigating this domain.

This book is more than an aggregation of knowledge. It epitomizes the expertise and adaptability of current computational researchers and accentuates the potential of metaheuristics. For those unfamiliar with the term, envision metaheuristics as high-level strategists that steer a multitude of heuristic methodologies toward their zenith. They offer the requisite tools to address complex challenges where conventional algorithms might be inadequate.

Throughout the book, you will find a wide range of applications and potential uses of metaheuristics that span across domains from machine learning to the cutting-edge fields of sustainability, communication, and networking. It is fascinating to note that the algorithms aren't just theoretical entities; they resonate with pressing real-world challenges. For instance, consider the pivotal role of metaheuristics in life-saving applications like breast cancer detection, or in ensuring security through anomaly identification in surveillance systems and botnet attack detection.

Moreover, as we delve deeper, we witness the subtle yet profound synergies between metaheuristics and contemporary technological innovations. The chapters dedicated to the advancements in 5G and 6G communication, and the future of autonomous vehicles, are prime examples. These sections underline the intricate balance and interdependence of the challenges we face today and the innovative solutions metaheuristics can offer.

For researchers who dedicate their lives to exploration, practitioners at the frontline of technological innovations, and students who look with hopeful eyes toward the future, this book will be a pivotal tool. Let it guide you, as it did for me, through the mesmerizing world of algorithms and their real-world applications.

**Diego Alberto Oliva**
*Universidad de Guadalajara, Mexico*

# Preface

While compiling this book, we were guided by a singular vision: to sculpt a resource that seamlessly melds the theoretical intricacies of metaheuristics with their myriad practical applications. Our aspiration was to produce a reference that not only delves deeply into the subject, but is also accessible to readers across spectra, offering a holistic understanding that is both profound and practical.

With every chapter, we strived to weave a narrative, oscillating between the vast expanse of the topic and the intricate minutiae that define it. The book commences with a foundational introduction, leading readers through the labyrinthine world of metaheuristics. Going forward, the narrative transitions, diving deeper into their multifaceted applications—spanning from the dynamic domain of machine learning to the ever-evolving spheres of technology, sustainability, and the intricate web of communication networks.

Metaheuristics present a promising solution to many formidable optimization conundrums. Yet, their true allure comes not just from their theoretical promise but their practical prowess. This book attempts to unveil this allure, transforming nebulous algorithms into tangible entities with real-world resonances—whether in the life-saving realm of healthcare or the cutting-edge world of vehicular communications.

We extend our endless gratitude to the brilliant authors, reviewers, and countless others whose relentless dedication, insight, and expertise are evident in these pages. The editorial journey has been one of profound learning and growth for all involved. With each chapter, we have gleaned new perspectives, and we hope this book becomes a wellspring of knowledge, inspiration, and introspection for both scholars and professionals.

In closing, we offer our sincere thanks to the Scrivener and Wiley publishing teams for their help with this book. We entreat you to immerse your intellect and curiosity in the mesmerizing world of metaheuristics and their applications. Here's to an enlightening reading journey ahead!

Kanak Kalita
Narayanan Ganesh
S. Balamurugan

# Metaheuristic Algorithms and Their Applications in Different Fields: A Comprehensive Review

**Abrar Yaqoob[1]\*, Navneet Kumar Verma[2] and Rabia Musheer Aziz[1]**

[1]*School of Advanced Science and Language, VIT Bhopal University, Kothrikalan, Sehore, India*
[2]*State Planning Institute (New Division), Planning Department Lucknow, Utter Pradesh, India*

## Abstract

A potent method for resolving challenging optimization issues is provided by metaheuristic algorithms, which are heuristic optimization approaches. They provide an effective technique to explore huge solution spaces and identify close to ideal or optimal solutions. They are iterative and often inspired by natural or social processes. This study provides comprehensive information on metaheuristic algorithms and the many areas in which they are used. Heuristic optimization algorithms are well-known for their success in handling challenging optimization issues. They are a potent tool for problem-solving. Twenty well-known metaheuristic algorithms, such as the tabu search, particle swarm optimization, ant colony optimization, genetic algorithms, simulated annealing, and harmony search, are included in the article. The article extensively explores the applications of these algorithms in diverse domains such as engineering, finance, logistics, and computer science. It underscores particular instances where metaheuristic algorithms have found utility, such as optimizing structural design, controlling dynamic systems, enhancing manufacturing processes, managing supply chains, and addressing problems in artificial intelligence, data mining, and software engineering. The paper provides a thorough insight into the versatile deployment of metaheuristic algorithms across different sectors, highlighting their capacity to tackle complex optimization problems across a wide range of real-world scenarios.

*Keywords:* Optimization, metaheuristics, machine learning, swarm intelligence

---

\**Corresponding author*: Abraryaqoob77@gmail.com

---

Kanak Kalita, Narayanan Ganesh and S. Balamurugan (eds.) Metaheuristics for Machine Learning: Algorithms and Applications, (1–36) © 2024 Scrivener Publishing LLC

## 1.1   Introduction

Metaheuristics represent a category of optimization methods widely employed to tackle intricate challenges in diverse domains such as engineering, economics, computer science, and operations research. These adaptable techniques are designed to locate favorable solutions by exploring an extensive array of possibilities and avoiding stagnation in suboptimal outcomes [1]. The roots and advancement of metaheuristics can be traced back to the early 1950s when George Dantzig introduced the simplex approach for linear programming [2]. This innovative technique marked a pivotal point in optimization and paved the way for the emergence of subsequent optimization algorithms. Nonetheless, the simplex method's applicability is confined to linear programming issues and does not extend to nonlinear problems. In the latter part of the 1950s, John Holland devised the genetic algorithm, drawing inspiration from concepts of natural selection and evolution [3]. The genetic algorithm assembles a set of potential solutions and iteratively enhances this set through genetic operations like mutation, crossover, and selection [4]. The genetic algorithm was a major milestone in the development of metaheuristics and opened up new possibilities for resolving difficult optimization issues. During the 1980s and 1990s, the field of metaheuristics experienced significant expansion and the emergence of numerous novel algorithms. These techniques, which include simulated annealing (SA), tabu search (TS), ant colony optimization (ACO), particle swarm optimization (PSO), and differential evolution (DE), were created expressly to deal with a variety of optimization issues. They drew inspiration from concepts like simulated annealing, tabu search, swarm intelligence, and evolutionary algorithms [5].

The term "meta-" in metaheuristic algorithms indicates a higher level of operation beyond simple heuristics, leading to enhanced performance. These algorithms balance local search and global exploration by using randomness to provide a range of solutions. Despite the fact that metaheuristics are frequently employed, there is not a single definition of heuristics and metaheuristics in academic literature, and some academics even use the terms synonymously. However, it is currently fashionable to classify as metaheuristics all algorithms of a stochastic nature that utilize randomness and comprehensive exploration across the entire system. Metaheuristic algorithms are ideally suited for global optimization and nonlinear modeling because randomization is a useful method for switching from local to global search. As a result, almost all metaheuristic algorithms can be used to solve issues involving nonlinear optimization at the global level [6].

In recent years, the study of metaheuristics has developed over time and new algorithms are being developed that combine different concepts and techniques from various fields such as machine learning, deep learning, and data science. The development and evolution of metaheuristics have made significant contributions to solving complex optimization problems and have led to the development of powerful tools for decision-making in various domains [7]. In order to find solutions in a huge search area, metaheuristic algorithms are founded on the idea of mimicking the behaviors of natural or artificial systems. These algorithms are particularly valuable for tackling problems that are challenging or impossible to solve using traditional optimization methods. Typically, metaheuristic algorithms involve iterations and a series of steps that modify a potential solution until an acceptable one is discovered. Unlike other optimization techniques that may become stuck in local optimal solutions, metaheuristic algorithms are designed to explore the entire search space. They also exhibit resilience to noise or uncertainty in the optimization problem. The adaptability and plasticity of metaheuristic algorithms are two of their main features. They can be modified to take into account certain limitations or goals of the current task and are applicable to a wide variety of optimization situations. However, for complex problems with extensive search spaces, these algorithms may converge slowly toward an optimal solution, and there is no guarantee that they will find the global optimum. Metaheuristic algorithms find extensive application in various fields including engineering, finance, logistics, and computer science. They have been successfully employed in solving diverse problems such as optimizing design, control, and manufacturing processes, portfolio selection, and risk management strategies [8].

## 1.2    Types of Metaheuristic Algorithms

We shall outline some of the most popular metaheuristic methods in this section.

### 1.2.1    Genetic Algorithms

Genetic algorithms (GAs) fit to a cluster of metaheuristic optimization techniques that draw inspiration from natural selection and genetics [9–11]. In order to find the optimal solution for a particular issue, the core idea underlying the GA is to mimic the evolutionary process. The genetic algorithm has the capability to address challenges spanning various fields such as biology, engineering, and finance [12–14]. In the methodology of the GA, a potential solution is denoted as a chromosome, or a collection of genes. Each gene within the context of the problem signifies an individual variable, and its value corresponds to the potential range of values that the variable can take [15, 16]. Subsequently, these chromosomes undergo genetic operations like mutation and crossover. This process can give rise to a fresh population of potential solutions, resulting in a novel set of potential outcomes [17–19].

The following are the major steps in the GA:

**Initialization:** The algorithm initializes a set of potential responses first. A chromosome is used to symbolize each solution, which is a string of genes randomly generated based on the problem domain [20].

**Evaluation:** The suitability of each chromosome is assessed based on the objective function of the problem. The quality of the solution is evaluated by the fitness function, and the objective is to optimize the fitness function by either maximizing or minimizing it, depending on the particular problem [21].

**Selection:** Chromosomes that possess higher fitness values are chosen to form a fresh population of potential solutions. Various techniques, such as roulette wheel selection, tournament selection, and rank-based selection, are employed for the selection process [22].

**Crossover:** The selected chromosomes are combined through crossover to generate new offspring chromosomes. The crossover operation exchanges the genetic information from the parent chromosomes and is utilized to generate novel solutions [23].

**Mutation:** The offspring chromosomes are subjected to mutation, which introduces random changes to the genetic information. Mutation aids in preserving diversity within the population and preventing the occurrence of local optima [24].

**Replacement:** As the child chromosomes multiply, a new population of potential solutions is formed and replaces the less fit members of the prior population.

**Termination:** The technique proceeds to iterate through the selection, crossover, mutation, and replacement phases

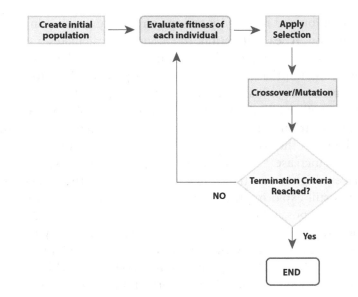

**Figure 1.1** Flowchart of the genetic algorithm.

until a specific termination condition is satisfied. Reaching a predetermined maximum for iterations is one scenario for termination, attaining a desired fitness value, or exceeding a predetermined computational time limit.

The GA has several advantages, such as being capable of solving complex issues, locating the global optimum, and being applicable to various domains. However, the GA also has some limitations, such as the need for a suitable fitness function, the possibility of premature convergence, and the high computational cost for complex problems. Figure 1.1 shows the flowchart of the genetic algorithm.

### 1.2.2  Simulated Annealing

Simulated annealing is a probabilistic method for optimizing complex multidimensional problems by seeking the global best solution. It draws inspiration from the metallurgical technique of annealing, which includes heating and gradually cooling a metal to enhance its strength and resilience [25]. Similarly, simulated annealing commences at an elevated temperature, enabling the algorithm to extensively investigate a vast array of possible solutions, and then slowly decreases the temperature to narrow down the search to the most promising areas. SA works by maintaining a current solution and repeatedly making small changes to it in search of a better solution. At each iteration, the algorithm calculates a cost function that measures how good the current solution is. The cost function can be any function that assigns a score to a potential solution, such as a distance metric or a likelihood function. Subsequently, the algorithm determines whether to embrace or disregard a new solution by utilizing a probability distribution that relies on the existing temperature and the disparity between the costs of the current and new solutions [26]. High temperatures increase SA's propensity to embrace novel solutions even if they have a higher cost than the current solution. This is because the algorithm is still exploring the space of potential solutions and needs to be open to new possibilities. As the temperature decreases, SA becomes increasingly discriminating and admits novel solutions solely if they surpass the existing solution. By employing this approach, SA prevents itself from becoming trapped in local peaks and eventually achieves convergence toward the global peak [27]. SA offers a notable benefit by effectively

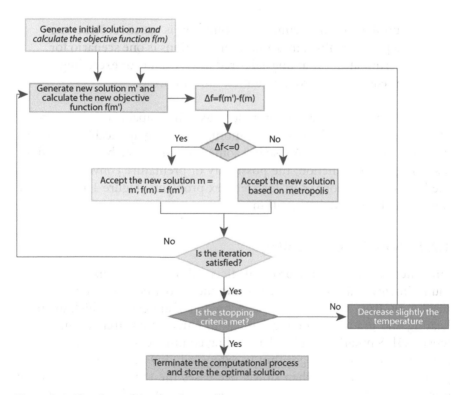

**Figure 1.2** Flowchart of simulated annealing.

addressing non-convex optimization problems, characterized by numerous local optima. By permitting the acceptance of solutions with greater costs, SA can navigate diverse areas within the solution space and prevent entrapment in local optima. Moreover, SA boasts ease of implementation and independence from cost function gradients, rendering it suitable for scenarios where the cost function lacks differentiability. However, SA does have some limitations. It can be slow to converge, especially for large or complex problems, and may require many iterations to find the global optimum. SA's effectiveness is also influenced by the decision of cooling schedule, which determines how quickly the temperature decreases. If the cooling schedule is too slow, the algorithm may take too long to converge, while if it is too fast, the algorithm may converge too quickly to a suboptimal solution [28, 29].

To put it briefly, simulated annealing is a highly effective optimization method that has the capability to address intricate problems, multidimensional problems with multiple local optima. It works by exploring the solution space and gradually narrowing down the search for the most promising regions. While it has some limitations, SA is a helpful tool for a variety of optimization issues in the real world. Figure 1.2 shows the flowchart of simulated annealing.

## 1.2.3 Particle Swarm Optimization

Particle swarm optimization is a technique for optimization that employs a population-based strategy to address a wide range of optimization problems. First introduced by Kennedy and Eberhart in 1995, this concept takes inspiration from the coordinated movements observed in the flocking of birds and the schooling of fish [30–32]. This algorithm emulates the social dynamics exhibited by these creatures, where each member learns from its own encounters and the experiences of its nearby peers, with the aim of discovering the best possible solution [33]. The PSO method begins by generating a population of particles, each of which acts as a potential solution to the optimization issue at hand. These particles, which have both a location and a velocity vector, are randomly distributed throughout the search space [34]. The location vector represents the particle's current solution, whereas the velocity vector represents the particle's moving direction and magnitude inside the search space. Through iterative steps, each particle's location and velocity vectors undergo constant modification and adjustment in the PSO algorithm, guided by its own best solution encountered thus far and the solutions of its neighboring particles [35]. Collaborative learning continues until a predetermined stopping condition

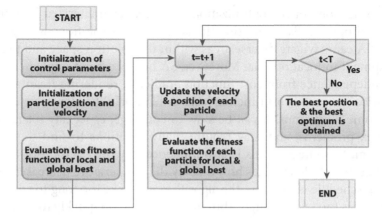

**Figure 1.3** Flowchart of the particle swarm optimization.

is met, such as when the desired outcome is attained or the maximum number of iterations has been reached. Compared to other optimization algorithms, the PSO algorithm boasts various advantages, including simplicity, rapid convergence, and robustness [36, 37]. PSO has found applications in diverse problem domains, spanning function optimization, neural network training, image processing, and feature selection. Nevertheless, the algorithm does come with certain limitations. These include the risk of premature convergence, where the algorithm may converge to suboptimal solutions prematurely, and challenges in effectively handling problems with high-dimensional spaces [38].

In general, the particle swarm optimization algorithm is a robust and effective optimization method capable of addressing numerous practical optimization problems. Its simplicity and intuitive approach make it an appealing choice compared to more intricate optimization methods. Figure 1.3 shows the flowchart of the particle swarm optimization.

### 1.2.4   Ant Colony Optimization

Ant colony optimization is a nature-inspired method that addresses difficult optimization problems by mimicking the behavior of ant colonies. The program takes its cues from the behavior of ant colonies, specifically the way ants communicate to discover the shortest path toward food sources. The fundamental idea behind the ACO is to simulate the foraging behavior of ants to solve optimization problems effectively. A simulated group of ants is put on a graph representing the problem space in the ACO. These ants navigate the graph by selecting the next node to visit based on the pheromone trails left behind by other ants. The strength of the phero-mone trail represents the quality of the solution that passed through that edge. As more ants traverse the same edge, the pheromone trail becomes stronger. This is similar to how ants communicate with each other in real life by leaving pheromone trails to signal the location of food sources [39, 40]. The ACO algorithm has several key parameters, such as the amount of pheromone each ant leaves, the rate at which pheromones evaporate, and the balance between exploiting the best solution and exploring new solutions. The optimal values of the parameters in the algorithm are deter-mined through a process of experimentation and refinement to obtain the best possible results for a specific problem [41].

The ACO has showcased impressive achievements in resolving diverse optimization challenges, including but not limited to the traveling sales-man problem, vehicle routing, and job scheduling. One notable advantage of the algorithm is its ability to swiftly discover favorable solutions, even

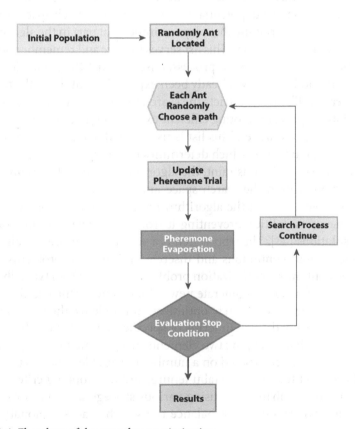

**Figure 1.4** Flowchart of the ant colony optimization.

when confronted with extensive search spaces. Furthermore, because the ACO belongs to the category of metaheuristic algorithms, it can be applied to a variety of situations without requiring a deep understanding of the underlying structure of those problems [42]. Figure 1.4 shows the flowchart of the ant colony optimization.

### 1.2.5   Tabu Search

The tabu search is a metaheuristic technique utilized for optimization problems, initially proposed by Fred Glover in 1986. It has gained significant popularity across diverse domains, including operations research, engineering, and computer science. The core concept behind the tabu search involves systematically traversing the search space by transitioning between different solutions in order to identify the optimal solution. However, unlike other local search algorithms, the tabu search incorporates a memory structure that records previous moves executed during the search. These data are then used to steer the search to potential places within the search space [43]. The tabu list, a memory structure that plays an important part in the algorithm, is at the heart of the tabu search. This list serves to store and remember previous moves made during the search process, ensuring that the algorithm avoids revisiting solutions that have already been explored. By utilizing the tabu list, the tabu search effectively restricts the search to new and unexplored regions of the solution space, promoting efficient exploration and preventing repetitive or redundant searches. This list is used to enforce a set of constraints, known as the tabu tenure, which determines how long a move is considered tabu. By imposing this constraint, the algorithm is compelled to investigate diverse regions within the search space and evade being trapped in local optima. This ensures that the algorithm remains dynamic and continually explores new possibilities, preventing it from being overly fixated on suboptimal solutions [43]. The tabu search is a versatile optimization algorithm applicable to both continuous and discrete optimization problems. When addressing continuous optimization problems, the algorithm typically uses a neighborhood function to generate new solutions by perturbing the present solution. In the event of discrete optimization problems, the neighborhood function is typically defined in terms of specific moves that can be made to the solution, such as swapping two elements in a permutation. The effectiveness of the tabu search is based on a number of variables, such as the choice of neighborhood function, the tabu tenure, and the stopping criterion. The algorithm can be enhanced by using various strategies, such as diversification and intensification, which balance the search space's exploitation and exploration [44].

The tabu search, a metaheuristic approach introduced by Fred Glover in 1986, is utilized for optimizing problems. Its application spans a wide array of domains, including operations research, engineering, and computer science, establishing it as a widely recognized technique. The fundamental principle of the tabu search involves a systematic traversal of the solution space, shifting between different solutions to ascertain the optimal one. Distinguishing itself from conventional local search algorithms, the tabu search incorporates a memory structure that logs prior moves executed during the search process. This stored information guides the search toward unexplored areas within the solution space [45]. Central to the tabu search is the tabu list, a pivotal memory structure. This list retains and recalls previous moves executed during the search, ensuring that revisiting already explored solutions is avoided. The tabu list effectively restricts the exploration to untrodden regions, preventing redundant searches and fostering efficient investigation. Governing the tabu list is the concept of the tabu tenure, setting the duration for which a move remains prohibited. This constraint compels the algorithm to explore diverse solution space regions, eluding entrapment in local optima. This dynamic approach continuously explores novel avenues, counteracting fixation on suboptimal solutions [46]. The tabu search is a versatile optimization algorithm suitable for both continuous and discrete optimization challenges. For continuous optimization, a neighborhood function is commonly used to generate new solutions by perturbing the current one. In the context of discrete optimization, the neighborhood function is typically defined by specific permissible moves, such as element swaps in a permutation. The efficacy of the tabu search hinges on factors like neighborhood function choice, tabu tenure, and the stopping criteria. The algorithm can be augmented through strategies like diversification and intensification, ensuring a balance between exploiting and exploring the search space.

In general, the tabu search is a robust and adaptable optimization technique that has demonstrated its effectiveness in addressing diverse problem sets. It can be employed independently or integrated into more intricate optimization algorithms. Its popularity stems from its versatility and straightforwardness, making it a favored option for tackling real-life challenges in various domains.

### 1.2.6 Differential Evolution

The DE is an optimization algorithm based on populations, originally created by Storn and Price in 1997 [47]. It fit to the category of evolutionary algorithms that iteratively grow a population of potential solutions to find the optimal solution. The algorithm adheres to the fundamental steps of mutation, crossover, and selection, which are key elements commonly shared among numerous evolutionary algorithms [48].

In the process of the differential evolution, a population of potential solutions undergoes iterative evolution through the implementation of the following sequential steps:

1. Initialization: A population of N possible solutions is produced at random.
2. Mutation: Involves randomly selecting three candidate solutions and modifying them to create a trial vector.
3. Crossover: It is a technique used in optimization algorithms to create a new candidate solution by combining the trial vector with the target vector.
4. Selection: If the new candidate solution has a higher fitness, it will take the place of the target vector.

The success of the differential evolution depends on the selection of the optimization technique's adjustable settings, such as mutation rate, crossover rate, and population size [49, 50]. Several variants of the DE have been proposed, including the SHADE (success history-based adaptive differential evolution) and JADE (adaptive differential evolution) algorithms, which incorporate adaptive control parameters to improve the algorithm's performance.

### 1.2.7   Harmony Search

The harmony search (HS) is an optimization technique motivated by the musical improvization process. Geem [125] had put forward the idea in 2001 and has now been used to solve several optimization issues. The techniques mimic the process of improvization by a group of musicians, where they adjust their pitches (or notes) to create harmony. In the HS, the choice variables of an optimization problem in high school are comparable to musical notes, and the value of the goal function reflects harmony [51].

Starting individuals of decision variable vectors (i.e., the notes) are used in the HS approaches and iteratively search for better solutions by generating new solutions through the following steps:

1. Harmony memory: A set of the best candidate solutions (i.e., the harmonies) is maintained.

2. Harmony creation: A potential solution is created by chance selecting values from the harmony memory.

3. Pitch adjustment: The values in the new candidate solution are adjusted with a probability based on a pitch adjustment rate.

4. Acceptance: The new candidate solution is accepted if it improves the objective function value.

The control variables, such as the harmony memory size, pitch adjustment rate, and number of iterations, affect how well the HS performs. The method follows the core phases of mutation, crossover, and selection, and the approach has been utilized to tackle diverse optimization challenges, such as managing water resources, designing structures, and operating power systems [52, 53].

## 1.2.8   Artificial Bee Colony

The artificial bee colony (ABC) is a population-based optimization method that draws inspiration from honey bees' feeding habits. Since its introduction by Karaboga in 2005, the technique has been used to solve a number of optimization issues [54]. The ABC mimics the foraging process of bees, where they search for food sources by visiting the flowers in the vicinity of the hive [55].

The artificial bee colony technique starts with an arbitrarily generated population of candidate solutions (i.e., food sources) and iteratively searches for better solutions by simulating the foraging process of bees through the following steps:

1. Phase of employed bees: The employed bees develop new candidate solutions by modifying the values of current solutions.

2. Phase of the onlooker bees: The onlooker bees choose the candidate solutions with the highest fitness values and send this information to the employed bees.

3. Phase of scout bees: The scout bees search for new candidate solutions by randomly generating new solutions.

The success of the ABC depends on the control parameters, such as the population size, the number of iterations, and the probability of abandoning a food source. The algorithm has been applied to a wide range of optimization problems, including image processing, wireless sensor networks, and fuzzy control systems [56].

## 1.2.9 Firefly Algorithm

A metaheuristic optimization technique called the firefly algorithm (FA) is based on how fireflies behave. Dr. Xin-She Yang first presented the FA in 2008. The social behavior of fireflies, which is characterized by their flashing light to attract mates or prey, served as an inspiration for the algorithm [57]. The firefly technique's primary role is to increase light intensity, and in order to maximize light intensity, fireflies travel toward the brighter fireflies. Starting with a random population of fireflies, using the goal function, the program calculates the light intensity of each firefly [58]. The movement of fireflies is governed by their attractiveness, which is determined by the brightness of their light, and the distance between them. The fireflies move toward the brighter fireflies and update their positions until the maximum light intensity is achieved [59]. Numerous optimization issues, including those involving machine learning, image processing, and function optimization, have been effectively solved using the firefly algorithm.

## 1.2.10 Gray Wolf Optimizer

The gray wolf optimizer (GWO) is a metaheuristic optimization system based on wolves' social structure and hunting techniques. The algorithm was developed in 2014 by Seyed Ali Mirjalili, Seyed Mohammad Mirjalili, and Andrew Lewis [60]. The optimization issue is viewed in the gray wolf optimizer as a wolf pack's prey–predator dynamic. The wolf population used by the method is randomly divided into four groups: alpha, beta, delta, and omega. While the omega wolf is the weakest and has the lowest fitness value, the alpha wolf assumes the role of the leader within the wolf pack and has the greatest fitness value [61–63]. The movement of the wolves is governed by three different types of hunting techniques: hunting for prey, following the alpha wolf, and surrounding the prey. The wolves adjust their locations based on these techniques until the optimal solution is accomplished. The gray wolf optimizer's application has been expanded to address a variety of optimization issues, such as function optimization, engineering design, and feature selection [64, 65].

## 1.2.11 Imperialist Competitive Algorithm

The imperialist competitive algorithm (ICA), a metaheuristic optimization method designed to address numerous optimization issues, was inspired by the political and economic rivalry of imperialist nations. Amir Hossein Gandomi and Ali Alavi introduced the method in 2010 [66]. In the imperialist competitive algorithm, the optimization problem is considered as a competition between empires. The algorithm starts with a random population of empires, which are categorized into two groups: imperialist and colonies. The imperialist empires have higher fitness values, and they expand their territories by annexing colonies. The movement of empires is governed by two different types of actions: assimilation and revolution. In the assimilation process, the imperialist empires try to improve the fitness of their colonies, while in the revolution process, the colonies rebel against their imperialist empires and become independent. Various optimization problems, including function optimization, image segmentation, and parameter estimation, have been effectively solved through the successful application of the imperialist competitive algorithm [67, 68].

### 1.2.12    Bat Algorithm

Xin-She Yang created the bat algorithm (BA) in 2010, which is a metaheuristic optimization technique used to tackle a variety of optimization challenges [69]. The bat algorithm is inspired by bats' echolocation activity, which uses ultrasonic noises to navigate and locate prey in the dark. It replicates the activity of bats in their hunt for prey in order to discover the best solution to a given optimization issue [70].

To solve an optimization problem using the bat algorithm, a population of bats is created in the search space with random placements and velocities. The bats move randomly, emitting frequencies proportional to their fitness values. Bats with better fitness emit higher-frequency sounds that attract other bats toward their position in the search space [71]. In adding to the frequency-based attraction mechanism, the bat algorithm includes a random walk component that allows the bats to explore uncharted regions of the search space. During each iteration, the algorithm updates the velocity and position of each bat using information on the best solution found thus far, as well as the loudness and frequency of its emitted signal. The algorithm iterates until it reaches a present stopping point, such as a maximum number of iterations or a goal fitness value [72].

### 1.2.13    Cuckoo Search

The cuckoo search, a metaheuristic optimization method inspired by the cuckoo bird reproductive behavior, was introduced in 2009 by Xin-She Yang and Suash Deb. Cuckoo birds use an unusual approach in which they deposit their eggs in the nests of other bird species, leaving the host birds to care for and rear their children [73]. The cuckoo search algorithm imitates the foraging behavior of cuckoos as they search for food, employing the strategy of brood parasitism. The objective is to discover the optimal solution for an optimization problem. The technique commences by initializing a population of cuckoos with random positions and velocities. Subsequently, each cuckoo deposits an egg in a nest that is chosen randomly, with the likelihood of selecting a specific nest being proportionate to its fitness level [74–76]. The cuckoo search algorithm incorporates a random walk element, allowing the cuckoos to explore unexplored regions within the search space. During each iteration, the algorithm adjusts the position and speed of each cuckoo based on the best solution found thus far and the potential for uncovering a superior solution by depositing an egg in a new nest. To enhance the solution quality by exploring the vicinity of the current answer, the algorithm also integrates a local search component. The process persists until a predetermined stopping condition is fulfilled, such as reaching the maximum iteration count or achieving the desired fitness level [77, 78].

## 1.2.14  Flower Pollination Algorithm

The flower pollination algorithm (FPA), created by Xin-She Yang in 2012, is a metaheuristic optimization algorithm that draws pollinators like butterflies and bees with their aroma [79]. The flower pollination algorithm emulates flower pollination behaviors to discern the optimal solution for a given problem. In 2012, Xin-She Yang introduced this algorithm, a metaheuristic optimization technique inspired by the way flowers attract pollinators like butterflies and bees through their fragrance. This involves initializing a group of flowers with random positions and fragrances. Each flower releases a fragrance that draws pollinators, with the likelihood of attraction determined by its fitness level. A random walk element is also integrated, enabling pollinators to explore novel sections of the search space [80]. Throughout each iteration, the flower pollination algorithm adjusts the position and fragrance of each flower based on the current best solution and the probability of enticing new pollinators to potentially uncover an improved solution. Furthermore, the algorithm incorporates a local search component that investigates the neighboring vicinity to enhance solution quality. The algorithm continues until a predefined stopping condition is met, which could be achieving a specific fitness target or reaching the maximum iteration count [81].

## 1.2.15     Krill Herd Algorithm

In 2012, Amir H. Gandomi and Amir H. Alavi introduced the krill herd algorithm (KHA), a metaheuristic optimization technique inspired by the coordinated motions and interplays of krill within their oceanic habitat. This algorithm endeavors to replicate the herding conduct of krill as they forage for sustenance and navigate survival challenges, all with the aim of identifying the finest solution for a specified problem [82].

The krill herd algorithm emulates the synchronized movements and interactions of krill in their pursuit of nourishment and companionship, striving to pinpoint the optimal solution for a given task. Commencing with the creation of a krill population featuring random positions and velocities, each individual krill engages in random movements across the search space. The course and speed of these movements are shaped by forces of attraction, repulsion from other krill, and environmental influences [83].

Depending on the best solution found thus far, the impact of other krill and the environment and the location and velocity of each krill are adjusted by the algorithm at each iteration. The technique also has a random walk component that enables krill to explore new regions of the search space [84]. The algorithm continues to run until a predefined stopping condition is met, such as a predetermined number of iterations or a predetermined goal fitness value [85].

## 1.2.16     Whale Optimization Algorithm

In 2016, Seyedali Mirjalili and Andrew Lewis introduced the whale optimization algorithm (WOA), a metaheuristic optimization technique. This concept drew inspiration from the hunting behaviors of humpback whales, characterized by a blend of independent and cooperative movements and vocalizations [86]. The core concept of the whale optimization algorithm is to replicate the foraging conduct of humpback whales as they seek sustenance, aiming to uncover the optimal solution for a particular problem. The algorithm commences by establishing a group of whales, each assigned random positions and velocities. Subsequently, every whale undertakes random movements across the search space, with the course and speed influenced by the forces of attraction, repulsion exerted by other whales, and environmental conditions [87]. Throughout each iteration, the whale optimization algorithm modifies the positions and velocities of individual whales based on the current best solution and the effects of other whales and the environment. Moreover, the algorithm integrates a random walk aspect to facilitate exploration of uncharted regions within the search space. Termination of the algorithm occurs upon meeting predefined cessation criteria, such as attaining the maximum iteration count or reaching a desired fitness level [88–90].

### 1.2.17   Glowworm Swarm Optimization

The glowworm swarm optimization (GSO) is an optimization technique inspired by nature and was introduced by Kalyanmoy Deb and Samir Dasgupta in 2006. It draws inspiration from the bioluminescent communication exhibited by fireflies and glowworms to emulate the coordinated behavior of swarms [91]. The glowworm swarm optimization serves as a metaheuristic optimization algorithm that replicates the bioluminescent actions of glowworms as they navigate their surroundings in pursuit of sustenance and companionship, all with the aim of identifying the optimal solution for a given problem. Commencing with the creation of a group of glowworms, each assigned random positions and luminosities, every glowworm emits light that attracts other individuals, with the degree of attraction being proportional to both the luminosity and the distance of neighboring glowworms [92]. Throughout each iteration, the glowworm swarm optimization algorithm updates the position and luminosity of each glowworm based on the likelihood of drawing new glowworms and the best solution attained up to that point. A random walk component is also integrated into the algorithm, allowing glowworms to venture into unexplored territories of the search space. The algorithm's execution continues until reaching a specific termination criterion, such as achieving a target fitness level or reaching the maximum permissible number of iterations [93].

### 1.2.18   Cat Swarm Optimization

The cat swarm optimization (CSO) method, which is a metaheuristic optimization algorithm based on the cooperative hunting behavior of a colony of cats, was first proposed by Ying Tan and Yuhui Shi in 2006. The method is modeled after the collaboration and communication that occur among cats while they are hunting [94]. The fundamental concept behind the cat swarm optimization involves emulating the collective hunting actions of a group of cats to ascertain the finest solution for a given problem. The approach commences by placing and endowing a population of cats with random positions and velocities. Subsequently, each cat undertakes randomized movements within the search space, wherein the course and speed of movement are influenced by the forces of attraction and repulsion exerted by fellow cats, alongside environmental variables [95].

In each iteration of the cat swarm optimization algorithm, adjustments are made to the positions and velocities of the cats based on the prevailing best solution, impact of other cats, and environmental conditions. Furthermore, a random walk element is infused into the algorithm, granting cats the capability to explore previously uncharted territories within the search space. This optimization process continues until a predetermined halting criterion, such as reaching a desired fitness threshold or attaining the maximum allowable number of iterations, is met. This algorithm was introduced by Ying Tan and Yuhui Shi in 2006, with inspiration drawn from the collaborative hunting demeanor of cats [96].

## 1.2.19    Grasshopper Optimization Algorithm

The grasshopper optimization algorithm (GOA), created in 2014 by Seyedali Mirjalili and Andrew Lewis, is a nature-inspired optimization algorithm that imitates the swarming behavior of grasshoppers. The GOA bases its optimization on the collective behavior of grasshoppers, which involves interpersonal communication and cooperation [97].

Throughout each iteration of the grasshopper optimization algorithm, adjustments are made to the position and velocity of every grasshopper, guided by the prevailing best solution and the influences stemming from fellow grasshoppers and environmental factors. Moreover, a random walk attribute is introduced, empowering grasshoppers to explore and uncover previously unexplored sectors within the search space [98, 99]. This algorithm persists until a predetermined cessation criterion is satisfied, such as reaching a maximum iteration count or achieving a designated fitness target.

## 1.2.20    Moth–Flame Optimization

The moth–flame optimization (MFO) algorithm draws inspiration from the natural behavior of moths, which exhibit an inherent attraction to flames and utilize celestial cues for navigation. This technique emulates the search pattern of moths, with the goal of uncovering the most optimal solution for a specific problem [100].

In the initial stages of the optimization procedure, the algorithm commences by generating a cluster of moths, each assigned random positions and luminosities. Subsequent to this, every moth traverses the search space via randomized movements, adjusting its velocity and trajectory based on two key factors: its inclination toward the brightest moth and the impact of environmental conditions [101]. As the moth–flame optimization algorithm progresses through each iteration, the position and luminosity of each moth are updated. These adjustments hinge upon the current best solution achieved and the attraction toward the brightest moth. Additionally, the algorithm incorporates a random walk feature to allow moths to explore new areas of the search space. The algorithm stops when a predefined stopping criterion is achieved, such as reaching a target fitness value or a maximum number of iterations [102].

Apart from this algorithm, several other algorithms like the sine cosine algorithm [103, 104], dragonfly algorithm [105, 106], and symbiotic organism search [107, 108] have widely been used in literature.

## 1.3  Application of Metaheuristic Algorithms

Hu *et al.* presented the crisscross optimisation arithmetic optimization algorithm (CSOAOA), an improved hybrid arithmetic optimization algorithm that seeks to solve the constraints of the original arithmetic optimization algorithm (AOA). The CSOAOA combines numerous strategies to enhance the speed at which convergence occurs, search efficiency, and calculation accuracy of the AOA, including the point set strategy, optimal neighborhood learning approach, and crisscross strategy. In terms of precision, convergence rate, and solution quality, the testing findings revealed that the CSOAOA outperformed other optimization algorithms, proving its potential as a viable approach for handling complicated engineering optimization issues [109].

Ghafil and Jármai proposed the dynamic differential annealed optimization (DDAO) in 2020, a unique metaheuristic optimization technique that uses random search and simulated annealing. The algorithm's efficacy was evaluated on 51 benchmark functions, and it beat many well-known optimization techniques, confirming its higher performance. The DDAO successfully converged to the global minimum of two real-world engineering optimization problems and produced a better feasible solution for the spring design problem than several other algorithms [110].

In 2022, Zhao *et al.* introduced a novel swarm intelligence optimization algorithm known as the dandelion optimizer (DO). This algorithm imitates the flight patterns of dandelion seeds and comprises three distinct stages: rising, descending, and landing. Each stage is characterized by its own set of rules and attributes. During the falling and landing stages, the algorithm simulates the seed's journey. Brownian motion and a Levy random walk were employed, and the efficiency of the differential evolution (DO) was evaluated using the CEC 2017 benchmark functions, and its performance was compared against nine other nature-inspired metaheuristic algorithms. The DO exhibited superior optimization accuracy, stability, convergence, and scalability, outperforming the competing algorithms. The study further demonstrated the robustness and exceptional performance of the DO by applying it to solve four real-world optimization problems [111].

The smart flower optimization algorithm (SFOA) is a metaheuristic optimization algorithm created by Sattar *et al.* (2021) that is inspired by the heliotropic motions of immature sunflowers as well as growth mechanisms based on sun-tracking and the biological clock. The success of the method is proven by benchmark testing utilizing CEC 2015 and comparisons with other optimization algorithms, which indicated improved optimization efficiency and performance. In addition, the SFOA was applied to real-world engineering design issues, yielding encouraging results and demonstrating its utility in addressing problems with unknown search spaces [112].

Azizi *et al.* introduced a novel metaheuristic algorithm named the fire hawk optimizer (FHO) in 2023. The FHO draws inspiration from the foraging behavior of fire hawks and exhibits remarkable efficiency in optimizing problems. Through comprehensive benchmarking against 233 mathematical test functions and two Competition on Evolutionary Computation (CEC) problems, the FHO outperformed other metaheuristic algorithms. Furthermore, the algorithm's efficacy was demonstrated in solving real-size structural frames, yielding promising outcomes and emphasizing its potential for addressing real-world problems. This research not only contributes to the advancement of metaheuristic algorithms but also underscores the capabilities of nature-inspired approaches [113].

In 2020, Ghasemian *et al.* introduced a new metaheuristic algorithm inspired by human behavior to address urbanization and improve the quality of life. The algorithm incorporates combined searching and population management strategies, and evaluation results demonstrate its superiority over other high-performing algorithms in a majority of search spaces [114].

Abollah Ansar *et al.* (2020) developed a hybrid metaheuristic algorithm for predicting corporate bankruptcy by combining the magnetic optimization algorithm (MOA) with the particle swarm optimization. The resulting algorithm, the MOA-PSO, was utilized to train an artificial neural network (ANN) for bankruptcy prediction and was found to outperform four existing algorithms, achieving an accuracy rate of 99.7%. Numerous optimization strategies have their benefits, and hybrid algorithms have proven to be useful in solving complicated problems more quickly and accurately [115].

Using a combination of artificial neural networks and optimization algorithms based on metaheuristics, Farahani *et al.* conducted a research study in 2022 with the goal of anticipating the Tehran Price Index (TEPIX). To determine the main market determinants influencing the stock market, the inquiry used a variety of algorithms, including GA, HS, PSO, MFO, and WOA. The outcomes showed that, in comparison to the traditional ANN model, the combined algorithms exhibited improved prediction skills. It is noteworthy that the study identified the whale optimization algorithm as the most precise technique for forecasting TEPIX [116].

In their 2022 research, Hadi Gholizadeh *et al.* introduced an environmentally friendly approach to the reverse logistics process for polystyrene disposable items. This method addresses uncertainties in demand and recovery costs by employing a mixed-integer nonlinear programming (MINLP) model. To tackle the problem, the researchers employed heuristic methods such as simulated annealing, cross-entropy, and genetic algorithms to generate initial solutions. Subsequently, they utilized the response surface method, robust optimization, and Taguchi method to refine the algorithm's performance. By comparing the heuristics' effectiveness with robust optimization using the best–worst technique and conducting a case study, the study confirmed the model's viability and highlighted the efficacy of optimization techniques in enhancing algorithmic performance. This work offers an ecologically sound approach to reverse logistics while showcasing the positive impact of optimization methods on algorithmic efficiency [117].

A hybrid metaheuristic method combining the discrete particle swarm optimization (DPSO) and the Harris hawks optimization (HHO) with three improvement strategies was first presented by Yan *et al.* in 2023. The purpose was to address the location routing problem (LRP) in the distribution of relief supplies in the immediate aftermath of disasters. They validated their proposed multiobjective model using a case study on COVID-19 in Wuhan, showing that the algorithm outperformed previous metaheuristic algorithms in terms of accuracy and the capacity to avoid local optima.

This study offers a viable method for planning disaster response that will optimize the distribution of relief supplies [118].

Yang *et al.* (2022) talked about the importance of information systems (ISs) in logistics and distribution management and suggested using the metaheuristic techniques (MHTs) to efficiently handle information across the supply chain. The study emphasized the value of cooperation, coordination, information-sharing, and communication among supply chain actors and stated that metaheuristics can be helpful in solving challenging logistical issues. The paper highlights the role of advanced decision support systems and the development of information and communication technology in adapting to the challenges of integration [119].

Adel Pourghader Chobar *et al.* (2022) focused on reverse logistics planning in response, recovery, and reconstruction phases during earthquakes, where a large amount of waste is generated. The problem is multiobjective and uncertain, which is solved using the non dominated sorting algorithm (NSGA-II) metaheuristic algorithm. The study indicates that increasing the capacity reduces the number of distribution centers needed but may lead to increased transportation costs. The case study is based on Tehran city [120].

Simran Gibson *et al.* published a review of the literature on identifying spam emails with machine learning algorithms and bio-inspired optimization strategies in 2020. On seven different email datasets, the researchers used numerous machine learning models, including Naive bayes, support vector machine, random forest, decision tree, and multilayer perceptron, along with feature extraction and preprocessing processes. The performance of the classifiers was improved by using bio-inspired techniques such as the particle swarm optimization and the genetic algorithm. The analysis found that the multinomial naive Bayes model, optimized with the genetic algorithm, performed better across several criteria. Furthermore, the scientists conducted a comparison with different machine learning and bio-inspired models to establish the best technique [121].

Oyelade *et al.* (2022) introduced a novel optimization algorithm named the Ebola optimization search algorithm (EOSA) that is inspired by the Ebola virus disease propagation mechanism. The technique was evaluated using two sets of benchmark functions, including both conventional and limited IEEE-CEC benchmark functions, by fusing the SEIR-HVQD mathematical model with the propagation model. The outcomes demonstrated that the EOSA beat popular metaheuristic algorithms including the artificial bee colony algorithm, genetic algorithm, and particle swarm optimization algorithm. The method was also used to resolve the issue of hyperparameter optimization in the categorization of digital mammography images, with a level of 96.0% accuracy [122].

The difficulty of resource scheduling for client tasks in the cloud environment, which has grown in popularity over the past 10 years, was the topic of the study by Bindu *et al.* (2020). To cut down on energy use, costs, and time, they created the optimal sequential ant colony optimisation algorithm (OSACO), an optimized scheduling method that takes into account the quality of service (QoS) requirements of customers. The OSACO algorithm was compared to other algorithms, and simulation results demonstrated its efficacy in resource scheduling optimization [123].

**Table 1.1** Strengths and weaknesses of metaheuristic algorithms.

| Strengths | Weaknesses |
| --- | --- |
| Metaheuristic algorithms are flexible and can be applied to a wide range of optimization problems. They can also be easily adapted to specific problem constraints or objectives. | Metaheuristic algorithms may converge slowly to an optimal solution, particularly for complex problems with a large search space. |
| Metaheuristic algorithms are designed to explore the entire search space, unlike other optimization techniques that may get stuck in local optima. | There is no guarantee that a metaheuristic algorithm will find the global optimum. |
| Unlike some optimization methods, metaheuristic algorithms do not require the computation of derivatives or gradients of the objective function. | Metaheuristic algorithms often require careful selection of algorithm parameters, which can be a time-consuming and difficult process. |
| Metaheuristic algorithms are usually robust to noise or uncertainty in the optimization problem. | Metaheuristic algorithms often involve complex mathematical operations, making it difficult to understand how they arrive at a solution. |
| Many metaheuristic algorithms can be parallelized, allowing the use of high-performance computing resources to solve complex problems. | In some cases, metaheuristic algorithms may overfit the training data, resulting in a suboptimal solution. |

Gharehchopogh (2022) discusses the incorporation of quantum computing (QC) concepts into metaheuristic algorithms and the ensuing development of quantum-inspired metaheuristic algorithms. The paper highlights the benefits of using QC-inspired metaheuristic algorithms in solving numerical and combinational optimization problems, achieving superior performance compared to conventional metaheuristic algorithms. The article presents a comprehensive review of the various applications of QC in metaheuristics, their classification in optimization problems, and their use in science and engineering. The study provides valuable insights into the potential of QC-inspired metaheuristic algorithms in solving optimization problems [124].

From the above discussion on different metaheuristic algorithms, we find that there are several strengths and weaknesses that are important to consider when choosing an optimization method. Some of the strengths and weaknesses of metaheuristic algorithms are shown in Table 1.1.

## 1.4  Future Direction

In the coming years, metaheuristic algorithms are anticipated to evolve along several trajectories. One promising path involves the creation of hybrid metaheuristic algorithms, which amalgamate the strengths of multiple techniques to enhance performance and resilience. Another trajectory involves adapting metaheuristics to grapple with optimization challenges posed by vast amounts of data, addressing the computational hurdles presented by extensive datasets. Moreover, the parallel and distributed implementation of metaheuristic algorithms can harness computational resources and expedite the optimization process. Subsequent research should also emphasize dynamic and multiobjective optimization, where metaheuristics can adjust to shifting problem conditions and manage numerous conflicting objectives simultaneously. Additionally, the call for explainable artificial intelligence (AI) necessitates metaheuristic algorithms that not only optimize but also shed light on decision-making processes. Real-time optimization demands metaheuristics that swiftly converge to nearly optimal solutions within strict time constraints.

Lastly, delving into innovative applications in domains like renewable energy, healthcare, smart cities, and cybersecurity will broaden the horizons of metaheuristic algorithms. By advancing in these directions, metaheuristics can persist in providing potent tools for resolving intricate optimization problems across diverse domains.

## 1.5 Conclusion

In summary, this article presents a comprehensive overview of metaheuristic algorithms and their broad spectrum of applications across diverse domains. The paper outlines well-known metaheuristic algorithms and underscores their efficacy in tackling intricate optimization issues. It extensively surveys the utilization of metaheuristic algorithms in engineering, finance, logistics, computer science, and related fields. The provided instances of employing these algorithms for tasks like devising optimal structures, governing dynamic systems, refining manufacturing procedures, orchestrating supply chains, and resolving challenges in artificial intelligence, data mining, and software engineering serve as concrete demonstrations of their capability to address complex problems across a variety of contexts. In essence, the paper underscores the significance and adaptability of metaheuristic algorithms in surmounting optimization hurdles in different spheres and offers a comprehensive comprehension of their practical application.

## References

1. Kvasov, D.E. and Mukhametzhanov, M.S., Metaheuristic vs. deterministic global optimization algorithms: The univariate case. *Appl. Math. Comput.*, 318, 245–259, 2018, doi: 10.1016/j.amc.2017.05.014.
2. Sinuany-Stern, Z., Foundations of operations research: From linear programming to data envelopment analysis. *Eur. J. Oper. Res.*, 306, 3, 1069–1080, 2023, doi: 10.1016/j.ejor.2022.10.046.
3. Ghneamat, R., *Genetic algorithms and application to adaptive automata for game theory*, Al-Balqa University, As-Salt, Jordan, 2005.
4. Holland, J.H., Genetic algorithms. *Sci. Am.*, 267, 1, 66–72, 1992, doi: 10.1038/scientificamerican0792-66.
5. Hammouche, K. *et al.*, A comparative study of various meta-heuristic techniques applied to the multilevel thresholding problem. *Eng. Appl. Artif. Intell.*, 23, 5, 676–688, 2010, doi: 10.1016/j.engappai.2009.09.011.
6. Gandomi, A.H. *et al.*, Metaheuristic algorithms in modeling and optimization, in: *Metaheuristic Appl. Struct. Infrastruct.*, pp. 1–24, 2013, doi:10.1016/b978-0-12-398364-0.00001-2.
7. Bandaru, S. and Deb, K., Metaheuristic techniques, in: *Decis. Sci.*, pp. 693–750, 2016, doi:10.1201/9781315183176-12.
8. Yang, X.-S., *Engineering optimization: An introduction with metaheuristic applications.* John Wiley & Sons, Hoboken, 2010, https://doi.org/10.1002/9780470640425.

9. Katoch, S. *et al.*, A review on genetic algorithm: Past, present, and future. *Multimed. Tools Appl.*, 80, 5, 8091–8126, 2021, doi: 10.1007/s11042-020-10139-6.
10. Slowik, A. and Kwasnicka, H., Evolutionary algorithms and their applications to engineering problems. *Neural Comput. Appl.*, 32, 16, 12363–12379, 2020, doi: 10.1007/s00521-020-04832-8.
11. Ghadai, R.K. and Kalita, K., Accurate estimation of DLC thin film hardness using genetic programming. *Int. J. Mater. Res.*, 111, 6, 453–462, 2020, doi: 10.3139/146.111911.
12. Ghadai, R.K. *et al.*, Genetically optimized diamond-like carbon thin film coatings. *Mater. Manuf. Processes*, 34, 13, 1476–1487, 2019, doi: 10.1080/10426914.2019.1594273.
13. Kalita, K. *et al.*, Robust genetically optimized skew laminates. *Proc. Inst. Mech. Eng. C*, 233, 1, 146–159, 2019, doi: 10.1177/0954406218756943.
14. Kalita, K. *et al.*, Genetic programming assisted multi-scale optimization for multi-objective dynamic performance of laminated composites: The advantage of a more elementary-level analysis. *Neural Comput. Appl.*, 32, 12, 7969–7993, 2020, doi: 10.1007/s00521-019-04280-z.
15. Kalita, K. *et al.*, Data-driven genetic programming-based symbolic regression metamodels for EDM process, in: *Data-Driven Optimization of Manufacturing Processes*, IGI Global, Scopus. USA, 2020, doi: 10.4018/978-1-7998-7206-1.ch009.
16. Kalita, K. *et al.*, Sensitivity analysis of GFRP composite drilling parameters and genetic algorithm-based optimization. *Int. J. Appl. Metaheuristic Comput.*, 13, 1, 1–17, 2022.
17. Kumar, V. *et al.*, A hybrid genetic programming-grey wolf optimizer approach for process optimization of biodiesel production. *Processes*, 9, 3, 442, 2021, doi: 10.3390/pr9030442.
18. Pal, S. *et al.*, Optimization of frequency separation of laminated shells carrying transversely distributed mass using genetic algorithm. *J. Vib. Control*, 2023, doi: 10.1177/10775463231190277.
19. Pal, S. *et al.*, Genetic algorithm-based fundamental frequency optimization of laminated composite shells carrying distributed mass. *J. Inst. Eng. (India) Ser. C*, 103, 3, 389–401, 2022, doi: 10.1007/s40032-021-00801-9.
20. Todorovski, M. and Rajicic, D., An initialization procedure in solving optimal power flow by genetic algorithm. *IEEE Trans. Power Syst.*, 21, 2, 480–487, 2006, doi: 10.1109/TPWRS.2006.873120.
21. Ji, S. *et al.*, Optimal tolerance allocation based on fuzzy comprehensive evaluation and genetic algorithm. *Int. J. Adv. Manuf. Technol.*, 16, 7, 461–468, 2000, doi: 10.1007/s001700070053.
22. Kumar, M., Husian, M., Upreti, N., Gupta, D., Genetic algorithm: Review and application. *Int. J. Inf. Technol. Knowl. Manag.*, 2, 451–454, 2010.

23. Umbarkar, and Sheth, Crossover operators in genetic algorithms: A review. *ICTACT J. Soft Comput.*, 06, 1, 1083–1092, 2015, doi: 10.21917/ijsc.2015.0150.

24. Mirjalili, S. *et al.*, Genetic algorithm: Theory, literature review, and application in image reconstruction, in: *Studies in Computational Intelligence. Nature-Inspired Optimizers*, pp. 69–85, 2020, doi:10.1007/978-3-030-12127-3_5.

25. Suman, B. and Kumar, P., A survey of simulated annealing as a tool for single and multiobjective optimization. *J. Oper. Res. Soc.*, 57, 10, 1143–1160, 2006, doi: 10.1057/palgrave.jors.2602068.

26. Amine, K., Multiobjective simulated annealing: Principles and algorithm variants. *Adv. Oper. Res.*, 2019, 1–13, 2019, doi: 10.1155/2019/8134674.

27. Eglese, R.W., Simulated annealing: A tool for operational research. *Eur. J. Oper. Res.*, 46, 3, 271–281, 1990, doi: 10.1016/0377-2217(90)90001-R.

28. Baykasoğlu, A. and Gindy, N.N.Z., A simulated annealing algorithm for dynamic layout problem. *Comput. Oper. Res.*, 28, 14, 1403–1426, 2001, doi: 10.1016/S0305-0548(00)00049-6.

29. Ming, C. and Raghav, N., Simulated annealing for mixture distribution analysis and its applications to reliability testing, in: *Simul. Annealing*, 2008, doi:10.5772/5834.

30. Banks, A. *et al.*, A review of particle swarm optimization. Part I: Background and development. *Nat. Comput.*, 6, 4, 467–484, 2007, doi: 10.1007/s11047-007-9049-5.

31. Kalita, K. *et al.*, Optimizing drilling induced delamination in GFRP composites using genetic algorithm & particle swarm optimization. *Adv. Compos. Lett.*, 27, 1, 1–9, 2018.

32. Shankar, R. *et al.*, Hybridized particle swarm - Gravitational search algorithm for process optimization. *Processes*, 10, 3, 616, 2022, doi: 10.3390/pr10030616.

33. Jain, N.K. *et al.*, A review of particle swarm optimization. *J. Inst. Eng. (India) Ser. B*, 99, 4, 407–411, 2018, doi: 10.1007/s40031-018-0323-y.

34. Ganesh, N. *et al.*, Multi-objective high-fidelity optimization using NSGA-III and MO-RPSOLC. *Comput. Model. Eng. Sci.*, 129, 2, 443–464, 2021, doi: 10.32604/cmes.2021.014960.

35. Kalita, K. *et al.*, Optimizing process parameters for laser beam micro-marking using genetic algorithm and particle swarm optimization. *Mater. Manuf. Processes*, 32, 10, 1101–1108, 2017, doi: 10.1080/10426914.2017.1303156.

36. Wang, D. *et al.*, Particle swarm optimization algorithm: An overview. *Soft Comput.*, 22, 2, 387–408, 2018, doi: 10.1007/s00500-016-2474-6.

37. Narayanan, G. *et al.*, PSO-tuned support vector machine metamodels for assessment of turbulent flows in pipe bends. *Eng. Comput.*, 37, 3, 981–1001, 2019, doi: 10.1108/EC-05-2019-0244.

38. Poli, R. *et al.*, Particle swarm optimization. *Swarm Intell.*, 1, 1, 33–57, 2007, doi: 10.1007/s11721-007-0002-0.

39. Dorigo, M. and Blum, C., Ant colony optimization theory: A survey. *Theor. Comput. Sci.*, 344, 2-3, 243–278, 2005, doi: 10.1016/j. tcs.2005.05.020.
40. Blum, C., Ant colony optimization: Introduction and recent trends. *Phys. Life Rev.*, 2, 4, 353–373, 2005, doi: 10.1016/j.plrev.2005.10.001.
41. Maniezzo, V. and Carbonaro, A., Ant colony optimization: An overview, in: *Operations Research/Computer Science Interfaces Series.* pp. 469–492, 2002, doi:10.1007/978-1-4615-1507-4_21.
42. Dorigo, M. and Stutzle, T., *Ant Colony Optimization.* MIT Press, Cambridge, UK, 2004.
43. Glover, F., Tabu search and adaptive memory programming—Advances, applications and challenges, in: *Operations Research/Computer Science Interfaces Series.* pp. 1–75, 1997, doi:10.1007/978-1-4615-4102-8_1.
44. Cangalovic, M. M., Kovacevic-Vujcic, V. V., Ivanovic, L., Drazic, M., Asic, M. D., Tabu search: A brief survey and some real-life applications. *Yugosl. J. Oper. Res.*, 6, 1, 5–18, 1996.
45. Jaeggi, D.M. *et al.*, The development of a multi-objective Tabu Search algorithm for continuous optimisation problems. *Eur. J. Oper. Res.*, 185, 3, 1192–1212, 2008, doi: 10.1016/j.ejor.2006.06.048.
46. Glover, F., Tabu search for nonlinear and parametric optimization (with links to genetic algorithms). *Discrete Appl. Math.*, 49, 1-3, 231–255, 1994, doi: 10.1016/0166-218X(94)90211-9.
47. Fleetwood, K., An introduction to differential evolution, in: *Proc. Mathematics and Statistics of Complex Systems (MASCOS) One Day Symposium*, Brisbane, Australia, pp. 785–791, 2004.
48. Bilal, M. *et al.*, Differential evolution: A review of more than two decades of research. *Eng. Appl. Artif. Intell.*, 90, 103479, 2020, doi: 10.1016/j. engappai.2020.103479.
49. Ganesh, N. *et al.*, Efficient feature selection using weighted superposition attraction optimization algorithm. *Appl. Sci. MDPI*, 13, 5, 3223, 2023, doi: 10.3390/app13053223.
50. Panigrahi, B.K., Suganthan, P.N., Das, S., Dash, S.S., Swarm, evolutionary, and memetic computing. In *Proceedings of the Third International Conference SEMCCO*, pp. 16–18, Springer, Chennai, India, December 2010.
51. Alia, O.M. and Mandava, R., The variants of the harmony search algorithm: An overview. *Artif. Intell. Rev.*, 36, 1, 49–68, 2011, doi: 10.1007/s10462-010-9201-y.
52. Guo, Z. *et al.*, Adaptive harmony search with best-based search strategy. *Soft Comput.*, 22, 4, 1335–1349, 2018, doi: 10.1007/s00500-016-2424-3.
53. Yadav, P. *et al.*, An intelligent tuned harmony search algorithm for optimization. *Inf. Sci.*, 196, 47–72, 2012, doi: 10.1016/j.ins.2011.12.035.
54. Kaur, G. and Oberoi, A., Novel approach for brain tumor detection based on naïve bayes classification. In *Data Management, Analytics and Innovation*, pp. 451–462, Springer, Singapore, 2020.

55. Karaboga, D. and Basturk, B., A powerful and efficient algorithm for numerical function optimization: Artificial bee colony (ABC) algorithm. *J. Glob. Optim.*, 39, 3, 459–471, 2007, doi: 10.1007/s10898-007-9149-x.

56. Karaboga, D. and Ozturk, C., A novel clustering approach: Artificial bee colony (ABC) algorithm. *Appl. Soft Comput.*, 11, 1, 652–657, 2011, doi: 10.1016/j.asoc.2009.12.025.

57. Yang, X.-S. and He, X.-S., Why the firefly algorithm works?. *Nature-Inspired Algorithms and Applied Optimization*, pp. 245–259, Springer, 2018.

58. Yang, X.-S., Nature-inspired optimization algorithms: Challenges and open problems. *J. Comput. Sci.*, 46, 101104, 2020, doi: 10.1016/j.jocs.2020.101104.

59. Osaba, E. and Yang, X.S. (Eds.), Applied optimization and swarm intelligence, in: *Springer Tracts in Nature-Inspired Computing*, Springer, Singapore, 2021.

60. Mirjalili, S. *et al.*, Grey wolf optimizer. *Adv. Eng. Software*, Barking, London, England, 69, 46–61, 2014, doi: 10.1016/j.advengsoft.2013.12.007.

61. Faris, H. *et al.*, Grey wolf optimizer: A review of recent variants and applications. *Neural Comput. Appl.*, 30, 2, 413–435, 2018, doi: 10.1007/s00521-017-3272-5.

62. Rajendran, S. *et al.*, A conceptual comparison of six nature-inspired metaheuristic algorithms in process optimization. *Processes*, 10, 2, 197, 2022, doi: 10.3390/pr10020197.

63. Kalita, K. *et al.*, A hybrid TOPSIS-PR-GWO approach for multi-objective process parameter optimization. *Process Integr. Optim. Sustain.*, 6, 4, 1011–1026, 2022, doi: 10.1007/s41660-022-00256-0.

64. Kalita, K. *et al.*, Grey wolf optimizer-based design of ventilated brake disc. *J. Braz. Soc. Mech. Sci. Eng.*, 43, 8, 405, 2021, doi: 10.1007/s40430-021-03125-y.

65. Tu, Q. *et al.*, Hierarchy strengthened grey wolf optimizer for numerical optimization and feature selection. *IEEE Access Pract. Innov. Open Solut.*, 7, 78012–78028, 2019, doi: 10.1109/ACCESS.2019.2921793.

66. Hosseini, S. and Al Khaled, A., A survey on the imperialist competitive algorithm metaheuristic: Implementation in engineering domain and directions for future research. *Appl. Soft Comput.*, 24, 1078–1094, 2014, doi: 10.1016/j.asoc.2014.08.024.

67. Lucas, C. *et al.*, Application of an imperialist competitive algorithm to the design of a linear induction motor. *Energy Convers. Manage.*, 51, 7, 1407–1411, 2010, doi: 10.1016/j.enconman.2010.01.014.

68. Ebtehaj, I. and Bonakdari, H., Comparison of genetic algorithm and imperialist competitive algorithms in predicting bed load transport in clean pipe. *Water Sci. Technol.*, 70, 10, 1695–1701, 2014, doi: 10.2166/wst.2014.434.

69. Yang, X.-S., A new metaheuristic bat-inspired algorithm, in: *Studies in Computational Intelligence*. Nature Inspired Cooperative Strategies for

Optimization (NICSO 2010), pp. 65–74, 2010, doi:10.1007/978-3-642-12538-6_6.

70. Yang, X.-S. and Hossein Gandomi, A., Bat algorithm: A novel approach for global engineering optimization. *Eng. Comput.*, 29, 5, 464–483, 2012, doi: 10.1108/02644401211235834.

71. Mirjalili, S. *et al.*, Binary bat algorithm. *Neural Comput. Appl.*, 25, 3-4, 663–681, 2014, doi: 10.1007/s00521-013-1525-5.

72. Fister, I. *et al.*, Bat algorithm: Recent advances. Presented at the *2014 IEEE 15th International Symposium on Computational Intelligence and Informatics (CINTI)*, Budapest, vol. 2014, IEEE, 2014, Nov., doi: 10.1109/CINTI.2014.7028669.

73. Yaqoob, A. *et al.*, A review on nature-inspired algorithms for cancer disease prediction and classification. *Mathematics*, 11, 5, 1081, 2023, doi: 10.3390/math11051081.

74. Yang, X.-S. and Deb, S., Cuckoo search: Recent advances and applications. *Neural Comput. Appl.*, 24, 1, 169–174, 2014, doi: 10.1007/s00521-013-1367-1.

75. Gandomi, A.H. *et al.*, Cuckoo search algorithm: A metaheuristic approach to solve structural optimization problems. *Eng. Comput.*, 29, 1, 17–35, 2013, doi: 10.1007/s00366-011-0241-y.

76. Kalita, K. *et al.*, Optimizing frequencies of skew composite laminates with metaheuristic algorithms. *Eng. Comput.*, 36, 2, 741–761, 2020, doi: 10.1007/s00366-019-00728-x.

77. Kalita, K. *et al.*, A comparative study on the metaheuristic-based optimization of skew composite laminates. *Eng. Comput.* Springer, 38, 4, 3549–3566, 2022, doi: 10.1007/s00366-021-01401-y.

78. Valian, E. *et al.*, Improved cuckoo search for reliability optimization problems. *Comput. Ind. Eng.*, 64, 1, 459–468, 2013, doi: 10.1016/j.cie.2012.07.011.

79. Yang, X.-S., Flower pollination algorithm for global optimization, in: *Lecture Notes in Computer Science*. Unconventional Computation and Natural Computation, pp. 240–249, 2012, doi: 10.1007/978-3-642-32894-7_27.

80. Abdel-Basset, M. and Shawky, L.A., Flower pollination algorithm: A comprehensive review. *Artif. Intell. Rev.*, 52, 4, 2533–2557, 2019, doi: 10.1007/s10462-018-9624-4.

81. Yang, X.S. (Ed.), *Nature-Inspired Algorithms and Applied Optimization*, vol. 744, Springer, Berlin/Heidelberg, Germany, 2017.

82. Hossein, A. and Hossein, A., A new bio-inspired optimization algorithm. *Commun. Nonlinear Sci. Numer. Simul.*, 17, 12, 4831–4845, 2012, doi: 10.1016/j.cnsns.2012.05.010.

83. La, A., Al-betar, M.A., Awadallah, M.A., Tajudin, A., Mohammad, L., A comprehensive review: Krill Herd algorithm (KH) and its applications. *Appl. Soft Comput. J.*, 49, 437–446, 2016, doi: 10.1016/j.asoc.2016.08.041.

84. Abualigah, L.M.Q., *Feature selection and enhanced krill herd algorithm for text document clustering*, Springer, Berlin/Heidelberg, Germany, 2019.

85. Wang, G.-G. *et al.*, Hybrid krill herd algorithm with differential evolution for global numerical optimization. *Neural Comput. Appl.*, 25, 2, 297–308, 2014, doi: 10.1007/s00521-013-1485-9.

86. Mirjalili, S. and Lewis, A., The whale optimization algorithm. *Adv. Eng. Software Barking*, London, England, 95, 51–67, 2016, doi: 10.1016/j.advengsoft.2016.01.008.

87. Mohammed, H.M. *et al.*, A systematic and meta-analysis survey of whale optimization algorithm. *Comput. Intell. Neurosci.*, 2019, 8718571, 2019, doi: 10.1155/2019/8718571.

88. Rana, N. *et al.*, Whale optimization algorithm: A systematic review of contemporary applications, modifications and developments. *Neural Comput. Appl.*, 32, 20, 16245–16277, 2020, doi: 10.1007/s00521-020-04849-z.

89. Kalita, K. *et al.*, A comparative study on multi-objective pareto optimization of WEDM process using nature-inspired metaheuristic algorithms. *Int. J. Interact. Des. Manuf.*, 17, 2, 499–516, 2023, doi: 10.1007/s12008-022-01007-8.

90. Shanmugasundar, G. *et al.*, Optimization of variable stiffness joint in robot manipulator using a novel NSWOA-Marcos approach. *Processes*, 10, 6, 1074, 2022, doi: 10.3390/pr10061074.

91. Ab Wahab, M.N. *et al.*, A comprehensive review of swarm optimization algorithms. *PLoS One*, 10, 5, e0122827, 2015, doi: 10.1371/journal.pone.0122827.

92. Puttamadappa, and Parameshachari, Demand side management of small scale loads in a smart grid using glow-worm swarm optimization technique. *Microprocess. Microsyst.*, 71, 102886, 2019, doi: 10.1016/j.micpro.2019.102886.

93. Kalaiselvi, T. *et al.*, A review on glowworm swarm. *Optimization*, 3, 2, 49–56, 2017.

94. Tsai, P.-W. and Istanda, V., Review on cat swarm optimization algorithms. Presented at the 2013 *3rd International Conference on Consumer Electronics, Communications and Networks (CECNet)*, 2013, Nov., vol. 2013, Xianning, China, doi: 10.1109/CECNet.2013.6703394.

95. Ahmed, A.M. *et al.*, Cat swarm optimization algorithm – A survey and performance evaluation. *Comput. Intell. Neurosci.*, 2020, 4854895, 2020, doi: 10.1155/2020/4854895.

96. Darwish, A., Bio-inspired computing: Algorithms review, deep analysis, and the scope of applications. *Future Computing Inform. J.*, 3, 2, 231–246, 2018, doi: 10.1016/j.fcij.2018.06.001.

97. Saremi, S. *et al.*, Grasshopper optimisation algorithm: Theory and application, in: *Adv. Eng. Softw.*, vol. 105, pp. 30–47, Barking, London, England, 2017, doi: 10.1016/j.advengsoft.2017.01.004.

98. Pijarski, P. and Kacejko, P., A new metaheuristic optimization method: The algorithm of the innovative gunner (AIG). *Eng. Optim.*, 51, 12, 2049–2068, 2019, doi: 10.1080/0305215X.2019.1565282.

99. Joshi, M. *et al.*, A conceptual comparison of dragonfly algorithm variants for CEC-2021 global optimization problems. *Arab. J. Sci. Eng.*, 48, 2, 1563–1593, 2023, doi: 10.1007/s13369-022-06880-9.

100. Shehab, M. *et al.*, Moth–flame optimization algorithm: Variants and applications. *Neural Comput. Appl.*, 32, 14, 9859–9884, 2020, doi: 10.1007/s00521-019-04570-6.

101. Mirjalili, S., Moth-flame optimization algorithm: A novel nature-inspired heuristic paradigm. *Knowl. Based Syst.*, 89, 228–249, 2015, doi: 10.1016/j.knosys.2015.07.006.

102. Khurma, R.A. *et al.*, An enhanced evolutionary software defect prediction method using island moth flame optimization. *Mathematics*, 9, 15, 1722, 2021, doi: 10.3390/math9151722.

103. Narayanan, R.C. *et al.*, A novel many-objective sine cosine algorithm (MaOSCA) for engineering. *Appl. Math.*, 11, 10, 2301, 2023.

104. Priyadarshini, J. *et al.*, Analyzing physics-inspired metaheuristic algorithms in feature selection with K-nearest-neighbor. *Appl. Sci.*, 13, 2, 906, 2023, doi: 10.3390/app13020906.

105. Joshi, M. *et al.*, Comparison of NSGA-II, MOALO and MODA for multi-objective optimization of micro-machining processes. *Mater. (Basel)*, 14, 17, 5109, 2021, doi: 10.3390/ma14175109.

106. Kalita, K. *et al.*, A novel MOALO-MODA ensemble approach for multi-objective optimization of machining parameters for metal matrix composites. *Multiscale Multidiscip. Model. Exp. Des.*, 6, 1, 179–197, 2023, doi: 10.1007/s41939-022-00138-5.

107. Ganesh, N. *et al.*, Efficient feature selection using weighted superposition attraction optimization algorithm. *Appl. Sci.*, 13, 5, 3223, 2023, doi: 10.3390/app13053223.

108. Ganesh, N. *et al.*, A novel decomposition-based multi-objective symbiotic organism search optimization algorithm. *Mathematics*, 11, 8, 1898, 2023, doi: 10.3390/math11081898.

109. Hu, G. *et al.*, An enhanced hybrid arithmetic optimization algorithm for engineering applications. *Comput. Methods Appl. Mech. Eng.*, 394, 114901), 2022, doi: 10.1016/j.cma.2022.114901.

110. Ghafil, H.N. and Jármai, K., Dynamic differential annealed optimization: New metaheuristic optimization algorithm for engineering applications. *Appl. Soft Comput.*, 93, 106392, 2020, doi: 10.1016/j.asoc.2020.106392.

111. Zhao, S. *et al.*, Dandelion optimizer: A nature-inspired metaheuristic algorithm for engineering applications. *Eng. Appl. Artif. Intell.*, 114, 105075, 2022, doi: 10.1016/j.engappai.2022.105075.
112. Sattar, D. and Salim, R., A smart metaheuristic algorithm for solving engineering problems. *Eng. Comput.*, 37, 3, 2389–2417, 2021, doi: 10.1007/s00366-020-00951-x.
113. Azizi, M. *et al.*, Fire hawk optimizer: A novel metaheuristic algorithm. *Artif. Intell. Rev.*, 56, 1, 287–363, 2023, doi: 10.1007/s10462-022-10173-w.
114. Ansari, A. *et al.*, A hybrid metaheuristic method in training artificial neural network for bankruptcy prediction. *IEEE Access*, 8, 176640–176650, 2020, doi: 10.1109/ACCESS.2020.3026529.
115. Chobar, A.P. *et al.*, Multi-objective hub-spoke network design of perishable tourism products using combination machine learning and meta-heuristic algorithms. *Environ. Dev. Sustain.*, 1–28, 2022, doi: 10.1007/s10668-022-02350-2.
116. Ghasemian, H. *et al.*, Human urbanization algorithm: A novel meta-heuristic approach. *Math. Comput. Simul.*, 178, 1–15, 2020, doi: 10.1016/j.matcom.2020.05.023.
117. Gholizadeh, H. *et al.*, Fuzzy data-driven scenario-based robust data envelopment analysis for prediction and optimisation of an electrical discharge machine's parameters. *Expert Syst. Appl.*, 193, 116419, 2022, doi: 10.1016/j.eswa.2021.116419.
118. Gibson, S. *et al.*, Detecting spam email with machine learning optimized with bio-inspired metaheuristic algorithms. *IEEE Access*, 8, 187914–187932, 2020, doi: 10.1109/ACCESS.2020.3030751.
119. Peng, B., Digital leadership: State governance in the era of digital technology. *Cult. Sci.*, 5, 4, 210–225, 2022, doi: 10.1177/2096608321989835.
120. Shahvaroughi Farahani, M. and Razavi Hajiagha, S.H., Forecasting stock price using integrated artificial neural network and metaheuristic algorithms compared to time series models. *Soft Comput.*, 25, 13, 8483–8513, 2021, doi: 10.1007/s00500-021-05775-5.
121. Yan, T. *et al.*, A hybrid metaheuristic algorithm for the multi-objective location-routing problem in the early post-disaster stage. *J. Ind. Manage. Optim.*, 19, 6, 4663–4691, 2023, doi: 10.3934/jimo.2022145.
122. Bindu, G.B. *et al.*, Optimized resource scheduling using the meta heuristic algorithm in cloud computing. *IAENG Int. J. Comput. Sci.*, 47, 3, 360–366, 2020.
123. Gharehchopogh, F.S., Quantum-inspired metaheuristic algorithms: Comprehensive survey and classification. *Artif. Intell. Rev.*, 56, 6, 5479–5543, 2023, doi: 10.1007/s10462-022-10280-8.

124. Oyelade, O.N. *et al.*, Ebola optimization search algorithm: A new nature-inspired metaheuristic optimization algorithm. *IEEE Access*, 10, 16150–16177, 2022, doi: 10.1109/ACCESS.2022.3147821.
125. Geem, Z.W. (Ed.), *Music-Inspired Harmony Search Algorithm: Theory and Applications*, vol. 191, Springer, Berlin/Heidelberg, Germany, 2009.

# A Comprehensive Review of Metaheuristics for Hyperparameter Optimization in Machine Learning

**Ramachandran Narayanan[1]\* and Narayanan Ganesh[2]**

[1]*Department of Computer Science and Engineering, Sona College of Technology,*
*Salem, India*
[2]*School of Computer Science & Engineering, Vellore Institute of Technology,*
*Chennai, India*

## Abstract

Hyperparameter optimization is a critical step in the development and fine-tuning of machine learning (ML) models. Metaheuristic optimization techniques have gained significant popularity for addressing this challenge due to their ability to search the hyperparameter space efficiently. In this review, we present a detailed analysis of various metaheuristic techniques for hyperparameter optimization in ML, encompassing population-based, single solution-based, and hybrid approaches. We explore the application of metaheuristics in Bayesian optimization and neural architecture search, two prominent areas within the field. Moreover, we provide a comparative analysis of these techniques based on established criteria and evaluate their performance in diverse ML applications. Finally, we discuss future directions and open challenges with special emphasis on the opportunities for improvement in metaheuristics. Other crucial issues like adaptability to new ML paradigms, computational complexity, and scalability issues are also discussed critically. This review aims to provide researchers and practitioners with a comprehensive understanding of the state-of-the-art metaheuristic optimization techniques for hyperparameter tuning, thereby facilitating informed decisions and advancements in the field.

*Keywords*: Metaheuristics, hyperparameter tuning, machine learning, population-based techniques, hybrid techniques

*\*Corresponding author*: narayananrc@sonatech.ac.in

Kanak Kalita, Narayanan Ganesh and S. Balamurugan (eds.) Metaheuristics for Machine Learning: Algorithms and Applications, (37–72) © 2024 Scrivener Publishing LLC

## 2.1   Introduction

Hyperparameter optimization (HPO) is an integral aspect of machine learning (ML) advancements—the idea of which revolves around finding the optimum values of parameters that are externally set by the user or the model and are not learned by the machine learning model during the training phase [1]. These are called hyperparameters, and they hold great power in determining the performance of the ML model that has been designed to solve a complex problem at hand. The optimization is not an easy job itself and faces critical challenges due to the large data space that needs to be sorted and simplified and the inherent nonlinear constraints. Metaheuristic algorithms that can provide effective routes for fast and decisive HPO serve as an enabling beacon of light for this task. This paper provides a consolidated and detailed review of these algorithms and techniques and provides a complete insight into the approaches that govern the systematic routes to reach the desired optimization while expanding on the scope and potential of the growing applications of metaheuristics.

### 2.1.1   Background and Motivation

Hyperparameter optimization (HPO) is rapidly becoming a trending global force in the machine learning (ML) development community, and harnessing its power using metaheuristic algorithms is becoming a new priority at the industrial level. This prominent change in R&D methods for obtaining more efficient solutions in much lesser time by minimizing iterations conducted for complex optimization problems demands effective metaheuristic integration for higher yields. The detail and scale of data and data structures follow an ever-increasing profile, and to support the growing race of enormous bit streams in every system, intelligent models need to be developed to select optimized parameters to save on computation time. Hutter *et al.* [2] have highlighted this potential area for growth, and the paper describes various metaheuristic algorithms and approaches for enabling automated machine learning. Developed on similar grounds, this comprehensive review aims to provide in-depth insight into the state-of-the-art metaheuristic optimization algorithms for HPO in ML to facilitate R&D efforts and accelerate the growth of this newly strengthening phenomenon.

### 2.1.2   Scope of the Review

This review encompasses a discussion of a wide range of metaheuristic optimization algorithms that can be used directly or as building blocks to enable

HPO. These include the broad categories of the genetic algorithms (GAs), particle swarm optimization (PSO), differential evolution (DE), animal colony and group behavior-based models, tabu search (TS), harmony search (HS), simulated annealing (SA), etc. The paper not only mentions the types of the algorithms but comments on their pros and cons, conducts a comparative analysis with other types, discusses their efficacy and efficiency in relation to real-life scenario applications, and gauges their performance using various parameters when integrated for HPO roles. This is brought together by sifting through a vast compilation of research journals to form the literature basis, such as this comparative analysis for approaches like the grid search, manual search, and random search cited in Bergstra and Bengio [3]. This review also offers guidelines for choosing the best-suited metaheuristic algorithm depending on the demand of the application and offers insight into general standard practices for dealing with complex HPO problems.

### 2.1.3 Organization of the Paper

This paper has been intelligently divided into 12 sections, each highlighting a core concept or application set in the field of HPO or associated topics. Section 2.1 is the overall introduction to the paper, its background and motivation, the scope of the review, and the organizational structure of the contents. Section 2.2 discusses the fundamentals of HPO, while section 2.3 dives into an overview of various metaheuristic optimization techniques. Sections 2.4, 2.5, and 2.6 explore the subcategories of the techniques further, taking on population-based, single solution-based, and hybrid metaheuristic techniques. Sections 2.7 and 2.8 are focused on applying metaheuristic applications in Bayesian optimization and neural architecture search. Section 2.9 compares different techniques that are employed at the broader industrial level using factors such as applications and performance characteristics. Section 2.10 discusses the applications that are brought about by the integration of metaheuristics into machine learning models, and section 2.11 discusses future prospects and possible fields that hold great potential in embracing metaheuristics and HPO while addressing challenges and threats posed to the expansion of ML. Section 2.12 rounds off the review with a consolidated conclusion to comment on the paper and to bridge any gaps in ideas for future research and development.

## 2.2 Fundamentals of Hyperparameter Optimization

HPO can be considered to be the most fundamental step in designing an efficient methodology for forming a smart and complete ML algorithm.

Neglecting to optimize hyperparameters tends to increase the overall runs needed in the learning phase, causes persistent inaccuracies and errors to remain stagnant in the code, plagues the speed of the program, and consumes resources that hold the potential to handle more data and efficiently process other commands. HPO is a sensitive and tedious task, with the challenges mainly originating from the nature of the datasets, including the vast high-dimensional search space and the non-linear constraints in the system. Section 2.2 provides an overview of hyperparameters, their importance, insight into the performance metrics used for HPO, and the challenges associated with HPO.

### 2.2.1   Introduction to Hyperparameters

Hyperparameters differ from ordinary input variables or parameters in the way they are addressed to the ML model system. While a regular parameter set is inherent to the data available to the ML model and is learned during the execution of the training phase, hyperparameters are selected by the user or by the governing algorithm. Hyperparameters form the basis for HPO and can control the overall behavior of the algorithm model, its convergence rate and performance, and the ability for generalization. Popular examples of hyperparameters that are frequently employed in applications include the rate of machine learning, the batch size, the number of hidden layers and sub-layers, and the number of neurons in the sub-layers.

### 2.2.2   Importance of Hyperparameter Optimization

HPO is a critical need in today's world of smart and automated process optimization and technological process or system design. Traditionally, HPO was conducted by humans—with all of the cumbersome calculations being done by hand [4]. As demonstrated by the authors of Bergstra *et al.* [5], modern CPU clusters and GPU modules can be programmed using various algorithm-based approaches, i.e., using random search and greedy sequential methods to automate HPO, yielding remarkable results even for complicated systems such as neural networks and deep belief networks (DBNs) [6, 7]. Optimizing hyperparameters can directly reflect a great increase in enhancing the performance, capability, and utility of such ML models [8]. Additionally, it can reduce the model training time, boost convergence accuracy, and help impart better generalization ability. These improvements can lower the rate and magnitude of the inherent error that is output by the model and can also increase performance metric statistics such as F1 scores [9].

### 2.2.3    Performance Metrics for Hyperparameter Optimization

Performance metrics are indicator statistics that are employed to evaluate the performance, effectiveness, and efficiency of various hyperparameter settings in the HPO process. A few metrics that are frequently used in correlation to HPO include accuracy, precision, F1 score, recall, and area under the receiver operating characteristic curve (AUC-ROC). These metrics also form the basis to assess the ability of a model to generalize unseen data. While conventional user-dependent HPO approaches had their performance slumps, modern research efforts have yielded fruitful results in boosting the overall effectiveness, accuracy, and convergence rate of the process [10]. Thornton *et al.* [11] have employed a fully automated Bayesian optimization approach for boosting the performance of HPO in simultaneously selecting the learning algorithm and associated hyperparameters. This was enabled by taking into account various feature selection techniques (a combination of three search and eight evaluator methods) and WEKA-implemented classification approaches with two ensemble methods, 10 meta-methods, 27 base classifiers, and individual hyperparameter settings for each classifier. Snoek *et al.* [12] have researched gaining higher tunability performance for HPO by varying the nature of a Gaussian process, the type of kernel, and the treatment of hyperparameters. This was enabled by integrating Bayesian optimization techniques.

### 2.2.4    Challenges in Hyperparameter Optimization

HPO is a newly developing methodology and faces new and unique challenges at present, including the increasingly accumulating dimensions of the search space data, the huge periods required for intensive computations, and the cost of the needed hardware to perform well. Domhan *et al.* [13] have worked to resolve the issue of poor HPO algorithm performance and delayed run termination on large and complex datasets with the help of learning curve extrapolation via probabilistic models. Additionally, the challenge to tune hyperparameter sets is an emerging issue that has proven to be slightly technical to be dealt with. Probst *et al.* [14] have researched the latter and have evaluated the problem of tuning from a statistical standpoint. In addition, the paper acts as a guide for quantifying the tunability of hyperparameters for HPO. The existence of several local optima also adds to the difficulty of finding an optimal solution, and this is a direct consequence of the non-convexity of the objective function.

## 2.3   Overview of Metaheuristic Optimization Techniques

Metaheuristic algorithm-based optimization techniques have gained popularity in recent years in the ML development industry—being an effective approach for solving evolving complex problems, with the list including HPO. Section 2.3 dives deeper into the world of metaheuristics to form a basis of the fundamental concepts needed to grasp its definition, characteristics, and classification.

### 2.3.1   Definition and Characteristics of Metaheuristics

Metaheuristics are problem-solving techniques or procedures that provide a flexible approach to solving optimization problems. Their superiority over the regular class of heuristic algorithms is apparent by the prefix added up front in the word itself as explained by Gandomi *et al.* [15] who define the term "meta" as "beyond or higher level." These algorithms are robust in nature, are easy to implement into existing pieces of code, and can be applied to a wide range of optimization problems, including HPO. They are algorithms that explore the given search space in incremental steps and guide the search based on a heuristic criterion to find a good solution—the convergence quality of which is often defined by the user.

They are characterized by their ability to escape local optima during the search phase and by their adaptability in handling complex and dynamic optimization problems. Gendreau *et al.* [16] have extensively researched the field of metaheuristics to compile their review paper and have keenly highlighted important concepts and properties of the algorithms. These include the ideas of intensification and diversification. Intensification is the act of concentrating the search on areas that are likely to contain good solutions, while diversification involves exploring different areas of the search space to prevent getting trapped in suboptimal solutions. Researchers working on metaheuristics use these two strategies together to find better-quality solutions more efficiently.

### 2.3.2   Classification of Metaheuristic Techniques

Metaheuristic techniques are generally inspired by forces of nature, animal social behavior, and other observable phenomena that might be natural, artificial, or digital and might exist at the macro or micro scale.

For simplicity, metaheuristics can be categorized into three broad types, i.e., population-based, single solution-based, and hybrid metaheuristics.

Population-based metaheuristics iteratively improve a population of solutions for optimization. These are built upon the principles of natural selection and the survival of the fittest. Popular examples of population-based metaheuristics include the genetic algorithms, differential evolution, and particle swarm optimization.

Single solution-based metaheuristics focus on improving a single solution by iteratively exploring its neighborhood as opposed to a population solution set. These techniques are particularly useful when convergence to a sole solution is required and the state is proving to be difficult to obtain under regular conditions. Examples of single solution-based metaheuristics include simulated annealing, tabu search, harmony search, and bat algorithm (BA).

Hybrid metaheuristics are the pinnacle of modern developments in the world of metaheuristics. These techniques are based on the combination of two or more metaheuristics to harvest synergized benefits. This results in improved inclusivity, performance, and accuracy when compared to the characteristics of a single-parent term involved. For example, the ant colony optimization (ACO) can be combined with a local search-based algorithm to improve the quality of the solutions obtained.

Presenting another classification perspective, Abdel-Basset et al. [17] employ two major classification methods for segregating metaheuristics. The first divides them into metaphor-based and non-metaphor-based metaheuristics, and the second method divides them into the lines of improved, adaptive, and hybridized metaheuristics.

The range and versatility of metaheuristics cannot be defined, since new forms are continuously being developed and rolled out around the clock. It is important to note that no metaheuristic technique can be considered universal, and the real challenge in today's world is finding the right algorithm and the right proportions to get things done.

## 2.4  Population-Based Metaheuristic Techniques

Section 2.4 of this paper focuses on population-based metaheuristic techniques that are the foremost picks for HPO applications, including the go-to options and new innovative emerging methods. While each of them is unique in its own sense, these algorithms explore a set of candidate solutions called a population and gradually improve the solutions in each run by iteratively applying selection, crossover, mutation, and other operators. A few important population-based metaheuristics are discussed below.

## 2.4.1   Genetic Algorithms

The genetic algorithms are robust metaheuristics based on the principles of natural selection, evolution, and genetics [18–20]. These algorithms use a population of candidate solutions that evolve and refine over time to form generations, and this is achieved through selection, crossover, and mutation operations [21, 22]. To demonstrate the versatility of the GA under the most unique applications, Di Francescomarino *et al.* [23] have developed a predictive process monitoring framework integrated with the GA to forecast the performance of ongoing businesses, basing the study on traces of past successes [24, 25].

## 2.4.2   Particle Swarm Optimization

The particle swarm optimization simulates the behavior of social animals such as birds and fish that move and huddle in swarms or groups [26] in order to find the best-fitting solution for the given scenario [27, 28]. The PSO maintains a population of particles in focus and observes their movements and mutual interactions as they move through the search space to yield results [29–32]. The PSO has been shown to be effective in HPO for various machine learning algorithms as revealed by Lorenzo *et al.* [33] in the research paper who successfully obtained a high classification accuracy for the case of CIFAR-10 machine vision datasets, an integral part of a deep neural network (DNN) study.

## 2.4.3   Differential Evolution

The differential evolution is an optimization technique that uses a population of candidate solutions and differential operators to explore the search space. Just like the rest, the DE updates the population of solutions iteratively to improve the accuracy of the results until the satisfactory convergence criterion is reached. The DE has proven its utility under the toughest scenarios, such as in the case mentioned by Zulfiqar *et al.* [34] who have employed an adaptive differential evolution (ADE) algorithm with a support vector machine (SVM) to estimate the demand capacity of an electrical distribution grid system. Combined with a multivariate empirical modal decomposition (MEMD) algorithm, the MEMD-ADE-SVM forecasting model delivered a high accuracy of 93.145% and offered great stability and a faster convergence rate than conventional approaches.

### 2.4.4 Ant Colony Optimization

The ant colony optimization is a population-based metaheuristic technique inspired by the foraging behavior of ants that swarm the search space and choose a hyperparameter set. Each generation of these digital ants deposits pheromones to guide existing and subsequent ants toward high-potential holding areas, guiding the search effectively and speeding up the optimization process. Lohvithee *et al.* [35] integrated the ACO for optimizing X-ray computed tomography (XCT) reconstruction and found the algorithm to have over 10 times faster convergence than regular cross-validation methods.

### 2.4.5 Biogeography-Based Optimization

The biogeography-based optimization (BBO) is based on mathematical equations that explain the geographical distribution of organisms, and the same analogy is applied to dataset populations for hunting optimal solutions. In this technique, the search space is represented as a set of islands, and the immigration and emigration rates between the islands are used to update the candidate solutions. Simon [36] have validated the accuracy of the BBO on a set of 14 standard benchmarks and have demonstrated its performance in comparison with seven popular biology-based optimization algorithms such as the GA and PSO.

### 2.4.6 Cuckoo Search

The cuckoo search (CS) is an emerging metaheuristic technique inspired by the natural brood parasitic behavior of cuckoo birds [37]. The technique is based on generating a population of candidate solutions through a combination of random walk and Lévy flight methodology for exploring the search space [38, 39]. Yang and Deb [40] have successfully validated the newly developed technique against test function checks and found it superior to existing genetic and PSO algorithms for multimodal objective functions.

### 2.4.7 Gray Wolf Optimizer

The gray wolf optimizer (GWO) is a metaheuristic technique inspired by the hunting behavior of gray wolves. Replicating the territorial behavior of wolves, the technique divides the search space into territories, and a social hierarchy of four types of gray wolves (i.e., alpha, beta, delta, and omega) is used to update the population of candidate solutions. This is done in accordance with the hunting behavior of the animals who hunt in packs [41, 42]. According to Mirjalili *et al.* [43], the metaheuristic holds the capability of simulating three main steps of hunting: searching for prey, encircling the prey, and attacking the prey. The authors have also benchmarked on 29 renowned test functions and found the GWO to match mainstream metaheuristics such as the PSO and DE in terms of result characteristics [44, 45].

### 2.4.8 Whale Optimization Algorithm

The whale optimization algorithm (WOA) is an emerging metaheuristic technique that is based on employing three operators for emulating the hunting behavior of humpback whales including the search for prey, encircling the prey, and bubble-net foraging. The methodology involves generating a population of candidate solutions that is updated using three types of whales (i.e., leader, challenger, and follower) to explore the search space for best-fitting points [46]. Ashraf *et al.* [47] have overcome the intense challenge of conducting HPO for a deep deterministic policy gradient (DDPG) algorithm used to regulate autonomous driving control, obtaining maximized total rewards and maintaining a stable driving policy.

### 2.4.9 Recent Developments in Population-Based Metaheuristics

Population-based metaheuristics seem to have been saturated for single-objective optimization (SOO) owing to the consistent research efforts being made in the field in recent decades. Modern research developments have focused on the use of hybrid techniques, multi-objective optimization (MOO), and parallel computing to improve the performance of these techniques further [48]. As established earlier, hybrid techniques involve combining two or more metaheuristics to boost HPO performance and convergence rate. MOO differs from SOO in terms of setting goals and involves optimizing multiple objectives simultaneously. The quality and success of such developments can be seen in an example of a swarm intelligence-based artificial bee colony (ABC) metaheuristic algorithm. Karaboga and Basturk [49] have researched to demonstrate the use of ABC for optimizing multi-variable functions to yield promising results that outperformed the GA and PSO. Parallel computing involves using multiple processors to speed up the optimization process [50].

## 2.5   Single Solution-Based Metaheuristic Techniques

Section 2.5 discusses the strategy of single solution-based metaheuristics that aim to optimize a unitary solution instead of refining a whole population of candidates. These techniques are often chosen by coders when the solution space under evaluation is continuous, and there is no need for multiple solutions to exist in order to refine the quality of the resulting solution.

### 2.5.1   Simulated Annealing

Simulated annealing is a technique inspired by the physical process of annealing in metallurgy where a material (most often a metal) is heated and slowly allowed to cool to reach a low-energy state. Similarly, SA minimizes an objective function by gradually decreasing toward a global minimum in refining steps. As explained by the authors of [16], it accepts worse solutions in hill-climbing moves with a certain probability to escape local optima and decreases this probability over time—this being the inherent minimization property of the SA technique. SA is indeed a powerful tool to use, and this statement can be backed by the work of Kirkpatrick *et al.* [51] who solved the traveling salesman problem, a challenge that belongs to a set of nondeterministic polynomial time complete problem family, using SA.

### 2.5.2   Tabu Search

The tabu search is a local search-based technique that overcomes the inherent weakness of local search methods where the algorithm gets trapped between local optima. The TS does this by using what is called a tabu list, storing a directory of recently explored solutions in order to avoid revisiting them in the following iterations. It explores the neighborhood of the current solution and selects the best one that is not on the tabu list. It can escape local optima by allowing moves that worsen the objective function. Glover [52] have presented an in-depth review of the TS and exhibit the hill-climbing behavior of the TS in Figure 2.1 where multiple local optima can be seen and at times the cost did worsen in search for the next minima.

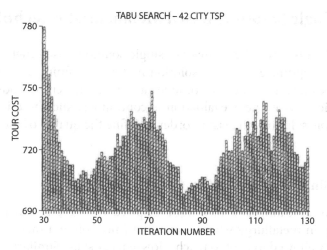

Figure 2.1 Tabu search for optimizing the tour cost for a city plotted vs. iterations [52].

### 2.5.3  Harmony Search

The harmony search is an emerging metaheuristic technique that is based on the music industry, simulating the improvisation process conducted by musicians to improve soundtracks. It generates a set of random solutions called harmony and improves them by iteratively selecting the best elements from other harmonies. Like the TS and other developed techniques, the HS can escape local optima by hill-climbing. Geem *et al.* [53] have reflected on the choice of the HS for HPO and solved the traveling salesman problem with great results using the HS.

### 2.5.4  Bat Algorithm

The bat algorithm (BA) is a newly developed metaheuristic generated by Yang [54]. It is inspired by the echolocation technique employed by bats to locate prey in the dark and works by generating a set of solutions that it then moves toward the best solution found so far. Keeping the hunt on, it introduces random walks to explore new regions of the solution space. The inventors have found it superior to the GA and PSO and intend on developing hybridized variants based on the BA.

### 2.5.5  Recent Developments in Single Solution-Based Metaheuristics

Single solution-based metaheuristics have been developed for improved local search performance in recent times, integrating the use of machine learning to escape local minima entrapment as proposed by Jaddi and Abdullah [55]. Additionally, the ever-continuing hybridization research efforts have borne fruit in improving single solution-based techniques in terms of accuracy and efficiency. These have led to various combinations, and the room for creativity seems to be endless. An example would be a hybridized synthesis of SA with the TS for improved exploration capability.

## 2.6  Hybrid Metaheuristic Techniques

Hybrid metaheuristic techniques have been briefly discussed earlier in this paper several times, all due to their strong presence and keen influence in today's metaheuristic approaches. Building a stronger foundation on the concept, these techniques can be formally introduced as an approach that combines two or more metaheuristic algorithms to synergize the strengths of each algorithm and overcome their weaknesses. It is important to note that while it is desired that the pair would be able to sufficiently bridge the gaps inherent to the individual components, it is not necessary to reach a perfect combination, and this requires trial and error between the choice of algorithms and in the degree of fractional composition. This section provides an overview of three commonly used hybrid metaheuristic techniques, i.e., GA-PSO, GA-SA, and PSO-TS hybrids.

### 2.6.1  Genetic Algorithm and Particle Swarm Optimization Hybrid

One of the most widely used hybrid metaheuristic techniques is the genetic algorithm and particle swarm optimization (GA-PSO) hybrid, combining the most fundamental algorithms to produce a robust and powerful output. Jeong *et al.* [56] aimed to improve the diversity of the GA and the convergence rate of the PSO with this combination. The GA-PSO hybrid technique was applied to two test functions, and after proper tuning, it was found that the search performance was raised by a satisfactory level. It is important to note that the GA-PSO hybrid has raised its status to hold popular applications in solving optimization problems for engineering design, scheduling, and image processing.

### 2.6.2  Genetic Algorithm and Simulated Annealing Hybrid

Another popular hybrid technique is the genetic algorithm and simulated annealing (GA-SA) hybrid. The GA-SA hybrid has been successfully applied to various optimization problems, including the traveling salesman problem, machine learning, and wireless sensor networks. Sanagooy Aghdam *et al.* [57] solved the challenge of optimized asset tracking that was to be done using radio frequency identification (RFID) systems. Using the pros of the GA, a multi-objective function was developed for maximizing the network coverage of the antennas, and using the pros of SA, the hyperparameters of the total cost, rate of tag reader collision, interference, and total energy consumption of the RFID antennas were minimized. The GA-SA hybrid metaheuristic allowed for savings (on average) in the total cost, making use of three types of readers with one, two, and four antenna ports in the most efficient way.

### 2.6.3 Tabu Search and Particle Swarm Optimization Hybrid

The tabu search and particle swarm optimization (TS-PSO) hybrid is another effective hybrid technique that combines the global search capabilities of the PSO with the local search capabilities of the TS. The TS-PSO hybrid has found great applicability to various optimization problems, including feature selection, image segmentation, and clustering. Zhang and Wu [58] conducted experiments on four test functions including Easom, Rosenbrock, Hump, and Rastrigin to validate the TS-PSO combination for increasing the probability of finding the optimal minima in the search space. It was discovered that the TS-PSO hybrid had higher performance than conventional standalone integrations of the GA, TS, and PSO for the same task.

### 2.6.4 Recent Developments in Hybrid Metaheuristics

The concept of hybridization itself is the ultimate direction of growth and development that has been selected for all preceding metaheuristics discussed above [59]. However, this did not rule out progress in the field of hybrid metaheuristics, and they have rapidly improved both vertically in detail and complexity and laterally in inclusivity. De *et al.* [60] have worked tirelessly to compile recent advances in hybrid metaheuristics, with the most notable research being conducted on developing hybrid algorithms for complex data clustering to raise computational intelligence.

## 2.7 Metaheuristics in Bayesian Optimization

Metaheuristics are gaining an increasing role in Bayesian optimization applications for solving complex optimization problems, including HPO.

Section 2.7 focuses to deliver insight into the fundamentals of Bayesian optimization and related concepts such as Gaussian process regression and acquisition functions. Lastly, recent developments in metaheuristic-based Bayesian optimization are discussed to provide a complete overview.

### 2.7.1   Background of Bayesian Optimization

Bayesian optimization is a search-guiding approach based on statistical methods for global optimization. It is the top choice for evaluating the objective function when it is complicated, non-differentiable, discontinuous, or time-consuming. The approach involves constructing a probabilistic model of the objective function and using it to make decisions about where to sample next, and this is done until the solution has been adequately refined. Bayesian optimization has proven to be highly resourceful for optimizing design choices. Shahriari *et al.* [61] have researched the technique at an industrial level and have analyzed the benefits that Bayesian optimization can produce in big data applications. They found it to provide a greater automation potential that has boosted both product quality and human productivity.

### 2.7.2   Gaussian Process Regression

Gaussian process regression is a statistical modeling technique that is often used in the Bayesian optimization to model the objective function. It involves constructing a Gaussian process (GP), which is a probabilistic model that can be used to make predictions about the function values at newly established input points. The model's predictions are not as accurate and require gauging for the level of confidence—marked by estimates. Being a versatile tool, GPs can be used to model both linear and nonlinear relationships between the input parameters and the corresponding output variables. The shape and behavior of the GP are governed by the estimated hyperparameters that were used to train the model [62, 63].

### 2.7.3   Acquisition Functions

Acquisition functions are used in Bayesian optimization as a tool to guide the decision process for locating regions for the next sampling. These functions incorporate a balance between exploration (the idea of sampling in regions where the function has high uncertainty) and exploitation (the idea of sampling in regions where the function is likely to be optimal and have

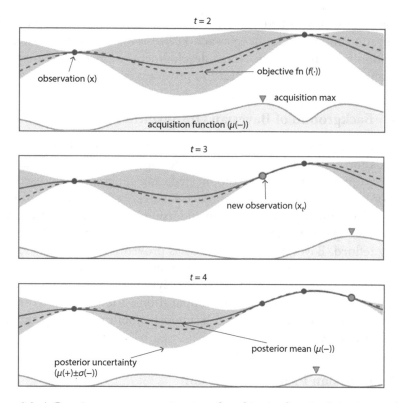

**Figure 2.2** A Gaussian process approximation of an objective function being iteratively refined over iterations. The green shaded region shows the acquisition function [64].

local maxima or minima). This can be seen in Figure 2.2 where the acquisition function is high in regions of high exploration and exploitation.

Common acquisition functions used in the Bayesian optimization technique include expected improvement (EI), probability of improvement (PI), Thompson sampling (TS), knowledge gradient (KG), and upper confidence bound (UCB).

### 2.7.4   Recent Developments in Metaheuristic-Based Bayesian Optimization

Recent developments in Bayesian optimization include the use of metaheuristics to optimize the acquisition function parameters and the development of efficient parallel algorithms. Many attempts have been made to enhance the effectiveness and broaden the scope of Bayesian optimization. It is important to note that GPs involved in Bayesian optimization tend to scale cubically with the number of observations, and this does create challenges in handling the objectives when several evaluations are needed per objective. Snoek *et al.* [65] have solved this parallelizing issue using linearly scaling deep neural networks as a competitive alternative to GP. Additionally, Brochu *et al.* [64] have researched to propose two developed extensions of Bayesian optimization: active user modeling with preferences and hierarchical reinforcement learning for improving the performance, inclusivity, and degree of control.

## 2.8   Metaheuristics in Neural Architecture Search

Neural architecture search (NAS) is a rapidly growing field that deals with finding the optimal architecture for neural networks. At present, the majority of neural architectures are created through manual development by human experts, which is prone to errors and can be a time-consuming process. Consequently, there is a growing demand for automated methods of neural architecture search, and metaheuristic algorithms have gained global attention due to their ability to efficiently explore a large search space and find optimal solutions. Section 2.8 aims to provide an introduction to NAS, highlight key applications of metaheuristics in NAS, and the recent developments in this emerging field.

### 2.8.1   Introduction to Neural Architecture Search

Neural architecture search is a technique used to automate machine learning and the search tasks for hunting optimal architectures of a neural network. NAS involves sifting through a large space of candidate architectures to search for the optimal element in the array that would give out the best performance for the given task at hand. Owing to the complexity of modern systems and the large bandwidth requirements, the search space can be very large, making the process computationally expensive and very exhaustive in terms of time and resources. Developments in metaheuristic algorithms have allowed efficient searches in the space to locate optima in the field of possible architectures.

### 2.8.2   Applications of Metaheuristics in Neural Architecture Search

Metaheuristic algorithms have been successfully applied in many NAS studies to find optimal neural network architectures. Some of the popular metaheuristic algorithms used in NAS include the GA, PSO, SA, and TS. Convolutional neural networks (CNNs), deep neural networks, and recurrent neural networks are examples of popular neural architectures that have been found to be highly compatible with metaheuristic integration for automating the search process for the ideal design. The authors of [66] have applied the GA on CIFAR10 to demonstrate the ability to search for network architectures via a small dataset experiment. The proposed solution allowed the GA to automatically learn the structure of deep convolutional neural networks [67]. The authors of [68] have found NAS methods to have outperformed manually designed architectures in areas of image classification, object detection, or semantic segmentation.

### 2.8.3    Recent Developments in Metaheuristic-Based Neural Architecture Search

Recent research has focused on improving the efficiency and accuracy of NAS with metaheuristic algorithms. One approach is to use a neural architecture search space that is more compact, allowing for a more efficient search. Additionally, there have been considerable research efforts on hybrid metaheuristic algorithms in recent times—aimed at combining the strengths of multiple metaheuristics to achieve better performance in NAS. Atop of the usual approaches, the authors of [69] have developed the GA-based NeuroEvolution of Augmenting Topologies (NEAT) that boasts increased efficiency over the current best fixed-topology methods for reinforcement learning tasks [70]. The major increase in performance efficiency can be attributed to employing a principled method of crossover of different topologies using speciation for protecting structural innovation and growing from minimal structures incrementally. The authors of [71] have introduced a novel algorithm called DARTS (Differentiable ARchiTecture Search) that is based on bilevel optimization, designed to take on the scalability challenge encountered by conventional architecture search methods. Instead of applying evolution or reinforcement learning over a discrete and non-differentiable search space, DARTS allows for continuous relaxation of the architecture representation to enable the use of gradient descent. The algorithm has proven itself on several leading benchmarks, yielding competitive results on CIFAR-10 and excelling in performance on PTB dataset (it is the name of a dataset, PTB stands for Physikalisch-Technische Bundesanstalt (PTB)). The algorithm has increased the overall efficiency of the architecture search process and has reduced the exploration time to a few GPU days only. Keeping with the boosted interest of researchers in the field of NAS in recent times, the continued exploration and advancement of metaheuristic algorithms in NAS hold great promise for the future.

## 2.9 Comparison of Metaheuristic Techniques for Hyperparameter Optimization

Countless metaheuristic techniques have been widely used for HPO in the defined context, but there has been no definition made so far to provide an insight into how each ranks in comparison and which algorithm is to be selected for a given problem. Therefore, there is a prominent need to evaluate and compare these techniques to determine the most effective ones, providing both a generalist view and a specific view under different cases. This section hence focuses on the comparison of the abovementioned metaheuristic techniques for HPO.

### 2.9.1   Criteria for Comparison

To perform a fair and objective comparison of metaheuristic techniques for HPO, it is essential to establish agreed-upon criteria for comparison that follows the defined objectives and scope of the desired application in which the metaheuristic will be implemented. These criteria include the efficiency, accuracy, and robustness of the techniques [72]. Efficiency refers to the smart use of computational resources required by the technique to obtain the optimal hyperparameters, wasting minimal time while doing so [73]. Accuracy is a measure of the trueness of the output of the metaheuristic technique in locating and identifying the optimized global value. The robustness of the algorithm is the ability to perform well under different conditions and for different types of models without requiring large changes to the code and without requiring excessive retraining altogether [74]. Choosing a unique approach, Blum and Roli [75] have researched the intensification and diversification (I&D) characteristics of commonly used metaheuristics and chose to use these as a comparative criterion for functional behaviors [76, 77].

### 2.9.2   Comparative Analysis of Metaheuristic Techniques

Based on existing literature and empirical relation-based research studies, it is difficult to conclude which metaheuristic technique is the best for HPO. In general, the GA and PSO have shown good performance on a wide range of hyperparameter optimization problems, while SA and DE

**Table 2.1** Breakdown of popular metaheuristics and their I&D components [75].

| Metaheuristics | I&D component |
| --- | --- |
| SA | acceptance criterion + cooling schedule |
| TS | neighbor choice (tabu lists) |
| | aspiration criterion |
| EC | recombination |
| | mutation |
| | selection |
| ACO | pheromone update |
| | probabilistics construction |
| ILS | black box local search |
| | kick-move |
| | acceptance criterion |
| VNS | black box local search |
| | neighborhood choice |
| | shaking phase |
| | acceptance criterion |
| GRASP | black box local search |
| | restricted candidate list |
| GLS | penalty function |

have shown promising results on specific problem domains. However, there always exists a need for in-depth analyses to support an empirical idea. Several studies have evaluated different metaheuristic algorithms and the way they process the search space to look for optima, and the results vary case by case, depending on the optimization problem and the specific hyperparameters being optimized. Table 2.1 summarizes the research findings of Blum and Roli [75], who have broken down the I&D components of the most frequently used metaheuristic techniques for a comparison of sub-methods and steps used in each [78].

While the study concluded with the identification of these subtasks and a guideline to run experiments to evaluate the differences originating due to the variations in these mechanisms, several other studies have followed through to further the vision.

**Table 2.2** Performance comparison of four different metaheuristics based on average, median and standard deviation [80].

| Algorithm | | Loss on LeNet-5 | Best value (loss) | Worst value (loss) |
|---|---|---|---|---|
| ABC | $f_{AVG}$ | 0.039988012 | 0.036257669 | **0.046849927** |
| | $f_{MEDIAN}$ | 0.039912244 | | |
| | $f_{STD}$ | 0.002684507 | | |
| ALO | $f_{AVG}$ | **0.038987691** | 0.03411367 | 0.043372824 |
| | $f_{MEDIAN}$ | **0.039091125** | | |
| | $f_{STD}$ | **0.002267059** | | |
| BA | $f_{AVG}$ | 0.041151504 | **0.03392095** | 0.04544504 |
| | $f_{MEDIAN}$ | 0.041771095 | | |
| | $f_{STD}$ | 0.00265998 | | |
| PSO | $f_{AVG}$ | 0.040463663 | 0.04651067 | 0.04651067 |
| | $f_{MEDIAN}$ | 0.039871245 | | |
| | $f_{STD}$ | 0.002462824 | | |

Traditionally, comparative analysis of metaheuristic techniques has been conducted through various benchmark problems, including optimization of the hyperparameters of convolutional neural networks, decision trees (DTs), and support vector machines [79]. Gaspar *et al.* [80] have studied the HPO for CNNs using four different metaheuristics, i.e., the particle swarm optimization, ant lion optimization (ALO), artificial bee colony, and bat algorithm. Each metaheuristic used the same CNN architecture and the same MNIST database—running 30 times to accumulate the needed data for comparison. It was found that the ALO stood out the best for the case of CNN optimization based on statistical parameters of mean, median, and standard deviation.

Another comparison can be attributed to the work of Ezugwu *et al.* [81] who have devoted their efforts to providing a differentiating insight on eight prominent algorithms, i.e., the particle swarm optimization, spotted hyena optimizer (SHO), gray wolf optimizer, ant colony optimization, whale optimization algorithm, gravitational search algorithm (GSA), moth–flame optimization (MFO), and bat algorithm. After running 23 benchmark tests and analyzing the exploration and exploitation of these algorithms' convergence curves, it was concluded that the SHO and GWO stood out from the rest in terms of the quality and accuracy of the global optima value.

### 2.9.3   Performance Evaluation of Metaheuristic Techniques

The performance evaluation of metaheuristics, specifically for the case of HPO, is usually conducted using benchmark datasets and ML models. This involves a comparison based on a variety of established and recognized metrics, including the accuracy of the resulting model's convergence speed, success rate, and quality of the final solution. The experiments' outcomes are subsequently evaluated to identify the merits and demerits of each technique. In certain cases, trade-offs between strong areas are required to reach a compromised overall performance needed for the given application, since no metaheuristic can generally perform well in all directions needed.

Continuing discussion on the previously stated study by Gaspar *et al.* [80], Table 2.2 shows the performance comparison of four algorithms based on the average mean, median, and standard deviation, tabulated across losses. The results show that the ALO performs the best among the rest in terms of the abovementioned metrics.

Another comparison metric for performance is the rate and ease of convergence, keeping with the least loss incurred. Figure 2.3 shows the convergence comparison of four metaheuristics based on the first 10 iterations that shows that the ALO and other algorithms stabilized in under two iterations while the ABC was found to be the worst for the given application, stabilizing after five iterations. It can also be seen that for the first 10 iterations, the ALO had the least overall losses incurred during the runs.

Similarly, the work of Ezugwu *et al.* [81] includes an evaluation for a convergence-based comparison of the eight renowned algorithms studied. Figure 2.4 shows the SHO and GWO converging in the least number of

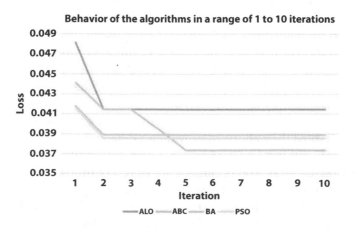

**Figure 2.3** Convergence comparison of four metaheuristics based on the first 10 iterations [80].

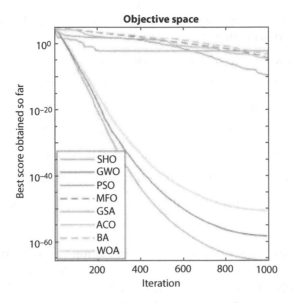

**Figure 2.4** Best score convergence profiles vs. iterations for eight renowned algorithms [81].

iterations—going below $10^{-20}$ in just over 200 iterations. The GSA can be seen to flatline after approximately 200 iterations after little initial decay, while the rest move out of the window for 1,000 iterations without reaching satisfactory convergence. The WOA proves to be the next best thing to the GWO in the benchmark test.

Sonmez [82] compared the performance of eight population-based metaheuristic algorithms (GA, ACO, PSO, ABC, GSA, firefly algorithm (FA), GWO, Jaya) for the application of optimal truss design evaluation in three-dimensional (3D) space. It was found that for double-layer grid (DLG) designs with over 53 variables, the PSO, GSA, and FA converged poorly and were highly sensitive to increment compared to the rest. Overall, the GWO, JAYA, and ABC had better results for runs having over 20 dimensional variables, as shown in Table 2.3 that shows the performance comparison of eight population-based metaheuristics for the DLG truss problem below.

It was also discovered that the nature and count of control parameters can be another influencing factor in gauging performance and would require additional studies.

At times, choosing the best-performing algorithm becomes highly necessary. Such is the case of critical applications that are highly sensitive. This includes fraudulent bank transaction detection, taken up by Tayebi and Kafhali [83]. The paper involves the performance comparison of industry-leading metaheuristic algorithms including the GA, DE, ABC,

**Table 2.3** Performance comparison of eight population-based metaheuristics for the DLG truss problem [82].

|  | GA | ACO | PSO | ABC | GSA | FA | GWO | JAYA |
|---|---|---|---|---|---|---|---|---|
| $\phi_{best}$ (tons) | 32.154 | 33.721 | 73.255 | 29.994 | 169.431 | 66.612 | 28.769 | 34.703 |
| Viol | 1.3E – 08 | 0 | 0 | 0 | 0 | 0 | 0 | 0 |
| $\bar{\phi}$(tons) | 37.34 | 46.38 | 95.30 | 34.57 | 183.06 | 92.55 | 29.45 | 50.29 |
| σ (tons) | 3.06 | 10.63 | 10.33 | 2.75 | 10.73 | 15.53 | 0.41 | 8.23 |
| # SA | 54,110 | 53,010 | 53,000 | 53,045 | 53,000 | 53,000 | 53,000 | 53,050 |
| Time (h) | 0.268 | 0.267 | 0.247 | 0.239 | 0.203 | 0.203 | 0.262 | 0.263 |

GWO, PSO, teaching learning-based optimization (TLBO), and GS, with a range of ML models such as decision tree, mlp classifier (MLP), k-nearest neighbors (KNN), logistic regression (LR), random forest (RF), support vector machine classifier, and AdaBoost (AD). The optimizers were compared based on accuracy, precision, recall, F1 score, and the area under the ROC curve (AUC) metrics.

The most important characteristic of global optima is accuracy. According to Figure 2.5, different metaheuristic techniques have varying performances for different ML models. LR produced the same results for most metaheuristic techniques except the PSO, while the DT provided higher accuracy compared to using the grid search (GS). RF performed better when using the ABC, DE, and TLBO. The SVM had better accuracy using the TLBO, while AD showed better accuracy using the GS. Meanwhile, MLP had better accuracy using the GA and GS, and KNN demonstrated better accuracy using the GA.

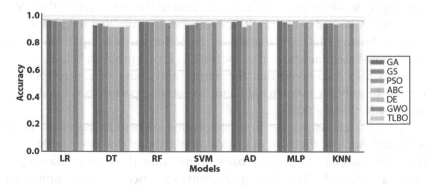

**Figure 2.5** Accuracy of metaheuristics for different ML models [83].

Therefore, it can be concluded that there are high variations in the overall performance of metaheuristics, affected strongly by several parameters, the nature of the application, and the type of ML model being used. While it may be possible to collectively group tasks and applications of similar nature and see what algorithm generally stands out the best for each, it is still a better practice to run personalized trial-and-error routines for the task at hand.

## 2.10   Applications of Metaheuristics in Machine Learning

Metaheuristics play an important role in automating processes in the digital industry, including ML. Machine learning is a rapidly growing field that aims to create intelligent algorithms capable of learning from datasets and making decisions or predictions based on newly acquired information. Section 2.10 focuses to discuss various applications of metaheuristics in the broad categories of ML, including supervised, unsupervised, reinforcement, and deep learning for integrating HPO in intelligent systems.

### 2.10.1   Supervised Learning

Supervised learning is an ML technique that is frequently employed to train a model in applications where the program is to discern between easily predictable outcomes. These usually have a consistency built-in such as a recurring pattern or progressive sequence. The technique is enabled by providing the system with inputs and their corresponding outputs (the concept of labeled data) in order to establish functional relations between the two. This trained function can then be applied to make predictions on unseen data. Metaheuristics have been applied in the supervised learning domains mainly for feature selection (FS) [84, 85], training ANNs and SNNs, HPO, and for model selection (MS). Javanshir et al. [86] have used a metaheuristic-based supervised learning technique for training spiking neural networks (SNNs), overcoming the challenge of discontinuities and the non-differentiable inherent nature of the spiking neuron (SN). Metaheuristics such as the HS, CS, DE, PSO, GA, ABC, and gene expression (GE) were implemented to run the trials, with the CS standing out from the rest to exhibit the best performance across four classification benchmarks. Turning toward HPO, Xian et al. [87] have improved a sine cosine algorithm (SCA) for finding global optima by integrating a teacher supervision learning (TSL) model. The hybridized TSL-SCA has better population control and distributivity, higher convergence speed, and balanced exploration and exploitation. The TSL-SCA proved to be more competitive than the DE, PSO, MFO, CS, and WOA algorithm types.

## 2.10.2   Unsupervised Learning

Unsupervised learning differs from the supervised mode in terms of data labels. It needs to be smart enough to identify patterns or structures in the data while training the model using unlabeled data. Metaheuristic algorithms have been used for clustering, dimensionality reduction, and anomaly detection in unsupervised learning. Clustering, being the most important application of all, involves grouping similar data points together for means of easier handling and efficiency for pattern finding. Metaheuristic algorithms possess the ability to optimize this process smoothly, and several research efforts have been dedicated in this direction. Jahwar and Abdulazeez [88] have discussed the use of SI approaches, including the PSO, ACO, and ABC for K-means clustering, with the PSO performing the best. Similarly, Kaur and Kumar [89] have devised a new water wave optimization (WWO)-based metaheuristic to solve the clustering problem. The WWO has been known to be effective in tackling constrained and unconstrained optimization issues but has a shortcoming that causes premature convergence. The authors have improved the algorithm with a modified search mechanism and decay operator and tested the new WWO in 13 benchmarks, gaining higher accuracy and F-score rates for clustering problems than usual metaheuristics.

## 2.10.3   Reinforcement Learning

Reinforcement learning involves training a model to adopt positive behaviors that are encouraged and reject negative ones that were discouraged by feedback received from the user. The model then makes decisions based on this feedback rewarding and correcting received. Reinforcement models require high-dimensional storage spaces and are computationally intensive, since they require data to be generally sorted into two classes as they operate in an accept/reject manner. Metaheuristic algorithms have been used for policy search, global optimization in HPO problems, and deep reinforcement learning. Seyyedabbasi [90] have combined a sand cat swarm optimization (SCSO) algorithm with integrated reinforcement learning to create an RL-SCSO metaheuristic hybrid for efficient exploration and exploitation for global optima in the search space. The study was validated on 20 benchmark tests, and the results were found appreciable. Seyyedabbasi *et al.* then rose the bar further in [91], developing three new hybrid metaheuristics, i.e., $RL_{I\text{-}GWO}$, $RL_{Ex\text{-}GWO}$, and $RL_{WOA}$. By implementing a control mechanism, the reward and penalty values for each action were obtained, and the algorithms were simulated over 30 benchmark functions to generate statistical data on their performance. It was found that the RL-based hybrids performed better than conventional algorithms in terms of exploration and exploitation abilities, with $RL_{WOA}$ outdoing the other two hybrids.

### 2.10.4    Deep Learning

Deep learning involves training deep neural networks to learn complex patterns in data. Metaheuristic algorithms have been used for various tasks in deep learning, including HPO, architecture search, and training DNNs. Tian and Fong [92] provide a comprehensive review of deep learning integration for DNNs, discussing the overall process, pros and cons, the importance and need of metaheuristic techniques, and the use of the GA and PSO for HPO in ANNs. In a similar effort, Rere *et al.* [93] present the use of SA to boost the performance of a CNN. Providing success with an implementation of an MNIST dataset, the proposed method did have to make an increased computation time trade-off. Another important discovery in the field is made by Kingma and Ba [94], who have created Adam, an algorithm that can handle first-order gradient-based optimization of stochastic objective functions. The research successfully demonstrated the versatility of the Adam algorithm that holds the ability to scale to large-scale high-dimensional machine learning problems, compares well against existing ML models to handle CNNs and DNNs, and can even efficiently solve practical deep learning problems.

## 2.11    Future Directions and Open Challenges

The field of metaheuristics is an emerging one, exploring new directions, taking new paths, and developing deep in a variety of unique ways. Entering into the world of ML opens up a lot more possibilities for the future, and just as more advanced techniques are developed and new applications are discovered, the need for improvement grows exponentially. This allows for R&D into metaheuristics to hold great potential. However, the pros come with cons. Branched-out opportunities in new ventures also pose an increased number of open challenges that must be conquered to fully master metaheuristics and their true abilities. These include challenges of complex model training, high-dimensional data handling, and ANN and DNN optimization.

### 2.11.1   Opportunities for Improvement in Metaheuristics

Metaheuristic algorithms have remarkably proven themselves to be useful tools for optimization problems in ML, but there is always room for improvement. The development of new metaheuristic techniques that can address the challenges of high-dimensional data and complex optimization landscapes is the foremost approach. Refining the art of creating better-hybridized algorithms stands second in the list – finding the right algorithms to combine and in the right proportions. Ting *et al.* [95] have discussed the past, present, and future of hybrid metaheuristics, extending hope for wider research horizons and countless possibilities of research and development to harness infinite opportunities. Lastly, improving existing algorithms in terms of inclusivity and capabilities remains a forever green task that is to remain a continual growth process till the end of time. Areas of growing metaheuristic applications include advanced quantum computing applications, nanotechnology, NFT and cryptocurrency transactions, space exploration simulations, and others.

### 2.11.2   Adapting Metaheuristics to New Machine Learning Paradigms

As ML continues to evolve, new paradigms are emerging that require the development of new optimization techniques to keep up with industrial benchmarks and with the intense competition in the global markets. Philosophies such as lean entrepreneurship, and other resource-managing methodologies require utmost optimization throughout all processes involved in the producer-to-consumer chain. Pairing metaheuristics with techniques such as continual learning, cognitive computing, quantum machine learning, adversarial machine learning, explainable AI, federated learning, human-in-the-loop learning, meta-learning and more might be the key to major breakthroughs in the waiting. Developing metaheuristics that can work with these new ML paradigms will definitely be an important area of research in the future.

### 2.11.3    Addressing the Computational Complexity and Scalability

With the increasing size and complexity of ML models, scalability and computational efficiency become significant challenges to counter in the current digital era of smart optimization and control. Keeping with the trends, the future is likely to add more challenges in terms of increased bandwidth and dimensional requirements for processing and storage. Although time taking, this needs to be addressed and substantial efforts should be concentrated on the issue. Additionally, there is a need for more research on parallel and distributed metaheuristic algorithms to speed up HPO. There is also a need to develop metaheuristics that can synergize with newer computing architectures, such as GPUs and FPGAs to exploit hardware efficiently and speed up optimization.

## 2.12    Conclusion

It can be agreed that metaheuristic algorithms and HPO are inseparable ideas in today's digital world. With the rapid developments being made in the industrial and artificial technology sectors around the clock, it is becoming increasingly important for companies to outdo the competition and to keep on improving product quality and diversity while keeping factors such as costs and process time low. This is where HPO comes into play for finding global optima for process parameters to boost desired metrics. Throughout this paper, it was seen that manual optimization is indeed a laborious task and requires an eternity of corrections, iterations, and error finding. Metaheuristics are indeed a powerful tool that can be used as a real-life hack to execute HPO in a smart and efficient manner. To build a sound foundation, this review paper covered important concepts needed to comprehend the complete idea of HPO, including terms in the field of metaheuristics, ML, AI, etc., and also examined unique optimization techniques employed by various researchers. The paper has also identified several areas of future research for improving the performance of metaheuristics in ML and also discusses challenges that need to be conquered to keep the push going on. Overall, it can be said with high confidence that the field holds significant potential for improving the accuracy and efficiency of ML algorithms – through both innovation of newer techniques and by hybridizing combinations of existing variants, and can help to address the challenges associated with HPO, feature selection, and model selection.

# References

1. Gupta, K.K. *et al.*, Machine learning-based predictive modelling of biodiesel production-A comparative perspective. *Energies*, 14, 4, 1122, 2021, doi: 10.3390/en14041122.
2. Hutter, F., Kotthoff, L., Vanschoren, J., *Automated Machine Learning*, Springer: New York, NY, USA, 2019.
3. Bergstra, J. and Bengio, Y., Random search for hyper-parameter optimization. *J. Mach. Learn. Res.*, 13, 281–305, 2012.
4. Feurer, M. and Hutter, F., Hyperparameter optimization, in: *Automated Machine Learning: Methods, Systems, Challenges*, pp. 3–33, 2019, doi:10.1007/978-3-030-05318-5_1.
5. Bergstra, J.S., Bardenet, R., Bengio, Y., Kégl, B., Algorithms for hyper-parameter optimization. In *Advances in Neural Information Processing Systems 24*, J. Shawe-Taylor, R.S. Zemel, P.L. Bartlett, F. Pereira, K.Q. Weinberger (Eds.), pp. 2546–2554, Curran Associates, Inc., Granada, Spain, 2011.
6. Eggensperger, K., others, Towards an empirical foundation for assessing bayesian optimization of hyperparameters, in: *NIPS Workshop on Bayesian Optimization in Theory and Practice*, 2013.
7. Hutter, F. *et al.*, Sequential model-based optimization for general algorithm configuration, in: *Learning and Intelligent, Optimization: 5th International Conference, LION 5*, Rome, Italy, January 17-21, 2011, 2011, Selected Papers 5.
8. Falkner, S. *et al.*, BOHB: Robust and efficient hyperparameter optimization at scale, in: *International Conference on Machine Learning*, 2018.
9. Bergstra, J. *et al.*, Implementations of algorithms for hyper-parameter optimization, in: *NIPS Workshop on Bayesian Optimization*, 2011.
10. Chen, T. and Guestrin, C., Xgboost: A scalable tree boosting system, in: *Proc. 22nd ACM SIGKDD International Conference on Knowledge Discovery and Data Mining*, pp. 785–794, 2016, doi: 10.1145/2939672.2939785.
11. Thornton, C. *et al.*, Auto-WEKA: Combined selection and hyperparameter optimization of classification algorithms, in: *Proc. 19th ACM SIGKDD International Conference on Knowledge Discovery and Data Mining*, pp. 847–855, 2013, doi: 10.1145/2487575.2487629.
12. Snoek, J., Larochelle, H., Adams, R.P., Practical bayesian optimization of machine learning algorithms. in: *Proceedings of the 25th International Conference on Neural Information Processing Systems*, vol. 2, pp. 2951–2959, Granada, Spain, 20 November 2020.
13. Domhan, T. *et al.*, Speeding up automatic hyperparameter optimization of deep neural networks by extrapolation of learning curves, in: *Twenty-Fourth International Joint Conference on Artificial Intelligence*, 2015.
14. Probst, P. *et al.*, Tunability: Importance of hyperparameters of machine learning algorithms. *J. Mach. Learn. Res.*, 20, 1934–1965, 2019.
15. Gandomi, A.H. *et al.*, Metaheuristic algorithms in modeling and optimization, in: *Metaheuristic Appl. Struct. Infrastruct.*, vol. 1, 2013, doi:10.1016/B978-0-12-398364-0.00001-2.

16. Gendreau, M. and Potvin, J.-Y., Handbook of metaheuristics, in: International Series in Operations Research & Management Science, 2nd ed., M. Gendreau, J.-Y. Potvin (Eds.), p. 648, Springer US, Boston, MA, USA, 2010.

17. Abdel-Basset, M. *et al.*, Metaheuristic algorithms: A comprehensive review, in: *Comp. Intell. Multimedia Big Data Cloud Eng. Appl.*, pp. 185–231, 2018, doi:10.1016/B978-0-12-813314-9.00010-4.

18. Holland, J.H., *Adaptation in natural and artificial systems: An introductory analysis with applications to biology, control, and artificial intelligence*, MIT Press, Cambridge, MA, USA, 1975.

19. Kalita, K. *et al.*, Genetic programming-assisted multi-scale optimization for multi-objective dynamic performance of laminated composites: The advantage of more elementary-level analyses. *Neural Comput. Appl.*, 32, 12, 7969–7993, 2020, doi: 10.1007/s00521-019-04280-z.

20. Kalita, K. and Chakraborty, S., An efficient approach for metaheuristic-based optimization of composite laminates using genetic programming. *Int. J. Interact. Des. Manuf.*, 17, 2, 899–916, 2023, doi: 10.1007/s12008-022-01175-7.

21. Kalita, K. *et al.*, Optimizing drilling induced delamination in GFRP composites using genetic algorithm & particle swarm optimization. *Adv. Compos. Lett.*, 27, 1, 2018, doi: 10.1177/096369351802700101.

22. Kalita, K. *et al.*, Optimizing process parameters for laser beam micro-marking using genetic algorithm and particle swarm optimization. *Mater. Manuf. Processes*, 32, 10, 1101–1108, 2017, doi: 10.1080/10426914.2017.1303156.

23. Di Francescomarino, C.D. *et al.*, Genetic algorithms for hyperparameter optimization in predictive business process monitoring. *Inf. Syst.*, 74, 67–83, 2018, doi: 10.1016/j.is.2018.01.003.

24. Kalita, K. *et al.*, Parametric optimization of non-traditional machining processes using multi-criteria decision making techniques: Literature review and future directions. *Multiscale Multidiscip. Model. Exp. Des.*, 6, 1, 1–40, 2023, doi: 10.1007/s41939-022-00128-7.

25. Kalita, K. *et al.*, Robust genetically optimized skew laminates. *Proc. Inst. Mech. Eng. C*, 233, 1, 146–159, 2019, doi: 10.1177/0954406218756943.

26. Kennedy, J. and Eberhart, R., Particle swarm optimization, in: *Proc. ICNN' 95-International Conference on Neural Networks*, pp. 1942–1948, 1995, doi: 10.1109/ICNN.1995.488968.

27. Tasgetiren, M.F. *et al.*, Particle swarm optimization algorithm for single machine total weighted tardiness problem, in: *Proc. 2004 Congress on Evolutionary Computation*, 2004, (IEEE, Cat. No. 04TH8753).

28. Narayanan, G. *et al.*, PSO-tuned support vector machine metamodels for assessment of turbulent flows in pipe bends. *Eng. Comput.*, 37, 3, 981–1001, 2019, doi: 10.1108/EC-05-2019-0244.

29. Shankar, R. *et al.*, Hybridized particle swarm-Gravitational search algorithm for process optimization. *Processes*, 10, 3, 616, 2022, doi: 10.3390/pr10030616.

30. Price, K.V., Storn, R.M., Lampinen, J.A., *Differential evolution: A practical approach to global optimization*. Springer Science & Business Media, Berlin/ Heidelberg, Germany, 2006.

31. Kalita, K. *et al.*, A response surface modelling approach for multi-objective optimization of composite plates. *Steel Compos. Struct. Int. J.*, 32, 455–466, 2019.

32. Kalita, K. *et al.*, A comparative study on the metaheuristic-based optimization of skew composite laminates. *Eng. Comput.*, 38, 4, 3549–3566, 2022, doi: 10.1007/s00366-021-01401-y.

33. Lorenzo, P.R. *et al.*, Particle swarm optimization for hyper-parameter selection in deep neural networks, in: *Proc. Genetic and Evolutionary Computation Conference*, pp. 481–488, 2017, doi: 10.1145/3071178.3071208.

34. Zulfiqar, M. *et al.*, Hyperparameter optimization of support vector machine using adaptive differential evolution for electricity load forecasting. *Energy Rep.*, 8, 13333–13352, 2022, doi: 10.1016/j.egyr.2022.09.188.

35. Lohvithee, M. *et al.*, Ant colony-based hyperparameter optimisation in total variation reconstruction in X-ray computed tomography. *Sensors (Basel)*, 21, 2, 591, 2021, doi: 10.3390/s21020591.

36. Simon, D., Biogeography-based optimization. *IEEE Trans. Evol. Comput.*, 12, 6, 702–713, 2008, doi: 10.1109/TEVC.2008.919004.

37. Kalita, K. *et al.*, Optimizing frequencies of skew composite laminates with metaheuristic algorithms. *Eng. Comput.*, 36, 2, 741–761, 2020, doi: 10.1007/s00366-019-00728-x.

38. Kalita, K. *et al.*, Metamodel based multi-objective design optimization of laminated composite plates. *Struct. Eng. Mech. Int. J.*, 67, 301–310, 2018.

39. Kalita, K. *et al.*, Memetic cuckoo-search-based optimization in machining galvanized iron. *Mater. (Basel)*, 13, 14, 3047, 2020, doi: 10.3390/ma13143047.

40. Yang, X.-S. and Deb, S., Cuckoo search via Lévy flights, in: *World Congress on Nature & Biologically Inspired Computing (NaBIC)*, vol. 2009, 2009, doi: 10.1109/NABIC.2009.5393690.

41. Kalita, K. *et al.*, A hybrid TOPSIS-PR-GWO approach for multi-objective process parameter optimization. *Process Integr. Optim. Sustain.*, 6, 4, 1011–1026, 2022, doi: 10.1007/s41660-022-00256-0.

42. Kalita, K. *et al.*, A comprehensive review on high-fidelity and metamodel-based optimization of composite laminates. *Arch. Comput. Methods Eng.*, 29, 5, 3305–3340, 2022, doi: 10.1007/s11831-021-09699-z.

43. Mirjalili, S. *et al.*, Grey wolf optimizer. *Adv. Eng. Software*, 69, 46–61, 2014, doi: 10.1016/j.advengsoft.2013.12.007.

44. Kalita, K. *et al.*, Grey wolf optimizer-based design of ventilated brake disc. *J. Braz. Soc. Mech. Sci. Eng.*, 43, 8, 1–15, 2021, doi: 10.1007/s40430-021-03125-y.

45. Kumar, V. *et al.*, A hybrid genetic programming-gray wolf optimizer approach for process optimization of biodiesel production. *Processes*, 9, 3, 442, 2021, doi: 10.3390/pr9030442.

46. Shanmugasundar, G. *et al.*, Optimization of variable stiffness joint in robot manipulator using a novel NSWOA-Marcos approach. *Processes*, 10, 6, 1074, 2022, doi: 10.3390/pr10061074.

47. Ashraf, N.M. *et al.*, Optimizing hyperparameters of deep reinforcement learning for autonomous driving based on whale optimization algorithm. *PloS One*, 16, 6, e0252754, 2021, doi: 10.1371/journal.pone.0252754.

48. Kalita, K. *et al.*, A novel MOALO-MODA ensemble approach for multi-objective optimization of machining parameters for metal matrix composites. *Multiscale Multidiscip. Model. Exp. Des.*, 6, 1, 179–197, 2023, doi: 10.1007/s41939-022-00138-5.

49. Karaboga, D. and Basturk, B., A powerful and efficient algorithm for numerical function optimization: Artificial bee colony (ABC) algorithm. *J. Glob. Optim.*, 39, 3, 459–471, 2007, doi: 10.1007/s10898-007-9149-x.

50. Kaveh, A. and Talatahari, S., A novel heuristic optimization method: Charged system search. *Acta Mech.*, 213, 3-4, 267–289, 2010, doi: 10.1007/s00707-009-0270-4.

51. Kirkpatrick, S. *et al.*, Optimization by simulated annealing. *Science*, 220, 4598, 671–680, 1983, doi: 10.1126/science.220.4598.671.

52. Glover, F., Tabu search-part I. *ORSA J. Comput.*, 1, 3, 190–206, 1989, doi: 10.1287/ijoc.1.3.190.

53. Geem, Z.W. *et al.*, A new heuristic optimization algorithm: Harmony search. *Simulation*, 76, 60–68, 2001, doi: 10.1177/003754970107600201.

54. Yang, X.-S., A new metaheuristic bat-inspired algorithm, in: *Nature Inspired Cooperative Strategies for Optimization*, pp. 65–74, 2010, doi:10.1007/978-3-642-12538-6_6.

55. Jaddi, N.S. and Abdullah, S., Global search in single-solution-based meta-heuristics. *Data Technol. Appl.*, 54, 3, 275–296, 2020, doi: 10.1108/DTA-07-2019-0115.

56. Jeong, S. *et al.*, Development and investigation of efficient GA/PSO-hybrid algorithm applicable to real-world design optimization. *IEEE Comput. Intell. Mag.*, 4, 3, 36–44, 2009, doi: 10.1109/MCI.2009.933099.

57. Sanagooy Aghdam, A. *et al.*, A hybrid GA-SA multiobjective optimization and simulation for RFID network planning problem. *J. Appl. Res. Ind. Eng.*, 8, 1–25, 2021.

58. Zhang, Y. and Wu, L., A hybrid TS-PSO optimization algorithm. *J. Converg. Inf. Technol.*, 6, 5, 169–174, 2011, doi: 10.4156/jcit.vol6.issue5.18.

59. Liu, H. *et al.*, Chaotic dynamic characteristics in swarm intelligence. *Appl. Soft Comput.*, 7, 3, 1019–1026, 2007, doi: 10.1016/j.asoc.2006.10.006.

60. De, S., Dey, S., Bhattacharyya, S. *Recent advances in hybrid metaheuristics for data clustering*, John Wiley & Sons, Hoboken, NJ, USA, 2020.

61. Shahriari, B. *et al.*, Taking the human out of the loop: A review of Bayesian optimization. *Proc. IEEE*, 104, 1, 148–175, 2015, doi: 10.1109/JPROC.2015.2494218.

62. Bhattacharya, S. *et al.*, A comparative analysis on prediction performance of regression models during machining of composite materials. *Mater. (Basel)*, 14, 21, 6689, 2021, doi: 10.3390/ma14216689.
63. Jain, P. *et al.*, Random forest regression-based machine learning model for accurate estimation of fluid flow in curved pipes. *Processes*, 9, 11, 2095, 2021, doi: 10.3390/pr9112095.
64. Brochu, E. *et al.*, A tutorial on Bayesian optimization of expensive cost functions, with application to active user modeling and hierarchical reinforcement learning, arXiv Preprint ArXiv:1012.2599, 2010.
65. Snoek, J. *et al.*, Scalable bayesian optimization using deep neural networks, in: *International Conference on Machine Learning*, 2015.
66. Xie, L. and Yuille, A., Genetic CNN, in: *Proc. IEEE International Conference on Computer Vision*, pp. 1388–1397, 2017, doi: 10.1109/ICCV.2017.154.
67. Krizhevsky, A. *et al.*, Imagenet classification with deep convolutional neural networks. *Commun. ACM*, 60, 6, 84–90, 2017, doi: 10.1145/3065386.
68. Elsken, T. *et al.*, Neural architecture search: A survey. *J. Mach. Learn. Res.*, 20, 1997–2017, 2019, doi: 10.1007/978-3-030-05318-5_3.
69. Stanley, K.O. and Miikkulainen, R., Evolving neural networks through augmenting topologies. *Evol. Comput.*, 10, 2, 99–127, 2002, doi: 10.1162/106365602320169811.
70. Hansen, P. *et al.*, Variable neighbourhood search: Methods and applications. *Ann. Oper. Res.*, 175, 1, 367–407, 2010, doi: 10.1007/s10479-009-0657-6.
71. Liu, H. *et al.*, Darts: Differentiable architecture search, arXiv Preprint ArXiv:1806.09055, 2018.
72. Ying, C. *et al.*, NAS-Bench-101: Towards reproducible neural architecture search, in: *International Conference on Machine Learning*, 2019.
73. Narayanan, R.C. *et al.*, A novel many-objective sine-cosine algorithm (MaOSCA) for engineering applications. *Mathematics*, 11, 10, 2301, 2023, doi: 10.3390/math11102301.
74. Silver, D. *et al.*, Lanctot and others, Mastering the game of Go with deep neural networks and tree search. *Nature*, 529, 484–489, 2016, doi: 10.1038/nature16961.
75. Blum, C. and Roli, A., Metaheuristics in combinatorial optimization: Overview and conceptual comparison. *ACM Comput. Surv.*, 35, 3, 268–308, 2003, doi: 10.1145/937503.937505.
76. Ganesh, N. *et al.*, A novel decomposition-based multi-objective symbiotic organism search optimization algorithm. *Mathematics*, 11, 8, 1898, 2023, doi: 10.3390/math11081898.
77. Joshi, M. *et al.*, A conceptual comparison of dragonfly algorithm variants for CEC-2021 global optimization problems. *Arab. J. Sci. Eng.*, 48, 2, 1563–1593, 2023, doi: 10.1007/s13369-022-06880-9.
78. Shaik, K. *et al.*, Big data analytics framework using squirrel search optimized gradient boosted decision tree for heart disease diagnosis. *Appl. Sci.*, 13, 9, 5236, 2023, doi: 10.3390/app13095236.

79. Real, E. *et al.*, Regularized evolution for image classifier architecture search. *AAAI*, 33, 1, 4780–4789, 2019, doi: 10.1609/aaai.v33i01.33014780.

80. Gaspar, A. *et al.*, Hyperparameter optimization in a convolutional neural network using metaheuristic algorithms, in: *Metaheuristics in Machine Learning: Theory and Applications*, pp. 37–59, Springer, Boston, USA, 2021, doi: 10.1007/978-3-030-70542-8_2.

81. Ezugwu, A.E. *et al.*, A conceptual comparison of several metaheuristic algorithms on continuous optimisation problems. *Neural Comput. Appl.*, 32, 10, 6207–6251, 2020, doi: 10.1007/s00521-019-04132-w.

82. Sonmez, M., Performance comparison of metaheuristic algorithms for the optimal design of space trusses. *Arab. J. Sci. Eng.*, 43, 10, 5265–5281, 2018, doi: 10.1007/s13369-018-3080-y.

83. Tayebi, M. and El Kafhali, S., Performance analysis of metaheuristics based hyperparameters optimization for fraud transactions detection. *Evol. Intell.*, 1–22, 2022, doi: 10.1007/s12065-022-00764-5.

84. Priyadarshini, J. *et al.*, Analyzing physics-inspired metaheuristic algorithms in feature selection with K-nearest-neighbor. *Appl. Sci.*, 13, 2, 906, 2023, doi: 10.3390/app13020906.

85. Ganesh, N. *et al.*, Efficient feature selection using weighted superposition attraction optimization algorithm. *Appl. Sci.*, 13, 5, 3223, 2023, doi: 10.3390/app13053223.

86. Javanshir, A. *et al.*, Training spiking neural networks with metaheuristic algorithms. *Appl. Sci.*, 13, 8, 4809, 2023, doi: 10.3390/app13084809.

87. Xian, H. *et al.*, A modified sine cosine algorithm with teacher supervision learning for global optimization. *IEEE Access*, 9, 17744–17766, 2021, doi: 10.1109/ACCESS.2021.3054053.

88. Jahwar, A.F. and Abdulazeez, A.M., Meta-heuristic algorithms for K-means clustering: A review. *PalArchs J. Archaeol. Egypt Egyptol.*, 17, 12002–12020, 2020.

89. Kaur, A. and Kumar, Y., A new metaheuristic algorithm based on water wave optimization for data clustering. *Evol. Intell.*, 15, 1, 759–783, 2022, doi: 10.1007/s12065-020-00562-x.

90. Seyyedabbasi, A., A reinforcement learning-based metaheuristic algorithm for solving global optimization problems. *Adv. Eng. Software*, 178, 103411, 2023, doi: 10.1016/j.advengsoft.2023.103411.

91. Seyyedabbasi, A. *et al.*, Hybrid algorithms based on combining reinforcement learning and metaheuristic methods to solve global optimization problems. *Knowl. Based Syst.*, 223, 107044, 2021, doi: 10.1016/j.knosys.2021.107044.

92. Tian, Z. and Fong, S., Survey of meta-heuristic algorithms for deep learning training, in: *Optim. Algor.-Methods Appl.*, 2016, doi:10.5772/63785.

93. Rere, L.M.R. *et al.*, Simulated annealing algorithm for deep learning. *Proc. Comput. Sci.*, 72, 137–144, 2015, doi: 10.1016/j.procs.2015.12.114.

94. Kinga, D. and Adam, J.B., A method for stochastic optimization, in: *Proceedings of the International Conference on Learning Representations-ICLR*, vol. 5, p. 6, San Diego, CA, USA, 7–9 May 2015.

95. Ting, T.O. *et al.*, Hybrid metaheuristic algorithms: Past, present, and future, in: *Recent Advances in Swarm Intelligence and Evolutionary Computation*, pp. 71–83, 2015, doi:10.1007/978-3-319-13826-8_4.

# 3

# A Survey of Computer-Aided Diagnosis Systems for Breast Cancer Detection

**Charu Anant Rajput\*, Leninisha Shanmugam and Parkavi K.**

*School of Computer Science and Engineering, Vellore Institute of Technology,*
*Chennai, India*

## Abstract

Computer-aided diagnosis (CAD) has been the most critical and vital approach concerning the medical domain in recent times. Also, with the trend of telemedicine in place, the reliability and efficiency of CAD systems have become the need of the hour. Dedicated research concerning CAD systems for the detection of breast cancer is being promoted globally. However, given the vast range of imaging modalities and the availability of diverse datasets concerning the aforementioned domain, choosing the most efficient and optimum implementation methodology becomes a challenge. The proposed survey paper, therefore, aims to provide a comprehensive overview of all of the existing imaging modalities and their corresponding datasets. Apart from this, some notable works concerning each modality representing both the machine learning and deep learning domains would also be presented in order to give a head start for the upcoming novel research. The proposed work would shed light on all the possible categories of classifications that can be performed concerning the domain of breast cancer. We finally conclude by pointing out new possible research gaps, thereby opening up avenues for future upcoming research.

*Keywords*: Benign, malignant, *in situ*, invasive ductal carcinoma, CAD

## 3.1 Introduction

Various indications and abnormalities come up during image screening and may prove to be early indicators of breast cancer. On further deep-dwelling,

*\*Corresponding author*: charuanant.rajput2019@vitstudent.ac.in

Kanak Kalita, Narayanan Ganesh and S. Balamurugan (eds.) Metaheuristics for Machine Learning: Algorithms and Applications, (73–94) © 2024 Scrivener Publishing LLC

they are further classified into benign or malignant wherein malignant represents the potential danger of development into breast cancer shortly.

According to a recently conducted statistics study, one woman is diagnosed with breast cancer every 4 minutes according to the Indian context. Breast cancer is annually registering a figure of approximately 1,78,000 as of 2020 and has therefore even overtaken cervical cancer to become the leading cause of cancer among Indian women. The point to be noted is that, in cases of early diagnosis, the survival rates can increase up to 98%. However, the irony lies in the fact that approximately 50%–80% of breast cancer cases in India are detected in the advanced stages.

This makes it necessary to put some light on the potential indicators of breast cancer. The occurrence of calcifications and masses are considered to be red flags and thereby involves clinical interpretation for facilitating proper diagnosis and treatment. Chaudhury et al. [1] in his work has termed calcifications as calcium deposits found in the breast. Probable reasons are listed as aging, historical infections, and wounds and are not necessarily linked to calcium intake. Calcifications have two main categories, namely, macrocalcifications and microcalcifications, wherein the former is not risky while microcalcifications raise an early suspicion of breast cancer and thereby need multiple follow-up tests. These days, there are automated systems in place for detecting instances of calcifications in the input ultrasound scans. Chaudhury et al. [1] have discussed a novel segmentation approach that is postulated in terms of four phases. The first phase involves preprocessing wherein the input image is converted into a grayscale image. The image segmentation is done by the application of K-means, and the subsequent feature extraction is performed by making use of the gray-level co-occurrence matrix (GLCM). Finally, for performing the classification concerning normal cells and calcified cells, the model makes use of Hidden Markov Model (HMM) classification algorithm wherein resemblance has precedence over contextual knowledge for classification purposes. The aforementioned proposed work made use of ultrasound scans. Loizidou et al. [2] have further provided a scope of extension to the aforementioned work wherein the proposed work not only detects microcalcifications but also further classifies whether they are benign or suspicious by making use of temporally sequential mammograms. The proposed work emphasizes temporal subtraction as the main accuracy-building factor. The methodology initiates with the application of preprocessing techniques like pixel normalization and border removal subsequently followed by the image registration of the temporally prior scan. Temporal subtraction is followed thereafter and then comes feature extraction wherein different categories like shape features, intensity-based features, first order statistic features

(FOS), and GLCM features are extracted. Finally, for classification, different classifiers like linear discriminant analysis (LDA), kNN, naive Bayes, support vector machine (SVM), decision trees, and ensemble of decision trees are used.

Another significant indicator is the presence of masses or lumps in the breast scans. Here, too, the presence of CAD systems has provided support and reassurance to the manual practice being carried out presently. Jeong *et al.* [3] made use of three-dimensional ultrasound images to detect the masses. The proposed methodology made use of the 3D Hough transform for identifying the spherical hyperplanes in the input images. The recognized spheres are then converted into a circumscribing parallelepiped cube as mass lesion candidates, and then the final classification is done based on the geometrical overlapping. Hamed *et al.* [4] made use of the You Only Look Once (YOLO)-based CAD system that works on full-field and cropped mammograms. This is followed by the application of feature extractors like ResNet, VGG, and Inception. The system successfully detects mass location with an accuracy of 98% and also performs classification between benign and malignant with an accuracy of 95%.

The aforementioned discussion puts light on some early symptoms like calcifications and masses; however, another judgment category that plays a significant role in determining the role of treatment is deciding whether the cancer is in the invasive ductal carcinoma (IDC) phase or undergoing the *in situ* stage. In medical terms, *in situ* means that the cancerous cells are limited inside the milk ducts; however, IDC means that the cancerous cells have started spreading to the surrounding tissues.

Automated works concerning the aforementioned criteria majorly make use of the histopathological whole slide imaging (WSI) dataset. For instance, Celik *et al.* [5] have implemented the detection of IDC by making use of standard deep learning (DL) architectures like ResNet-50 and DenseNet-161. The training was performed over the last layers of the model, and the performance produced was almost the same wherein DenseNet produced an F-score of 92.38% and a balanced accuracy of 91.75%, whereas the ResNet model obtained an F-score of 94.11% and an accuracy of 90.96%; thus, it can be concluded that both models have performed considerably with the same efficiency. Bejnordi *et al.* [6] on the other hand have proposed a three-step approach for detecting the presence of Ductal Carcinoma *In Situ* (DCIS) in H&E-stained histopathological WSIs. The proposed algorithm performed multi-scale superpixel classification in an attempt to identify the epithelial regions. This is followed by graph-based clustering of the epithelium-labeled superpixels and the subsequent delineation of the ROIs. Finally, the segmented regions are classified as benign or DCIS. Lastly comes the CAD systems predicting the classification between benign and malignant, and according to the survey carried out, the majority of the research works are focused upon this classification modality.

Table 3.1 represents the definitions of all of the medical jargon described in the aforementioned discussion for the convenience of the readers. Hereafter, the structure of the paper is framed in the following order. Section 3.2 describes the methodology and ideology adopted for successfully surveying all of the research works concerning the medical domain of breast cancer detection. Section 3.3 gives an account of different imaging modalities considering both the biological and computational perspectives. Additionally, this section also describes all of the publicly available datasets corresponding to each of the imaging modalities mentioned. Additionally, a mention of all of the private datasets used in the papers included in the survey has also been represented. Section 3.4 gives an account of the research works systematically bifurcated based on the type of technique adopted, i.e., machine learning (ML) or deep learning. They have been further arranged

**Table 3.1** Summary of the medical jargon used.

| Medical term | Definition | Source |
|---|---|---|
| Calcification | Minute solid bits of calcium found in the breast region | Chaudhury *et al.* [1] |
| Masses | Excessive growth of tissues leads to the formation of round structures that are further classified based on the region of the formation. | Wook Jeong *et al.* [3] |
| Ductal carcinoma *in situ* | Represents the condition wherein the cancerous outgrowth is limited to the milk duct region | Bejnordi *et al.* [6] |
| Invasive ductal carcinoma | Represents the medical condition wherein the cancerous region starts spreading in the surrounding regions and is not limited to the duct region. | Celik *et al.* [5] |
| Benign | Cancer that is non-spreading in nature | Deblee *et al.* [7] |
| Malignant | Cancer tends to spread and affect other organs | Deblee *et al.* [7] |

based on the imaging modality employed for the work. Finally, we conclude in Section 3.5 by highlighting the research gaps identified across the survey, thereby opening up new avenues for future research.

## 3.2 Procedure for Research Survey

We surveyed research papers of recent years covering a span from 2019 to 2022. A few papers from 2016 were also included in the survey, keeping in mind the novelty and complexity of the proposed approach. These papers were evaluated keeping in mind the following parameters: *1) Imaging modality used, 2) Complexity and novelty of the proposed approach, 3) Nature of the dataset employed, 4) Nature of technique used, i.e., whether ML or DL.* The general search criteria for this survey made use of keywords like "automated breast cancer detection," "CAD systems using ML and (name of the imaging modality)," "CNN-based CAD systems for breast cancer detection," and "ROI segmentation-based papers for BC detection." The searches were carried out in acclaimed research databases and websites like *1) PubMed, 2) Science Direct, 3) IEEE Xplore Digital Library, 4) Google Scholar, and 5) MDPI (Multidisciplinary Digital Publishing Institute).* A few survey papers were also reviewed to analyze and understand the procedure for drafting a survey paper concerning the subject of breast cancer. The references and details concerning the datasets were obtained from Kaggle.

## 3.3 Imaging Modalities and Their Datasets

### 3.3.1 Histopathological WSI

This imaging modality involves taking samples of soft tissues from the suspicious regions with the help of surgical experts using fine-needle aspiration (FNA). According to Mahmood *et al.* [8], these extracted tissues are then pigmented and examined under a microscope for further diagnosis, classification, and assertion. These are then converted into digital records, as microscopic slides are perishable, which is indeed useful for the application of automated algorithms. The digitized copies not only help in portability and record-storing but also give an edge over manual examination using a microscope in terms of enhancing magnification flexibility and also help view different regions without much eye-straining. The disadvantage that is faced is during the processing phase. The WSI file is typically memory-intensive and cannot be fed into the processing/classification model. Typically, this requires cropping out the ROI and augmenting the image that can lead to loss of diagnostically critical information. But on medical grounds, this is the most preferred and reliable imaging modality used for confirming the diagnosis of breast cancer.

Some of the popular public datasets concerning the aforementioned imaging modality are as follows:

(i) *IDC Breast Histopathological Image Dataset*: This dataset contains approximately 277,524 RGB image patches of dimensions 50 × 50 pixels, and the primary aim is to identify the presence of invasive ductal carcinoma.

(ii) *BACH Grand Challenge (ICIAR 2018 conference)*: The acronym BACH stands for breast cancer histology images that essentially consist of 400+ labeled microscopy images, and the task is to perform classification corresponding to four classes: normal, benign, *in situ* carcinoma, and invasive carcinoma.

(iii) *BreakHis (Breast Cancer Histopathological Database)*: This dataset contains approximately 9,109 microscopic images wherein there were 2,480 benign and 5,429 malignant samples. These samples are available in the RGB mode with the dimensions 700 × 460 pixels.

(iv) *CAMELYON17*: This dataset is a part of the challenge for detecting and differentiating between the metastatic and normal regions, and the annotations are available on the lesion level and patient level. The dataset contains 1,000 slide images covering different sections of the lymph node.

(v) *PCam dataset (Patch Camelyon)*: This dataset contains approximately 327,680 images wherein the ROI patch region of dimension 96 × 96 pixels has been extracted and labeled based on the presence of metastatic tissue.

## 3.3.2   Digital Mammography

This imaging modality involves capturing the insides of the breast by exposing the area under examination to low doses of X-rays. It is similar to CT wherein the images are taken in slices and then assembled for getting the whole image. CAD systems examine abnormalities by assessing the overall density and morphological features of the abnormal areas. As opposed to histopathological WSI, here, there is no need for manual effort for the conversion of digitization; however, as far as CAD systems are concerned, the mammograms require a lot of image preprocessing and annotations before feeding into the classification model.

Some of the popular public datasets concerning the aforementioned imaging modality are as follows:

(i) *DDSM-400 and CBIS-DDSM:* These datasets are often used together to increase the volume of the input data. The dataset contains ROI-extracted images of dimensions 299 × 299 pixels with a sample size of 55,890 out of which 14% of the samples are positive for the presence of malignancy while the remaining 86% are negative. Preprocessing techniques like cropping, random flips, and rotations accompanied by resizing have been performed.

(ii) *MIAS Mammography (Mammographic Image Analysis Society):* The dataset contains approximately 327 images with detailed annotations describing: 1) the character of the background tissue, 2) the class of abnormality present, 3) the severity of abnormality, and 4) coordinate location of the abnormality. The dimensions of the samples are 1,024 pixels × 1,024 pixels.

### 3.3.3 Ultrasound

This imaging modality is normally used for capturing and examining early signs of cancer like masses and calcifications. It is complementary to both mammograms and MRI and therefore can be used for deep diving into the abnormalities detected by the aforementioned scans. For instance, ultrasonography is recommended for whether a detected breast mass is a fluid-filled cyst or a solid tumor. However, the classification concerning benign and malignant is not very clear using this imaging modality. As far as the CAD systems are concerned, effective and precise feature selection tends to be an issue because of inaccurate contour identification and segmentation of the ROI. Additionally, the majority of the works concerning the use of ultrasonography have represented the need for manual annotations for training purposes, and therefore, this imaging modality is not fully supportive of automation.

Some of the popular public datasets concerning the aforementioned imaging modality are as follows:

(i) *OASBUD (Open Access Series of Breast Ultrasonic Data):* The dataset contains US scans of approximately 100 patients wherein 52 of them are malignant and 48 are benign. Additionally, two perpendicular scans in the transverse and longitudinal directions were performed for each lesion.

(ii) *UDIAT:* The dataset contains 163 US images wherein 110 of them belong to the benign category and 53 of them are malignant. The dataset was acquired from UDIAT Diagnostic Center in Spain by making use of a Siemens ACUSON scanner.

(iii) *BUSI (Breast Ultrasound Images Dataset):* Contains approximately 780 ultrasound scan images of dimensions $500 \times 500$ pixels and are collected from approximately 600 patients. The images are categorized into three classes, namely, normal, benign, and malignant. This dataset was developed by Dhabyani *et al.* [9].

### 3.3.4   Magnetic Resonance Imaging

This imaging modality is primarily performed on high-risk women who cannot undergo procedures like mammography and ultrasonography because of the nature of their tumors. This technique is based on the absorption of radio frequencies by the cellular nuclei in the presence of magnetic fields. However, concerning their implementation using CAD systems, the main issue faced is the segmentation and separation of the breast region from the non-required body parts. Additionally, because of the use of different frequencies while imaging, complex feature fusion techniques have to be used for extracting useful diagnostic conclusions from the scans using classification models.

The majority of the works concerning this domain consist of a privately collected dataset from hospitals mainly because of the need for manual annotation by a radiologist. However, the point to be noted is that majority of these works make use of dynamically contrast-enhanced MRI (DCE-MRI). One such benchmark report describing the practices and preprocessing methods utilized while collecting this dataset has been put up by Witowski *et al.* [10].

### 3.3.5   Infrared Breast Thermal Images

This imaging modality is noninvasive and nonionizing and makes use of temperature distribution across the breast region for detecting abnormality. According to Venkatachalam *et al.* [11], thermography is based upon the fact that precancerous regions exhibit higher temperatures as compared to surrounding regions because of a high metabolic rate due to angiogenesis. This activity is captured using an infrared thermal camera. However, the main issues posed by this imaging modality as rightly identified and as worked upon by Venkatachalam in [11] are intensity inhomogeneity, ROI overlapping, poor contrast, and low signal-to-noise ratio (SNR).

A reference to a refined privately collected dataset as utilized by Venkatachalam *et al.* [11] is as follows:

The Infrared Breast Thermal Images (IBTI) dataset used for this research work was collected from "Harshmitra Super Speciality Cancer Centre and Research Institute," Trichy, Tamil Nadu, India, and consisted of images captured using the infrared camera DITI CX320 having a resolution of 320 × 240. It contained data collected from approximately 50 patients.

**Table 3.2** Advantages and disadvantages.

| Imaging modality | Advantages | Disadvantages |
|---|---|---|
| Histopathological WSI | Useful for minute observation and classification concerning *in situ* and invasive ductal carcinoma | Large resolutions make it difficult for processing purposes. |
| Digital mammography | Noninvasive and efficient for the detection of tumors and masses | The multitude of image preprocessing required |
| Ultrasound | Noninvasive and painless method of image screening | Radiologist expertise and mandatory manual annotation required |
| Magnetic resonance imaging (MRI) | Is the most detailed imaging modality and is preferred for women at the high-risk stage. | Use of complex feature fusion techniques for the purpose of extracting diagnostically critical information |
| Infrared breast thermal images (IBTI) | noninvasive, nonionizing imaging modality and is therefore potentially harmless. | Intensity inhomogeneity, ROI overlapping, poor contrast, low signal-to-noise ratio (SNR). |

Another public dataset being used is DMR-IR that has been published by Fluminense Federal University, Brazil. This dataset too contained an account collected from 50 patients where the images were captured by making use of a FLIR infrared camera having a resolution of 640 × 480 pixels.

A summary of different imaging modalities along with an account of their advantages and disadvantages is represented in Table 3.2. Figure 3.1

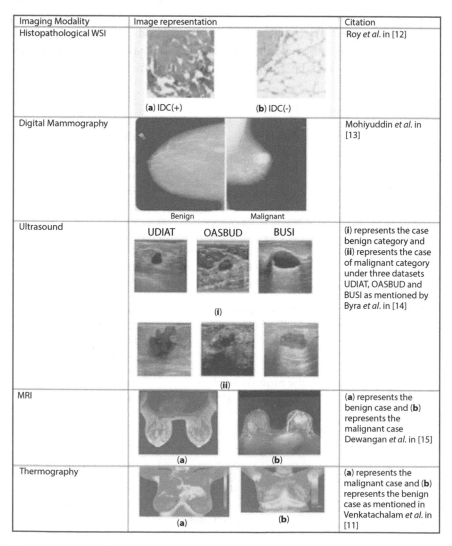

**Figure 3.1** Pictorial representation of the imaging modalities.

represents a pictorial representation of all of the aforementioned imaging modalities with the specification of benign and malignant.

## 3.4    Research Survey

This section gives a brief description of all of the notable research works concerning each imaging modality as mentioned in the aforementioned section. For the ease of identification of interest, these works have been systematically bifurcated depending on whether the proposed methodology was based on machine learning or deep learning.

### 3.4.1    Histopathological WSI

Given the complexity involved in the interpretation of the input image, most of the research works are based on deep-learning CNN models. However, an account of one of the noteworthy works involving the use of machine learning techniques is as follows.

#### 3.4.1.1    Machine Learning-Based Histopathological WSI

Roy *et al.* [12] have made use of ML classifiers and ensemble learning for drawing out the classification between IDC-positive and IDC-negative samples. The classification has been performed by the extraction of textural features like SIFT, SURF, and ORB. Haralick features are the statistical features that are taken into account for performing the classification. Pearson's coefficient has been used for weeding out the redundancy of features. The features thus extracted are subsequently fed into six classifiers, namely, random forest, extra trees, XGBoost, AdaBoost, CatBoost, and multilayer perceptron to present a comparative study. The proposed work concluded with the fact that CatBoost was able to deliver the highest accurate performance registering a figure of 92.55%. The proposed work made use of BreakHis dataset.

#### 3.4.1.2    Deep Learning-Based Histopathological WSI

Sanyal *et al.* [13] have based the proposed work on the BACH (Breast Cancer Histology Images) dataset that is posed as a challenge organized as a part of the ICIAR 2018 conference. The proposed methodology involves fine-tuning of principal and popular CNN architectures, namely, VGG 19, InceptionV3, Inception-ResNetv2, and ResNet-101 to extract classification critical and discriminative features. As a part of ensemble learning, XGBoost has been incorporated into the softmax layer for improving the classification performance. The work proposes a model performing four-class classification at the image and patch level. The classification categories are *in situ*, invasive, normal, and benign. The inference of image level is drawn from the fact that the individual patches together make an image and the classification at the image level is essentially made out by using the patches as participants during the voting procedure.

Das *et al.* [14] have proposed a methodology for automating the preprocessing stage wherein manual annotations are required. It makes use of a deep multiple instance learning-based CNN framework. Its working can be closely mapped to the popular bags of words approach that is adopted and widely used for sentiment analysis in the domain of natural language processing (NLP). Here, the input test images are represented as a bag of patches that are obtained during the training phase. The input test image is classified as benign if and only if all of the patches are benign and classified as malignant even if anyone of the patch comes out to be malignant. Additionally, the versatility of the proposed model has been represented by testing it on diverse and popular datasets like BreakHis, IUHPL, and UCSB, registering accuracy figures of 93.06%, 96.63%, and 95.83%, respectively.

Han *et al.* [15] have come up with a noteworthy methodology targeting the multi-classification problem involving the identification of subordinate classes of malignant tissues that are named ductal carcinoma, lobular carcinoma, adenosis, fibroadenoma, phyllodes tumor, tubular adenoma, mucinous carcinoma, and papillary carcinoma. The novelty of the proposed work is the introduction of a new deep learning model called the structured deep learning model that achieves an accuracy of 93.2%. The novelty of class structure-based deep convolutional neural network (CSDCNN) is that it systematically bypasses the stage involving feature engineering for the training process, and instead of that, it makes use of space distance constraints for classification.

### 3.4.2   Digital Mammogram

#### 3.4.2.1   Machine Learning-Based Digital Mammogram

Mohiyuddin *et al.* [16] have made use of the popular object detection algorithm YOLO for scanning digital mammograms and classifying them as malignant or benign. The proposed model aims to decrease the false positive rate (FPR) and false negative rate (FNR) while increasing Matthew's correlation coefficient (MCC). Initially, the preprocessing stage involves the removal of rough white borders and pectoral muscles. This is followed by the usage of contrast limited adaptive histogram equalization (CLAHE) for image enhancement. CLAHE is primarily used for viewing the hidden features wherein the image is fragmented into tiles and the adjacent tiles are then blended using bilinear interpolation for removing the false boundaries. The prepared data are then fed as input to the proposed model of YOLOv5 that utilizes all four versions of YOLOv5. This is followed by presenting a comparative study with YOLOv3 and faster RCNN. The accuracy produced as a result is a whopping 96.5%. The dataset used for the aforementioned work was CBIS-DDSM.

Darweesh *et al.* [17] have proposed a two-level hierarchical classification wherein the first classification is distinguishing between normal and abnormal tissues, while the second level dives deep into the abnormality for further classification as benign or malignant. Feature extraction in the first phase uses GLCM, while the second level makes use of local binary patterns (LBP). The point to be noted here is that random forest is employed as the classifier in both stages of classification. The first stage classification gives an accuracy of 97%, whereas the second stage classification gives an accuracy of 75%. The model together produces an overall accuracy of 85% and an MCC coefficient value of 0.76. MIAS was employed as the dataset for the aforementioned work.

### 3.4.2.2   Deep Learning-Based Digital Mammogram

Tsochatzidis *et al.* [18] have proposed a methodology to integrate mammographic segmentation information along with the input image to improve the diagnosis. This involves modification in each of the CNN layers such that the information of the input image along with the segmentation map is considered.

Either the segmentation maps can be established from the ground truth or an automatic segmentation system is put in place using U-Net, which by its features of upsampling, downsampling, and skip layers come up with the segmented lesion. Furthermore, a new loss function is introduced, which adds an extra term to the standard cross-entropy, aiming to steer the attention of the network toward the mass region, penalizing strong feature activations based on their location. The main CNN model thereafter employed is ResNet. DDSM-400 and CBIS-DDSM were used for implementing the proposed model.

Mohapatra *et al.* [19] have come up with a survey paper for analyzing and comparing the performance of various popular CNN architectures like AlexNet, VGG16, and ResNet. All these models were trained on the CBIS-DDSM dataset, and the ratio of 90:10 is used as the validation strategy. According to the observations, AlexNet emerged as the best-performing model, putting up an accuracy of 65% when fine-tuned and pretrained with weights. VGG16 and ResNet-50 registered accuracy figures of 65% and 61%, respectively, under the same circumstances.

### 3.4.3   Ultrasound

#### 3.4.3.1   Machine Learning-Based Ultrasound

Cheng et al. [20] have presented an effective survey about the techniques being used by CAD systems based on ultrasound images. The survey explores methods being applied for automated breast cancer detection under four main phases: 1) image preprocessing, 2) image segmentation, 3) feature extraction and selection, and 4) classification. The image preprocessing stage aims at targeting and solving image modality issues like low contrast and speckle interference. The techniques covered under the image segmentation phase are aimed at identifying and isolating the ROI. Under the section concerning feature extraction and selection, the author presents a detailed description of the most effective features that are detrimental to the accurate performance of classifiers. It is under the classifiers section that the application of popular machine learning techniques like linear discriminant analysis, logistic regression, Bayesian neural networks, and decision trees is discussed at length. The research works providing an application of the aforementioned techniques have also been pondered upon as a part of this survey.

Sadad et al. [21] have proposed a methodology that employs the use of ML-based classifiers like a decision tree and KNN. It makes use of Hilbert transform for the conversion of original ultrasound images into B-mode. These B-mode images are in turn used for ease of tumor identification and detection given the low contrast of the ultrasound images. Segmentation of the lesions is done using marker-controlled watershed transformation, and a hybrid set of features including shape and texture parameters is used for feature extraction. In addition to the public dataset OASBUD, the work also makes use of a private dataset collected from Baheya Hospital, Egypt.

#### 3.4.3.2   Deep Learning-Based Ultrasound

Byra [22] proposed novel changes in transfer learning techniques that are applied to CAD systems in the medical domain. Traditionally, transfer learning involves fine-tuning wherein the weights of pretrained networks are modified to address the given medical problem. However, fine-tuning becomes difficult in case the number of trainable parameters becomes large and therefore the work proposes a novel transfer learning technique based on deep representation scaling (DRS) that is inserted in between the CNN blocks for better flow of information. With the application of DRS, we need to just change the DRS parameters and significantly reduce the number of trainable parameters. To showcase the accuracy of the proposed model, the authors have implemented it to be used on a system of breast mass classification implemented upon a dataset of ultrasound images. Indeed, the method seems to be pretty effective to be implemented on other medical domains as well seeing it registering the accuracy figures of approximately 0.915.

Li *et al.* [23] have proposed an entirely novel CNN architecture for the detection of malignant lesions in ultrasound images. It is called BUSnet. This architecture has been specifically developed for effectively solving and terminating accuracy-depleting factors like speckle noise and acoustic shadow. ROI segmentation makes use of unsupervised region proposal and bounding box regression algorithms. The unsupervised region proposal method makes use of the Canny Edge Detector, while ResNet-50 serves as the backbone for the bounding box regression technique. Aggregation is used as the postprocessing technique that effectively integrates all of the regressive bounding boxes into one and thereby eliminates redundant information.

### 3.4.4    MRI-Based

#### 3.4.4.1    Machine Learning-Based MRI Analysis

Dewangan *et al.* [24] have proposed an ML-based approach by making use of MRI images. The novelty of the work lies in its preprocessing stage wherein an effective combination of Wiener and median filters is used. Together, this combination is named Wienmed filter. The combined application of these two filters ensures the replacement of the noisy neighborhood pixels, thereby improving the quality of the MRI breast image portion. Additionally, it also leads to the enhancement of some of the important image attributes that play a vital role during the classification process. After the preprocessing stage, the images are fed to the backpropagation recurrent Wienmed model that is used for performing the classification and identification of breast tumors in the image. GLCM is used for feature extraction. Additionally, the proposed work makes use of a hybrid algorithm called hybrid krill herd African buffalo optimization for improving classification accuracy. The accuracy thus produced is 99.6% with a 0.12%

lower error rate that is quite appreciable given the complexity of the dataset under examination. This work can further be explored for understanding the formulation and implementation of hybrid algorithms.

### 3.4.4.2   Deep Learning-Based MRI Analysis

Hu *et al.* in [25] have made a private dataset by acquiring examination samples over 8 years spanning from 2005 to 2013 at a medical institute. The MRI images have been collected in two sequences, DCE-MRI and T2-weighted. The extraction of features from these two sequences of MRI scan can be incorporated in the following three ways:

- Image fusion – fusing the DCE and T2w images for producing the RGB composite
- Feature fusion – merging the CNN features extracted from both the DCE and T2w images and then serving it to the SVM for classification
- Classifier fusion – Aggregation of the malignancy probability output from both the DCE and T2w via soft voting

The proposed work makes use of the feature fusion technique. ROI location has been done using fuzzy C-means with the provision of seed indication done manually. The identification of 4D characteristics concerning temporal and volumetric has been done uniquely for each frequency sequence. For DCE, maximum intensity projection (MIP) was performed over the images obtained from the second postcontrast subtraction. However, for the T2w sequence images, the largest lesion area was selected and cropped out. These were subsequently fed into a deep-learning CNN model for getting the results.

Ha and Vahedi [26] have proposed an automated tumor detection system based on hybrid CNN architecture and implementation of an improved deer hunting optimization algorithm (DHOA). The first phase involves preprocessing that involves normalization of the intensities followed by noise removal. The filter used here is based on the fuzzy-neural network as proposed by Ma *et al.* [27], and the primary aim here is the removal of acoustic noise. The novelty of the proposed work lies in the implementation of an improved version of the deer hunting optimization algorithm that is used in CNN architecture replacing the traditional back-propagation approach to reduce network error. The proposed work also makes use of Haralick texture and LBP for feature extraction.

Jiao *et al.* [28] have proposed an automated breast mass detection approach consisting of two main parts: breast region segmentation and breast mass detection. Here, for the segmentation approach, a DCNN model based on the U-Net++ framework has been used. The segmented parts are then fed into Faster RCNN that itself is composed of two modules. The first module is a DCNN used for region proposal, and the second module is a detector that generates output by using the proposed regions. ResNet 101 is used for feature extraction, and subsequently, the feature map so generated is considered by the region proposal network (RPN) to generate multiple coordinates, each of them being graded according to an objectness score. In this way, tumors having a diameter of less than 48 pixels are targeted and identified by the aforementioned methodology.

### 3.4.5  Thermography-Based

#### 3.4.5.1  *Machine Learning-Based Thermography Analysis*

Venkatachalam *et al.* [11] have proposed effective ROI segmentation from the relatively complex thermogram that suffers from issues like intensity inhomogeneity, ROI overlapping, poor contrast, and low SNR. The image preprocessing involves the conversion of pseudo-colored images to gray scale followed by the segmentation of non-breast regions. The left and right breasts are thereafter separated and undergo binary histogram difference thresholding (BHDT) for segmenting the contours exhibiting high-intensity inhomogeneity. The Multiscale Local Global Image Fitted (MLGFI) model is used for getting more clear segmentation results from the outputs produced after the application of BHDT. This procedure makes use of multiscale median filters, and according to the mathematical derivations presented, we get the image devoid of intensity inhomogeneity as a result. To prove the efficiency of the proposed segmentation approach, its performance is compared with state-of-art ML methods like Fuzzy C Means (FCM), Chan-Vese (CV-ACM), and K-means. Benign and malignant tissues exhibit significant differences corresponding to the area-based features (AFs) and average intensity-based features (AIFs), and therefore, the work proposes the computation of the absolute difference of the aforementioned features corresponding to the inflamed region and residual region. GLCM is used for extracting the textural features, and for classification, all of these features are fed into a support vector machine (SVM). The proposed work exhibits an accuracy of 91.5%.

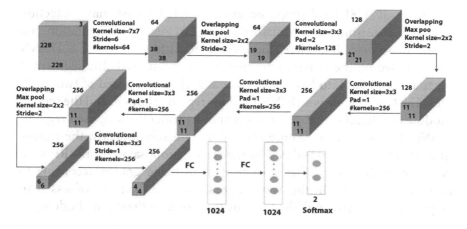

**Figure 3.2** CNN architecture as illustrated by Mohamed *et al.* in [29].

### 3.4.5.2  Deep Learning-Based Thermography Analysis

Mohamed *et al.* [29] have proposed an approach that can be systematically segmented into three phases, namely, image resizing, breast area segmentation, and classification. The thermal images are available of the size 640 × 480 pixels that can prove to be computationally intensive for processing, and therefore, the first phase involves resizing the input image to the dimension 280 × 280 pixels. This is followed by segmenting the breast area from other body parts that act as noise, and this is achieved by making use of the U-Net network structure. U-Net over a series of works has been proven effective for biomedical segmentation. The two-class classification concerning abnormal and normal areas is done using a CNN model that is indigenously developed and trained from scratch. The novelty, therefore, lies in the architecture of the proposed CNN model. The architecture diagram is shown in Figure 3.2.

Here, the use of transfer learning is not done as opposed to existing works and therefore indicates the novelty in the work. The proposed system is evaluated considering the measures of accuracy, sensitivity, and specificity and registers the figures 99.33%, 100%, and 98.67%, respectively. The figures put up are indeed impressive and commendable.

## 3.5  Conclusion

The paper discussed the characteristics of some of the most prominent imaging modalities that are used for breast cancer detection. It also presented a review of the characteristics of popular public datasets corresponding to each imaging modality so that the readers can infer and make informed choices concerning the dataset to be used for research. Additionally, some very notable works systematically segmented into sections concerning machine learning and deep learning have been presented as a source of reference so that the readers can imbibe and implement hybrid formulations from the aforementioned proposed methodologies.

There are still some relatively unexplored techniques and subjects that can open up new avenues for future research. Concerning histopathological WSI, the research can be extended for the formulation of efficient patch extraction techniques, thereby reducing the rate of misclassifications. Mammographic scans are majorly used for predicting whether a given mass is malignant or benign. However, the scope of multiclass classification is evident and must be explored. Research works concerning the use of ultrasound scans are mostly involved in mass detection, and the dataset used is also standard 2D scans. With the introduction of high-resolution US and 3D scans as rightly pointed out by Cheng et al. [20], research works implementable on these latest version datasets can be developed for the detection of microcalcifications. Lastly, in recent years, there has been a trend of using complementary imaging modalities (mammography with ultrasound scans for instance), and therefore, there arises a need for developing CAD systems implementable on mixed modality datasets.

From the survey, it has been noticed that most of the works based on medical image processing have preferred the use of deep learning techniques over machine learning. However, machine learning too can be employed over datasets for representing diagnostic parameters in numerical form as has been  represented in the dataset titled "Breast Cancer Wisconsin (Diagnostic) Data set" in Kaggle. It has the diagnosis based on 10 real-valued features like radius, texture, perimeter, concavity, and symmetry to name a few. This, therefore, opens up a new avenue for research concerning classification based on numerical diagnostic parameters.

## 3.6   Acknowledgment

I would like to extend my gratitude towards Dr. Girish N. Bedre (MD Radiation Oncology) of Shree Guruji Hospital, Nashik for giving his valuable insights and sharing information concerning the technical nuances of the imaging modalities discussed in this work. I would also like to thank my guide and co-author Dr. Leninisha Shanmugam for propelling my research efforts in the correct direction. Lastly, I would like to thank

Vellore Institute of Technology, Chennai for providing me with the opportunity and knowledge resources to carry forward my research.

# References

1. Chaudhury, S., Rakhra, M., Memon, N., Sau, K., Ayana, M.T., Breast cancer calcifications: Identification using a novel segmentation approach. *Comput. Math. Methods Med.*, 2021, 9905808, Oct. 2021, doi: 10.1155/2021/9905808.

2. Loizidou, K., Skouroumouni, G., Nikolaou, C., Pitris, C., An automated breast micro-calcification detection and classification technique using temporal subtraction of mammograms. *IEEE Access*, 8, 52785–52795, 2020, doi: 10.1109/ACCESS.2020.2980616.

3. Jeong, J.-W., Yu, D., Lee, S., Chang, J.M., Automated detection algorithm of breast masses in three-dimensional ultrasound images. *Healthc. Inform. Res.*, 22, 4, 293–298, Oct. 2016, doi: 10.4258/hir.2016.22.4.293.

4. Hamed, G., Marey, M., Amin, S.E., Tolba, M.F., Automated breast cancer detection and classification in full field digital mammograms using two full and cropped detection paths approach. *IEEE Access*, 9, 116898–116913, 2021, doi: 10.1109/ACCESS.2021.3105924.

5. Celik, Y., Talo, M., Yildirim, O., Karabatak, M., Acharya, U.R., Automated invasive ductal carcinoma detection based using deep transfer learning with whole-slide images. *Pattern Recognit. Lett.*, 133, 232–239, May 2020, doi: 10.1016/j.patrec.2020.03.011.

6. Ehteshami Bejnordi, B. *et al.*, Automated detection of DCIS in whole-slide H&E stained breast histopathology images. *IEEE Trans. Med. Imaging*, 35, 9, 2141–2150, Sep. 2016, doi: 10.1109/TMI.2016.2550620.

7. Debelee, T.G., Schwenker, F., Ibenthal, A., Yohannes, D., Survey of deep learning in breast cancer image analysis. *Evol. Syst.*, 11, 1, 143–163, Mar. 2020, doi: 10.1007/s12530-019-09297-2.

8. Mahmood, T., Li, J., Pei, Y., Akhtar, F., Imran, A., Rehman, K.U., A brief survey on breast cancer diagnostic with deep learning schemes using multi-image modalities. *IEEE Access*, 8, 165779–165809, 2020, doi: 10.1109/ACCESS.2020.3021343.

9. Al-Dhabyani, W., Gomaa, M., Khaled, H., Fahmy, A., Dataset of breast ultrasound images. *Data Brief*, 28, 104863, Feb. 2020, doi: 10.1016/j.dib.2019.104863.

10. Witowski, J. *et al.*, The NYU breast MRI dataset v1.0.

11. Venkatachalam, N., Shanmugam, L., Heltin, G.C., Govindarajan, G., Sasipriya, P., Enhanced segmentation of inflamed ROI to improve the accuracy of identifying benign and malignant cases in breast thermogram. *J. Oncol.*, 2021, 5566853, 2021, doi: 10.1155/2021/5566853.

12. Roy, S.D., Das, S., Kar, D., Schwenker, F., Sarkar, R., Computer aided breast cancer detection using ensembling of texture and statistical image features. *Sensors*, 21, 11, 3628, Art. no. 11, Jan. 2021, doi: 10.3390/s21113628.

13. Sanyal, R., Kar, D., Sarkar, R., Carcinoma type classification from high-resolution breast microscopy images using a hybrid ensemble of deep convolutional features and gradient boosting trees classifiers. *IEEE/ACM Trans. Comput. Biol. Bioinform.*, 19, 4, 2124–2136, Jul. 2022, doi: 10.1109/TCBB.2021.3071022.

14. Das, K., Conjeti, S., Chatterjee, J., Sheet, D., Detection of breast cancer from whole slide histopathological images using deep multiple instance CNN. *IEEE Access*, 8, 213502–213511, 2020, doi: 10.1109/ACCESS.2020.3040106.

15. Han, Z., Wei, B., Zheng, Y., Yin, Y., Li, K., Li, S., Breast cancer multi-classification from histopathological images with structured deep learning model. *Sci. Rep.*, 7, 1, 4172, Jun. 2017, doi: 10.1038/s41598-017-04075-z.

16. Mohiyuddin, A. *et al.*, Breast tumor detection and classification in mammogram images using modified YOLOv5 network. *Comput. Math. Methods Med.*, 2022, 1359019, Jan. 2022, doi: 10.1155/2022/1359019.

17. Darweesh, M.S. *et al.*, Early breast cancer diagnostics based on hierarchical machine learning classification for mammography images. *Cogent Eng.*, 8, 1, 1968324, Jan. 2021, doi: 10.1080/23311916.2021.1968324.

18. Tsochatzidis, L., Koutla, P., Costaridou, L., Pratikakis, I., Integrating segmentation information into CNN for breast cancer diagnosis of mammographic masses. *Comput. Methods Programs Biomed.*, 200, 105913, Mar. 2021, doi: 10.1016/j.cmpb.2020.105913.

19. Mohapatra, S., Muduly, S., Mohanty, S., Ravindra, J.V.R., Mohanty, S.N., Evaluation of deep learning models for detecting breast cancer using histopathological mammograms images. *Sustainable Oper. Comput.*, 3, 296–302, Jan. 2022, doi: 10.1016/j.susoc.2022.06.001.

20. Cheng, H.D., Shan, J., Ju, W., Guo, Y., Zhang, L., Automated breast cancer detection and classification using ultrasound images: A survey. *Pattern Recognit.*, 43, 1, 299–317, Jan. 2010, doi: 10.1016/j.patcog.2009.05.012.

21. Sadad, T., Hussain, A., Munir, A., Habib, M., Ali Khan, S., Hussain, S., Yang, S., Alawairdhi, M., Identification of breast malignancy by marker-controlled watershed transformation and hybrid feature set for healthcare. *Appl. Sci.*, 10, 6, 1900, 2020, https://doi.org/10.3390/app10061900.

22. Byra, M., Breast mass classification with transfer learning based on scaling of deep representations. *Biomed. Signal Process. Control*, 69, 102828, Aug. 2021, doi: 10.1016/j.bspc.2021.102828.

23. Li, Y., Gu, H., Wang, H., Qin, P., Wang, J., BUSnet: A deep learning model of breast tumor lesion detection for ultrasound images. *Front. Oncol.*, 12, 848271, 2022, Accessed: Dec. 17, 2022. [Online]. Available: https://www.frontiersin.org/articles/10.3389/fonc.2022.848271.

24. Dewangan, K.K., Dewangan, D.K., Sahu, S.P., Janghel, R., Breast cancer diagnosis in an early stage using novel deep learning with hybrid optimization

technique. *Multimed. Tools Appl.*, 81, 10, 13935–13960, 2022, doi: 10.1007/s11042-022-12385-2.

25. Hu, Q., Whitney, H.M., Giger, M.L., A deep learning methodology for improved breast cancer diagnosis using multiparametric MRI. *Sci. Rep.*, 10, 10536, 2020, https://doi.org/10.1038/s41598-020-67441-4.

26. Ha, W. and Vahedi, Z., Automatic breast tumor diagnosis in MRI based on a hybrid CNN and feature-based method using improved deer hunting optimization algorithm. *Comput. Intell. Neurosci.*, 2021, 5396327, Jul. 2021, doi: 10.1155/2021/5396327.

27. Ma, D., Shang, L., Tang, J., Bao, Y., Fu, J., Yin, J., Classifying breast cancer tissue by Raman spectroscopy with one-dimensional convolutional neural network. *Spectrochim. Acta A Mol. Biomol. Spectrosc.*, 256, 119732, Jul. 2021, doi: 10.1016/j.saa.2021.119732.

28. Jiao, H., Jiang, X., Pang, Z., Lin, X., Huang, Y., Li, L., Deep convolutional neural networks-based automatic breast segmentation and mass detection in DCE-MRI. *Comput. Math. Methods Med.*, 2020, 1–12, May 2020, doi: 10.1155/2020/2413706.

29. Mohamed, E.A., Rashed, E.A., Gaber, T., Karam, O., Deep learning model for fully automated breast cancer detection system from thermograms. *PLoS One*, 17, 1, e0262349, Jan. 2022, doi: 10.1371/journal.pone.0262349.

# 4

# Enhancing Feature Selection Through Metaheuristic Hybrid Cuckoo Search and Harris Hawks Optimization for Cancer Classification

**Abrar Yaqoob[1]\*, Navneet Kumar Verma[1], Rabia Musheer Aziz[2] and Akash Saxena[3]**

*[1]School of Advanced Science and Language, VIT Bhopal University, Kothrikalan, Sehore, India*
*[2]State Planning Institute (New Division), Planning Department Lucknow, Utter Pradesh, India*
*[3]School of Engineering and Technology, Central University of Haryana, Mahendergarh, India*

## Abstract

Gene expression platforms offer vast amounts of data that can be utilized for investigating diverse biological processes. However, due to the existence of redundant and irrelevant genes, it remains challenging to identify crucial genes from high-dimensional biological data. To overcome this obstacle, researchers have introduced different feature selection (FS) methods. Developing more efficient and accurate FS techniques is essential to select important genes for the classification of complex biological information with multiple dimensions for many purposes. To tackle the difficulty of selecting genes in high-dimensional biological datasets, a novel approach called the Harris hawks optimization and cuckoo search algorithm (HHOCSA) is proposed for commonly used machine learning classifiers such as K-nearest neighbors (KNN), support vector machine (SVM), and naive Bayes (NB). The effectiveness of the hybrid gene selection algorithm was assessed using six commonly used datasets and compared to other techniques for selecting features. The experimental findings demonstrate that the HHOCSA outperforms alternative methods when considering performance metrics of accuracy measures such as precision, sensitivity, and specificity. Furthermore, the HHOCSA

*\*Corresponding author*: abraryaqoob77@gmail.com

Kanak Kalita, Narayanan Ganesh and S. Balamurugan (eds.) Metaheuristics for Machine Learning: Algorithms and Applications, (95–134) © 2024 Scrivener Publishing LLC

approach proposed in this study is both computationally efficient and consistent in terms of variability when compared to the other methods. Therefore, the proposed hybrid algorithm can be used as a useful instrument for the classification of cancer datasets and can help medical professionals make better-informed decisions in cancer diagnosis.

*Keywords*: Harris hawks optimization and cuckoo search algorithm (HHOCSA), K-nearest neighbors (KNN), support vector machine (SVM), naive Bayes (NB)

## 4.1 Introduction

Cancer is a significant global health issue that affects populations across the globe, with millions of new cases diagnosed every year. While advances in medical technology have significantly improved cancer diagnosis and treatment, the complexity of the disease remains a challenge. Early and accurate diagnosis is crucial for successful treatment outcomes, and the potential of machine learning techniques is enormous in this area. In particular, gene expression microarray data analysis using machine learning has appeared as a promising tool for identifying cancer [1]. Machine learning models have been developed during the last 10 years as a result of the study of publicly accessible cancer data. Recently, models for classifying cancer types and diagnosing cancer in its early stages based on machine learning have been published [2]. Machine learning has greatly helped genetic data analysis. It has been put into use in several fields of biological sciences, mostly in the last 20 years. Making prediction models for identifying malignant growths from tumor tissue is among the most promising uses of machine learning.

Gene expression microarray data analysis involves the discovery of genes important for cancer categorization and diagnosis. Because of the vast number of genes involved and the complex nature of the data, which lead to a high-dimensional space, it becomes a challenging task. Selecting a group of genes that are most pertinent to the condition will increase the precision of cancer categorization. This process is known as feature selection, and it involves identifying a smaller set of characteristics that can accurately discriminate between cancer and non-cancer sample. The use of arrays to detect cancer is a newer area of intelligence analysis. The capacity of gene chip technology to examine hundreds of genes' expression patterns concurrently results in the development of unique profiles of biological processes. Researchers are examining the properties of microarray technology for classification of cancer, which may help to provide a deeper understanding of the disease.

Cancer classification issues are resolved by differentiating healthy and unhealthy samples using microarray organic phenomenon information. Microarray technology has the potential to provide a substantial technique for prognosis and diagnosis, which will also expand knowledge of the primary origins of cancer and open the door to the creation of innovative treatments. The majority of the alternatives (genes) are useless even though there are more possibilities (genes) in these data than there are samples, which results in an oversized visit classification accuracy. The method of factor selection was first used as a technique for categorization, comprises choosing the smallest group of genetic variants that are most relevant to the associated cluster. As a result, the classifier's ability to categorize samples precisely is improved. As a result, using heuristic methods to solve this problem is more effective. The two key concerns driving microarray research are the knowledge is limited or deficient, meaning there are often just a few dozen samples, and it is robust, meaning it encompasses many thousands of genes (features). Second, because genes seem to be either directly or indirectly associated, there is a great level of richness in the understanding of organic phenomena. These methods did not work effectively since conventional machine learning procedures function best when there are more samples than attributes. As they utilize various technical advancements in the fields of deep learning, machine learning, and artificial intelligence to aid healthcare professionals in quickly spotting abnormalities, these image-based medical systems can be highly helpful for the early identification of cancer. Sadly, this system's architecture demands a training set containing useful characteristics, yet the actual features acquired may be completely useless. Consequently, before a consequence, prior to categorization, relevant features with a high potential for discrimination are selected [3].

Feature selection encompasses various techniques, such as filter, wrapper, and embedded approaches. Filter methods prioritize characteristics determined by their significance to the desired outcome variable, while wrapper methods assess feature subsets using machine learning algorithms. Embedded methods integrate feature selection directly into the learning algorithm. All of these techniques possess their own advantages and limitations, and the selection of an appropriate method primarily relies on the characteristics of the dataset and the specific problem under consideration. Recently, various novel hybrid optimization algorithms have been proposed for the task of selecting relevant features in cancer classification. Hybrid algorithms combine two or more optimization techniques to achieve better performance than each individual technique.

The suggested method reduced the computing complexity of the Harris hawks optimization (HHO) exploitation process by using the cuckoo search (CS). Although the CS algorithm has a strong exploitation process, it is less successful than the HHO algorithm at discovering new ideal solutions. As a result, the CS algorithm's main shortcomings are its convergence issue and early discovery of the local optima. CS is an algorithm designed for optimization purposes that draws inspiration from the behavior of cuckoo birds. It operates by generating a population of potential solutions and creating new solutions by imitating the cuckoo's habit of deposition of eggs within the nests of different bird species. The algorithm incorporates a random walk to generate fresh candidate solutions, and the top-performing solutions are retained for the subsequent generation. On the other hand, HHO is another optimization algorithm rooted in the hunting behavior of Harris hawks. It involves a collective effort by a group of hawks to search for prey, with each hawk employing its own distinct strategy. The algorithm employs an integration of both local and global search methods, techniques to uncover the optimal solution. The combination of CS and HHO has been shown to be effective for feature selection in cancer classification. This hybrid algorithm combines the strengths of both CS and HHO to achieve better performance than either algorithm alone. The algorithm uses CS to generate candidate solutions, and HHO is used to refine the solutions and determine the most suitable set of features. The CSAHHO algorithm combines the HHO and CS algorithms to preserve the equilibrium between the period following the exploitation and exploration stages [3].

The recommended work contributes considerably to the following:

1. A novel hybrid algorithm, known as the HHOCSA (cuckoo search and Harris hawks optimizations), has been developed to specifically target cancer identification.
2. The suggested approach fixes the issue of minimal convergence of HHO.
3. The combination of HHO and CS algorithms is employed to keep the processes of extraction and exploration in balance.

This article will follow a structured approach to explore a specific topic. The *Introduction* will provide an overview of the research purpose and structure. Section 4.2 will cover related work, while Section 4.3 will introduce the unique research approach used. Section 4.4 will present the overview of the classifiers used in the proposed algorithm. Section 4.5 will provide an analysis and interpretation of the results and their potential

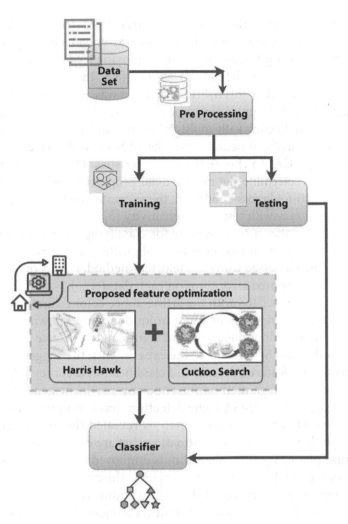

**Figure 4.1** The proposed research methodology.

consequences, while Section 4.6 will conclude the article by summarizing the key findings, discussing their significance, and providing recommendations for future research. Figure 4.1 shows the proposed methodological approach in broad strokes.

## 4.2 Related Work

Nanglia *et al.* developed a technique for categorizing cancer that included three basic components. The data were initially preprocessed in the first block, next using the SURF approach, features were retrieved from the second block. In the third block, the model was enhanced using a genetic algorithm, and using a neural network employing feed-forward and back-propagation techniques, the tumor was classified. The overall classification correctness achieved by this hybrid algorithm was an amazing 98.08% [4].

Sahu *et al.* created a prediction model by fusing learning strategies based on artificial intelligence with multivariate statistical methods. This study suggests using artificial neural networks (ANNs) with principal component analysis (PCA) to choose the characteristics. Data are preprocessed using PCA to determine the most crucial properties. Utilizing the WBC Dataset with 10-fold cross-validation, the suggested method demonstrated improved accuracy with respect to sensitivity [5].

A hybrid metaheuristic technique for classifying cancer was proposed by Motieghader *et al.* using the genetic algorithm and learning automata (GALA). When assessed using the selected method, GALA outperformed certain newly proposed algorithms on each dataset [6].

The benefits associated with the artificial bee colony algorithm and ant colony algorithm are combined in a unique method known as AC-ABC hybrid, created by Shunmugapriya and Kanmani to enhance feature selection. According to the findings of the experiments, the suggested method seeks to increase feature selection and classification accuracy [7].

A unique two-stage method for choosing pertinent genes for cancer classification, called MI-GA Gene Selection, has been proposed by Jansi Rani M. and Devaraj. First-stage analysis revealed the presence of genes with a high degree of mutual information that are connected to cancer. In the second phase, a genetic algorithm is employed to select a set of genes capable of accurately classifying cancer data. The classification process utilized a support vector machine (SVM). The findings reveal that the MI-GA method, as proposed, surpasses current techniques in terms of classification accuracy for ovarian, lung, and colon cancer datasets [8].

The mRMR-COA-HS is a two-step technique of gene selection that was developed by Elyasigomari *et al.* To find a significant set of genes, they first use the lowest redundancy and maximum relevance strategy. Following that, they employ a wrapper configuration made consisting of a support vector machine classifier and a brand-new cuckoo optimization technique called the harmony search (COA-HS). The maximum degree of categorization accuracy is guaranteed by this algorithm [9].

Jain *et al.* devised a hybrid approach for cancer classification that combines correlation-based feature selection with an improved binary particle swarm optimization. The model utilizes the naive Bayes classifier alongside stratified 10-fold cross-validation to classify biological samples with binary and multiclass malignancies. Consistently, the outcomes exhibit the superior performance of this model over seven other well-established strategies, regarding both classification precision and the quantity of selected genes [10].

Shahbeig *et al.* introduced a novel hybrid method for identifying crucial genes linked to the development of breast cancer. Their objective was to uncover the most concise gene set capable of achieving optimal levels of classification accuracy, sensitivity, and specificity. To achieve this, they merged the teaching learning-based optimization (TLBO) technique with a recently introduced mutant fuzzy adaptive particle swarm optimization method. Their approach produced encouraging outcomes, with a detection accuracy of 91.88%, sensitivity of 90.55%, and specificity of 93.33% when applied to microarray data for breast cancer detection [11].

Lu *et al.* utilized a hybrid method for feature selection, merging mutual information maximization (MIM) with an adaptive evolutionary algorithm. Their experimental results demonstrate that this approach effectively reduces the dimensionality of gene expression data and eliminates redundancies in the classification process. When compared to traditional feature selection methods, their generated gene expression dataset achieved the highest classification accuracy [12].

Naeem *et al.* demonstrated the precise diagnosis of liver cancer using machine learning algorithms. They integrated a dataset consisting of two-dimensional computed tomography images and magnetic resonance imaging. Through the application of 10-fold cross-validation, they assessed the performance of multilayer perceptron (MLP), support vector machine, random forest (RF), and J48 classifiers using an optimized hybrid-feature dataset. Notably, the MLP classifier showcased remarkable success, achieving an impressive accuracy of 99% [13].

Kharrat and Neji employed simulated annealing and genetic algorithm (SA-GA) techniques to generate the most optimal subset of features. The efficacy of this approach was assessed by employing two real datasets of magnetic resonance imaging for brain tumor analysis. Advanced methods like simulated annealing and genetic algorithms were compared to the suggested methodology. The outcomes showed that SAGA outperforms and computes more quickly than these approaches when used separately. With segmentation correctness rates of 97.82% and 0.74 for glioma tumors and 95.12% and 3.21% for pituitary malignancies, the analysis showed that the suggested method is superior to cutting-edge methodologies [14].

Zheng *et al.* presented a hybrid method for selecting feature subsets known as the maximum Pearson maximum distance enhanced whale optimization approach. This technique combines Pearson's correlation coefficient with a correlation distance-based MPMD filtering algorithm.

Maximum Pearson Maximum Distance (MPMD) utilizes two parameters to adjust the weights of relevance and redundancy. The effectiveness of the approach was assessed using 10 benchmark datasets from the UCI machine learning databases. The results highlighted its superiority over three existing wrapper strategies and one hybrid strategy in terms of classification accuracy [15].

Stephan *et al.* developed a hybridization of the artificial bee colony algorithm that blends the whale optimization's bubble net attacking strategy with the ABC's exploitative employee bee phase hybridization of artificial bee colony with whale optimisation (HAW). The exploratory phase of the HAW algorithm consists of a mutative initialization step, which improves upon the limited exploration capability of the standard ABC method. In the context of an ANN model, the HAW technique is utilized to simultaneously select features and optimize parameters. To create hybrid versions of HAW, three backpropagation learning algorithms (Levenberg–Marquart, robust backpropagation, and momentum-based gradient descent) are incorporated, resulting in HAW-LM, HAW-RP, and HAW-GD. The effectiveness of these hybrid variations is assessed using datasets related to breast cancer, including WBCD, WDBC, WPBC, DDSM, MIAS, and IN-breast, based on accuracy, complexity, and processing time. Among these, the HAW-RP variant, utilizing a low-complexity ANN model, achieves the highest accuracy with values of 99.2%, 98.5%, 96.3%, 98.8%, 98.7%, and 99.1% for the respective datasets [16].

In their examination of breast cancer, Khamparia *et al.* focus a lot of stress on the process of transfer learning. They used a modified version of the visual geometry group (VGG) (MVGG) on datasets that included 2D and 3D mammograms. According to the findings of their studies, the suggested hybrid transfer learning model's accuracy, which combines MVGG with ImageNet, is 94.3%. The MVGG design, which was the only one studied, had an accuracy rate of 89.8%. The recommended hybrid pretrained network is therefore superior to previous convolutional neural networks (CNNs) of a similar design. The authors give thorough explanations of these findings [17].

Shukla *et al.* have developed a unique hybrid framework named CMIMAGA to extract important indications from gene expression data. This method combines adaptive genetic algorithm and conditional mutual information maximization (CMIM). The method employs a wrapper approach as a straightforward filter, followed by the CMIM approach as a second filter, to exclude extraneous genes. The next step is to choose highly discriminating genes that can reliably diagnose tumors and malignancies using an adaptive genetic algorithm. As a fitness function, the system uses classifiers to choose these genes. In order to evaluate the effectiveness of the suggested method, six commonly employed microarray datasets were employed, alongside three classifiers: Extreme learning machine, support vector machine, and K-nearest neighbors (KNN) were employed for comparison purposes. The suggested method using ELM outperformed earlier filter and wrapper techniques, according to experimental findings, and achieved improved classification accuracy with fewer genes [18].

In order to classify microarray data with high dimensionality using artificial neural networks, Aziz R. *et al.* have developed a unique method for feature selection and extraction. The strategy uses artificial bee colonies (ABCs) as an optimization technique and as an extraction method, independent component analysis (ICA). By contrasting the ICA + ABC method with ICA and ABC alone and running rigorous testing on six gene expression microarray datasets, the study assesses the effectiveness of the procedure. Comparing the suggested approach to previous ICA-based bio-inspired algorithms and well-known filtering strategies, in terms of classification accuracy and the number of selected genes, it outperforms the current technique. The studies' findings show that the ICA + ABC algorithm improves an ANN classifier's classification accuracy rate, making it a potential method for resolving concerns using microarray data in the context of gene selection and the classification of cancer [19].

Kilicarslan *et al.* carried out an investigation utilizing three microarray datasets: ovarian, leukemia, and central nervous system (CNS). They employed autoencoder methods to reduce the dimensionality and employed support vector machines and convolutional neural networks for analysis. The leukemia dataset comprised 72 samples with 7,129 genes and two classes, while the ovarian and CNS datasets also contained 60 samples, 7,129 genes, and two classes. With bracket accuracy of 96.14 for ovarian datasets, 94.83 for leukemia datasets, and 65 for CNS datasets without dimension reduction, SVM shown good performance. The ovarian, leukemia, and CNS datasets' respective bracket accuracy for the proposed mixed system Relief-F CNN was 98.6, 99.86, and 83.95 [20].

Melekoodappattu and Subbian proposed utilizing extreme learning machines (ELMs) in conjunction with the fruit fly optimization algorithm (ELM-FOA) to modify the input weight. The objective is to achieve the optimal arrangement at the hidden layer of the ELM, enabling the analytical acquisition of the output. During ELM testing, FOA's perception and perfection are 97.5 and 100, respectively. The cutting-edge technology can describe calcium deposits and cancers with 99.04 delicacies. Through the utilization of advanced preprocessing and segmentation techniques, incorporating features from various point filters, and harnessing a robust classifier algorithm, this approach showcases outstanding performance [21].

Two novel CNN-SVM hybrid models have been developed by Keerthana *et al.* to classify dermoscopy pictures as benign or malignant lesions. Features are extracted by the primary and secondary CNN models, which are then merged and sent into the SVM classifier for classification. The efficacy of the proposed methodology is evaluated using expert dermatologist labeling. Using the ISBI 2016 dataset, the suggested models outperformed current CNN models and obtained an accuracy of 88.02% and 87.43%, respectively, outperforming traditional CNN models [22].

The literature survey brings to the conclusion that CSAHHO, a hybrid cuckoo search method with Harris hawks optimization, has not yet been used for cancer classification. Filling this gap is the main objective of the suggested inquiry. It is worth noting that despite the cuckoo search algorithm being an effective method, it has sluggish convergence and local minima stagnation. While HHO is better for obtaining global optimum, in some cases, it may have a low convergence problem. Moreover, no one solution can solve all optimization problems, according to the no free lunch (NFL) concept. The proposed hybrid algorithm was developed with this goal in mind.

## 4.3   Proposed Methodology

The methodology introduced in this paper involves several key steps, including data collection, data preprocessing, feature selection, training the model, evaluation, refinement, and final testing. The first step is to collect relevant data from various sources, followed by cleaning, normalizing, and transforming the data to make them suitable for analysis. Then, feature selection is conducted to identify the most crucial characteristics (features) that should be incorporated into the model. Once this is done, a hybrid algorithm is selected to use the data to train a machine learning model. The trained model is then assessed for its performance on a separate validation set, and any necessary changes are made based on the results obtained. To assess the model's generalization ability, it is tested on a different test set. By following this proposed methodology, the paper aims to build a robust and accurate model that can effectively address the problem.

### 4.3.1   Cuckoo Search Algorithm

The cuckoo bird's reproductive habits served as the inspiration for the optimization method used in computer science. The strategy makes use of a tactic known as Levy flying in place of random movements with a wide range and unexpected pattern, which would require a significant shift from the existing position [23, 24]. In order to ensure the survival of its young, the cuckoo lays its eggs in other birds' nests, causing the host birds to raise the cuckoo chicks as if they were their own [25, 26].

**Brood Parasitism**: Uses another bird's nest as its own, hides its eggs there, and then relies on the host bird to raise the young.
**Host Bird**: Owner of the host nest, responsible for raising and feeding the cuckoo chicks.
**Parasite Bird**: Birds that deposit eggs within the host bird nest.
**Levy Flight**: A levy flight is a physical phenomenon whose phase lengths follow the probability distribution with a pronounced tail known as the Levy distribution. Levy distribution is used to regulate the Levy flights' transition opportunity in the manner described below:
For $1 < \lambda \leq 3$

$$\text{We have } Levy \, (\lambda) \approx g^{\lambda} \tag{4.1}$$

The process of using Levy flights to generate random numbers comprises two parts from the perspective of implementation.

1. Uniform distribution-based random direction selection
2. Making decisions that follow the selected Levy distribution

**Random Walk**: Random process that describes a path that comprises a sequence of discrete constant length steps in random directions on some mathematical space (1D, 2D, or nD) such as integers.

Random Walk Equation:

$$S_i^{t+1} = E_i^t + \alpha \odot L(\lambda) \tag{4.2}$$

where $S_i^{t+1}$= new solution, $E_i^t$ = existing solution, $\alpha$ = *walk length*, $\odot$ = entry considerate multiplication, $L(\lambda)$ = Levy expositor.

The fundamental cuckoo search algorithm in pseudocode is developed based on these criteria. It is crucial to control the situation while seeking new solutions. Lévy flights, characterized by random walks, help prevent large movements that could lead to escaping the search area. The size of each step is determined by the scale of the problem, and this can be achieved by incorporating interest. Exploring the use of Lévy flight for optimization proves to be an intriguing topic for further investigation. For ease of use, as recommended by the authors, a common step size factor of 0.01 is employed.

| **Pseudocode for the cuckoo search** |
|---|
| 1. Receive the initial assignment as the input. |
| 2. Establish a baseline population based on assignment. |
| 3. While (stop requirement not satisfied) |
|     1) Select a cuckoo at random from Levy flights |
|     2) Examine its effectiveness/quality Fi |
|     3) Randomly select one nest out of n (let us say j). |
|     4) If (Fi > Fj) |
|     5) Substitute the new solution for j |
|     6) Unfavorable nests are discarded, and new ones are constructed |
|     7) Maintain the top solutions (or nests of excellent solutions) |
|     8) Order the answers to determine which is currently best. |
| 4. End while |
| 5. Report the best solution |

## 4.3.2   Harris Hawks Algorithm

Native to the southern Arizona region of the United States, the Harris hawk, is considered one of the most intelligent bird species largely due to its feeding habits. This raptor is known for its strong family ties, and research on animal behavior has revealed that Harris hawks actively support their group. In contrast to most other bird species, which hunt, attack, and eat prey individually, Harris hawks participate in group meals that gradually increase in size during nonbreeding months. Every member of a Harris hawk family takes part in the nightly feast [27].

Heidari *et al.* created a labeling algorithm called the HHO method, which imitates the behavior of Harris hawks in catching prey (2019). The Harris hawks have exceptional behaviors that help them detect and capture prey quickly. They use a technique called "7 killings" to weaken their prey before capturing it. This technique involves several tasks, including striking quickly to startle the prey, engaging in fast and identical dives to confuse the prey, and having a skilled hawk take the prepared victim. The prey is then distributed among the team. The HHO method uses similar strategies in searching for and attacking targets, combining exploratory and exploitative functions to achieve success [28].

Assume $T_{rabbit}(H)$ indicates where the prey is and $T(H)$ indicates where the hawks are. Equation 4.3, which considers the probability p, is used to calculate the positioning of the hawks during the exploration phase of the (H + 1) iteration. The locations of the other hawks and the prey are used to determine the position of the hawks for the (H + 1) iteration if p is less than 0.5 (rabbit). An estimated location is given for the (H + 1)-iteration. Similarly, for p >= 0.5 by randomly selecting hawks, as suggested by $T_{rabbit}(H)$.

$$T(H+1) = \{Trd(H) - rd1\,|\,Tr(H) - 2rd2T(H)\,|\,if\ p \geq 0.5\ Trabbit(H)$$
$$-Tm(H) - rd3(lb + rd4(ub - lb)if\ p < 0.5 \qquad (4.3)$$

where $rd_1$, $rd_2$, $rd_3$, $rd_4$, and p are the random variables and lb, ub represents lower and upr bounds, and $T_m(H)$ denotes the mean position and is calculated as follows:

$$T_m(H) = \frac{1}{PS} \sum_{i=1}^{PS} T(H) \qquad (4.4)$$

where PS represents population size.

When the energy level of the escaping rabbit (E) is considered, the HHO algorithm transitions from the exploration phase to the exploitation phase. This transition is symbolized as follows:

$$E = 2E_0(1 - H/Max - IT) \qquad (4.5)$$

where E0 is the rabbit's (the prey's) initial state of energy, randomly produced using a [-1, 1] range, and Max IT is the most iterations allowed. When $|E| > 1$, the hawks are looking in more areas to find where their prey is. According to this, the exploitation phase of the HHO discovery process starts at $|E| < 1$.

HHO is used to plan the rabbit's escape before the hawks' unexpected approach. Let n represent the possibility of a rabbit escaping successfully (n 0.5) or unsuccessfully (n >= 0.5) prior to the hawk's unexpected pounce. The hawks use a soft or harsh siege depending on whether the victim is able to escape successfully or not. The gentle siege is depicted in Equations 4.6–4.8 and took place when $|E| > = 0.5$.

$$T(H + 1) = \Delta T(H) - E\,|J \times T_{rabbit}(H) - T(H)| \qquad (4.6)$$

$$\Delta T(H) \; T_{rabbit}(H) - T(H) \tag{4.7}$$

$$J = 2(1 - rd) \tag{4.8}$$

where J is the rabbit's power of chance leaps, and rd is a random variable. Equation 4.9 illustrates a harsh siege that took place for |E|< 0.5.

$$T(H+1) = T(H) - K|\Delta T(H)| \tag{4.9}$$

The HHO method models the prey jumping frog for increasing fast diving using the Levy flight (FL) principle, which occurs for |E|>= 0 and n < 0.5. The hawks' ability to dive successfully or unsuccessfully is measured by the following:

$$Y = T_{rabbit}(H) - E\,|J \times T_{rabbit}(H) - T(H)| \tag{4.10}$$

When the dive in Equation 4.10 fails, hawks perform a dive based on Levy flying based on Equation 4.11.

$$Z = Y + W + Ly \,(Pdim) \tag{4.11}$$

where W is the random variable, and Pdim stands for the issue dimension. The Levy flight functn Ly is calculated as follows:

$$Ly(x) = 0.01 \times \frac{u \times \sigma}{|v|^{1/\beta}} \tag{4.12}$$

$$where \; \sigma = \left( \frac{\Gamma(1+\beta)\; Xsinsin\left(\dfrac{\prod \beta}{2}\right)}{\Gamma\left(\dfrac{1+\beta}{2}\right) X\; \beta\; X\; 2^{\frac{\beta-1}{2}}} \right)^{\frac{1}{\beta}} \tag{4.13}$$

where $\beta$ is a constant with a value of 1.5, u and v are random variables with a range of [0, 1]. Equations 4.10 and 4.11 are used to calculate the final step in updating the hawks' position for this dive.

$$T(H+1) = \{Y \text{ if } cos(Y) < cost(T(H)) Z \text{ if } cost(Z) < cost(T(H))$$

(4.14)

Similarly, Equation 4.15 computes the position of the hawks during the hard besiege phase with successive dives, and it does so for $|E| < 0.5$ and $n < 0.5$.

| Pseudocode for Harris Hawk |
|---|
| **Inputs: population size h and Max_iter**<br>1) **Initialize a population of h random hawks $x_i$ (i=1, ....h)**<br>2) **Calculate the fitness of each hawk**<br>3) **$X_{rabbit}$ = best position of minimum fitness**<br>4) **T=1**<br>5) **while(t<=Max_iter)**<br>  a) **Update E**<br>  b) **If ($|E| >= 1$)**<br>    i) **Update x(t+1)**<br>  c) **If ($|E| < 1$)**<br>  d) **If ($p >= 0.5$ && $|E| >= 0.5$)**<br>    i) **Update x(t+1)**<br>  e) **If ($p >= 0.5$ && $|E| < 0.5$)**<br>    i) **Update x(t+1)**<br>  f) **If ($p < 0.5$ && $|E| >= 0.5$)**<br>    i) **Update x(t+1) using soft besiege progressive rapid dives**<br>  g) **If ($p >= 0.5$ && $|E| >= 0.5$)**<br>    i) **Update x(t+1) using hard besiege progressive rapid dives**<br>  h) **If (fitness(x(t+1)) < fitness($x_{rabbit}$))**<br>    i) **Update $x_{rabbit}$ = x(t+1)**<br>6) **t++**<br>Output: **rabbit position $x_{rabbit}$** |

### 4.3.3 The Proposed Hybrid Algorithm

The suggested method for improving the convergence and effectiveness of the Harris hawks employs a combined algorithm called CSAHHO, which combines the cuckoo search algorithm and the Harris hawks optimization algorithm. By combining the process of updating the population mechanism of CSA with the integrated HHO's population update structure, the algorithm gains more flexibility to explore the population and achieve greater diversity. As a result, the CSAHHO approach enhances the capacity to explore and achieve a broader range of solutions. Figure 4.2 shows a hybrid flowchart of the HHO and CSA.

The following lists the CSAHHO implementation steps:

1. To specify the parameters, we need to assign values to the following: maximum iterations (Max IT), population size (Pop-size), number of feature variables, awareness probability, flight duration, and crossover rate.
2. Population Encoding: A binary encoding strategy was used to encode the population. In this approach, a binary string comprising of "0s" and "1s" is used to depict the population. When a value is "1," the feature is included, whereas it is excluded when the value is "0."
3. Fitness Function: By removing superfluous attributes, the suggested CSAHHO algorithm chooses an ideal feature set. With the aid of the fitness function, the algorithm accomplishes this task. The effectiveness of the classifier and the quantity of characteristics chosen are two competing goals that are integrated by the fitness function (FS). The convolutional neural network evaluates the performance of each chosen feature set. The feature set that the algorithm chooses offers maximum accuracy with the fewest features. Using Equation 4.15, the fitness Xi(t) of each individual within the population vector is computed.

$$Cost(x_i(t)) = (E_{xi(t)}) \times \left(1 + 0.5 \times \frac{FS}{N}\right)^2 \tag{4.15}$$

where cost($x_i$(t)) stands in for $X_i$(t) fitness value. $E_{(xi(t))}$ represents the performance rating assigned by the classifier. The term "FS/N" stands for the ratio of "selected features" to "total features."

Depending on the probability value (Pi) determined, it is necessary to decide whether to utilize CSA or HHO when updating the population for the hybrid CSAHHO model. The population update process is described in Equation 4.16, and the algorithm below provides the implementation stages.

$$P_i = \frac{costi}{\displaystyle\sum_{j=1}^{pop-size} costi} \tag{4.16}$$

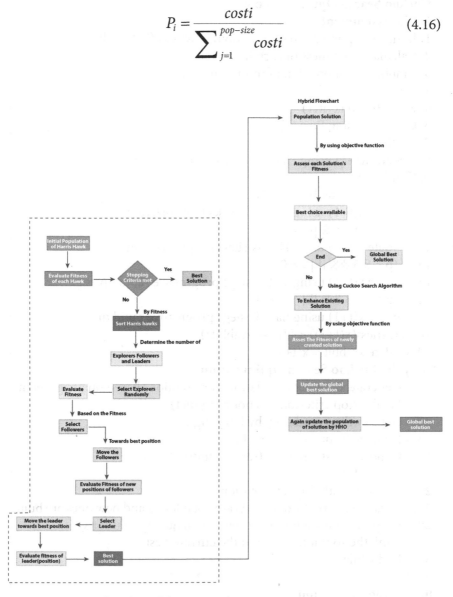

**Figure 4.2** Hybrid flowchart of the HHO and CSA.

**Hybrid CSAHHO Algorithm**

**Inputs:**
- **population size h**
- **Max_iter**
- **Harris Hawks Optimization pa**
- **Cuckoo Search Optimization n**
- **Initial assignment**
  **1.** Initialize a population of h random hawks xi (i=1, ….h)
  **2.** Calculate the fitness of each hawk
  **3.** Xrabbit = best position of minimum fitness
  **4.** T=1
  **5.** while(t<=Max_iter)
  **6.** Update E using Eq. (16)
  **7.** If (|E| >= 1)
  **8.** Update x(t+1) using Harris Hawks Optimization
  **9.** If (|E| < 1)
  **10.** If (p >= 0.5 && |E| >= 0.5)
  **11.** Update x(t+1) using Harris Hawks Optimization
  **12.** If (p >= 0.5 && |E| < 0.5)
  **13.** Update x(t+1) using Harris Hawks Optimization
  **14.** If (p < 0.5 && |E| >= 0.5)
  **15.** Update x(t+1) using soft besiege progressive rapid dives
  **16.** If (p >= 0.5 && |E| >= 0.5)
  **17.** Update x(t+1) using hard besiege progressive rapid dives
  **18.** If (fitness(x(t+1)) < fitness(xrabbit))
  **19.** Update xrabbit = x(t+1)

**Apply the Cuckoo Search Optimization**
  **20.** - Generate an initial population of n solutions based on assignment
  **21.** - While (stop criterion has not been met)
  **22.** - Get a cuckoo randomly by Levy flights
  **23.** - Evaluate its quality/fitness Fi
  **24.** - Choose a nest among n (say j), randomly
  **25.** - If (Fi > Fj)
  **26.** - Replace j with the new solution
  **27.** - A fraction (pa) of worse nests are abandoned and new ones are built
  **28.** - Keep the best solutions (or nests with quality solutions)
  **29.** - Rank the solutions and find the current best
  **30.** - End while
  **31.** t++

**Output: rabbit position**

### 4.3.4    Classifiers Used

#### 4.3.4.1    KNN Classifier

The K-nearest neighbor is an uncomplicated yet effective classification algorithm used for both tasks of binary and multiclass classification [29]. The functioning of the KNN algorithm involves identifying the k closest data points to the input point within the feature space and assigning the input point the class label that appears most frequently among those k points. The value of k is a hyperparameter that must be adjusted to achieve optimal performance. One notable advantage of KNN is its nonparametric nature, which means it does not rely on assumptions about the underlying data distribution. However, KNN is challenged by the curse of dimensionality, as its computational complexity increases with higher numbers of features [30, 31].

#### 4.3.4.2    SVM Classifier

The support vector machine is a widely used and influential classification algorithm in machine learning. SVM works by finding the best hyperplane that separates data points into different classes [32]. This hyperplane is selected to maximize the margin, which represents the distance between the hyperplane and the nearest points of each class. By employing the kernel trick, SVM is able to transform the input data into a higher-dimensional feature space, enabling the linear separation of data that are not linearly separable in the original space. Additionally, SVM exhibits robustness against overfitting and exhibits efficient performance even with high-dimensional data [33–35].

#### 4.3.4.3    NB Classifier

When it comes to text classification scenarios, naive Bayes (NB) is a simple and speedy algorithm that can be employed. The naive Bayes algorithm is based on the principles of Bayes' theorem and assumes that the features are conditionally independent when given the class label. NB gives the class that possesses the highest probability to the input data after calculating the posterior probabilities of each class given the input data. NB is a computationally efficient algorithm that performs well with little training data. In contrast, naive Bayes assumes feature independence, which may not be valid in reality and can result in suboptimal performance on specific datasets [36].

### 4.3.4.4   mRMR

The feature selection technique known as the mRMR, or minimal redundancy maximum relevance, is frequently employed in machine learning. In addition to minimizing redundancy among the chosen features. The objective of feature selection is to identify a subset of features that exhibit high relevance to the target variable. Peng *et al.* [49] introduced the mRMR algorithm in 2005, and it has since gained popularity as a feature selection technique. Relevance and redundancy are the two key requirements of the algorithm. While the redundancy criterion evaluates the degree of overlap between the chosen characteristics, the relevance criterion assesses the amount of information that a feature holds regarding the target variable [37]. The mRMR algorithm utilizes relevance and redundancy scores to rank features. The relevance score of a feature is determined by calculating its mutual information with the target variable. In this situation, it evaluates how much knowledge the characteristic offers about the target variable. The mutual information quantifies the reliance between two variables. A feature's redundancy score is calculated by measuring the average mutual information between the specific feature and all other chosen features. The redundancy score calculates how much the chosen features overlap one another. The algorithm chooses the characteristics with the highest relevance scores while minimizing redundancy among them after the features are sorted according to their relevance and redundancy scores. This is accomplished by gradually adding features to the chosen set while periodically assessing the set's level of redundancy. The algorithm stops accumulating features and returns the chosen set if the redundancy score is greater than a given threshold [38]. It has been demonstrated that the mRMR algorithm exhibits superior performance compared to alternative feature selection techniques in a number of applications, including text categorization and gene expression analysis. However, it is crucial to remember that the algorithm's success depends on the particular application and the selection of parameters, such as the redundancy score cutoff [39].

In conclusion, the mRMR stands as a widely recognized and popular approach for feature selection that balances the relevance and redundancy of the selected features. The algorithm assigns rankings to the features based on their relevance and redundancy scores and selects the features that maximize the relevance while minimizing the redundancy.

## 4.4    Experimental Setup

In this work, we sought to investigate the potential of this system for the analysis of complicated biological data using an HP laptop with an Intel Core i7 processor, 8 GB RAM, and a 512-GB SSD. Six cancer microarray datasets were analyzed in this study to see how effective the recommended approach was. The study, which focused on gene expression, employed six high-dimensional biological datasets that were collected from the online database Kent Ridge. The datasets contained information on high-grade gliomas for binary classification, colon cancer, acute leukemia, prostate cancer, lung cancer-II, and leukemia 2 for multiclassification (http://datam. i2r.astar.edu.sg/datasets/krbd/index.html). All of the details and characteristics of these six datasets are listed in Table 4.1.

**Table 4.1**  Information regarding the six cancer microarray data.

| Dataset | Classes | Genes | Class balance | No. of samples | Short description |
|---|---|---|---|---|---|
| Colon cancer | 2 | 2,000 | (22\40) | 62 | Colorectal cancer refers to the formation of cancerous cells in either the colon or rectum. This type of cancer can be recognized by a range of symptoms including the presence of blood in the stool, alterations in bowel movements, weight loss, and feelings of fatigue. |
| Acute leukemia | 2 | 7,129 | (47\25) | 72 | Acute leukemia is a group of severe symptoms linked to a leukemia diagnosis and can be categorized based on the myeloid or lymphoid lineage of the malignant cells. ALL and AML are the two classes. |

*(Continued)*

**Table 4.1** Information regarding the six cancer microarray data. (*Continued*)

| Dataset | Classes | Genes | Class balance | No. of samples | Short description |
|---------|---------|-------|---------------|----------------|-------------------|
| Prostate tumor | 2 | 12,600 | (50\52) | 102 | Prostate cancer is a male gland cancer that can develop slowly or aggressively and requires monitoring or other therapies. |
| High-grade glioma | 2 | 12,625 | (28\22) | 50 | High-grade gliomas are fast-growing brain tumors affecting people of all ages and include glioblastomas and anaplastic oligodendrogliomas. |
| Lung cancer II | 2 | 12,533 | (31\150) | 181 | The lymph nodes close to the affected lung contain cancer cells, and the tumor measures up to 5 cm. In addition, the lung may be completely or partially collapsed or inflamed, or the cancer may have spread to the primary airway and/or into the layer of the membrane covering the lung. Samples of malignant pleural mesothelioma and lung adenocarcinoma tissue acquired from stage II lung cancer. |

(*Continued*)

**Table 4.1** Information regarding the six cancer microarray data. (*Continued*)

| Dataset | Classes | Genes | Class balance | No. of samples | Short description |
|---------|---------|-------|---------------|----------------|-------------------|
| Leukemia 2 | 3 | 7,129 | (28\24\20) | 72 | Leukemia is a type of cancer that affects the blood and is marked by the rapid growth of abnormal blood cells. This abnormal growth primarily occurs in the bone marrow, which is responsible for producing most of the blood in the body. Leukemia cells are usually immature or underdeveloped white blood cells. The Leukemia 2 data collection comprises 28 samples of class 28 AML, 24 samples of ALL, and 20 samples of MLL. |

## 4.4.1   The Compared Algorithms

The CSAHHO algorithm, proposed in this study, has been compared to three other methods: mRMR, mRMR+CSA, and mRMR+HHO. Furthermore, a hybrid approach that combines both methods was also examined, the mRMR+CSAHHO, and has also been tested for comparison. The comparison was conducted based on the characteristics of the CSAHHO algorithm. To assess the effectiveness of each method, the classification outcomes were obtained by utilizing the genes selected through the respective methods.

**mRMR**: The classification outcomes are achieved using genes that have been chosen through the mRMR selection method.

**mRMR+CSA**: The classification outcomes are derived from genes that have been chosen through the mRMR+CSA selection process.

**mRMR+HHO:** The classification outcomes are derived from genes that have been selected using the mRMR+HHO method.

**mRMR+CSAHHO:** The classification outcomes are derived from genes selected using the hybrid method mRMR+CSAHHO.

### 4.4.2   Parameter Setting

The following table (Table 4.2) present the parameters used in our experimental implementation of the proposed technique, HHOCSA. In order to ensure a fair comparison, the gene selection process involved selecting the same top-ranked genes identified by the mRMR for each gene selection approach.

**Fitness function:** the proposed approach's effectiveness is evaluated by evaluating the accuracy of classification using SVM, KNN, and NB classifiers. When the current fitness value exceeds the previous value, the previous result is discarded and replaced with the current one. However, if the current fitness value is not better, the previous solution is retained. Ultimately,

**Table 4.2** Parameter settings of the proposed algorithm.

| Parameter | Value |
|---|---|
| Dimension | Number of genes selected with the mRMR algorithm |
| Maximum iterations | 100 |
| Lower bound (LB) and upper bound (UB) | 0 and 1 |
| Global phase fitness modification method | Harris hawks optimization (HHO) |
| No. Harris hawks (SearchAgents_no) | 10 and (K=5 and 10) |
| Number of iterations without improvement | 30 runs |
| Local phase fitness modification method | Cuckoo search algorithm (CSA) |
| Cuckoo search $\alpha$ step size | 1.0 and $(P_{a_{min}} = 0.25, P_{a_{max}} = 0.25)$ |
| Limit | 5 iterations |

the gene subset with the highest fitness value is chosen as the optimal solution for predictive purposes. The fitness function (fit) is defined as follows:

$$Fitness\ (f) = Accuracy\ (f)$$

## 4.5    Results and Discussion

We applied the proposed algorithm with the three most popular classifiers for the cancer classification problem section 4.5.1 Section 4.5.2 presents the experimental results using the SVM classifier, Section 4.5.3 showcases the experimental results using the NB classifier, and Section 4.5.4 demonstrates the experimental results using the KNN classifier.

### 4.5.1    Experimental Results of the Proposed Algorithm With the SVM Classifier

Table 4.3 provided information presenting a comprehensive analysis of various datasets and feature selection algorithms, employing both 5-fold and 10-fold cross-validation techniques. The mean accuracy values, accompanied by their respective standard deviations, illuminate on the performance of each combination. Notably, the results demonstrate that the utilization of feature selection algorithms yields higher accuracy rates compared to relying solely on the mRMR algorithm. Among the feature selection approaches, the mRMR+CSAHHO combination consistently stands out as the most effective, attaining remarkably high mean accuracy values ranging from 92.32% to a perfect 100% across different datasets. This compelling evidence suggests that integrating feature selection techniques into the classification models significantly enhances their predictive capabilities, offering valuable insights into the underlying patterns of the data. Provided information presents a comprehensive analysis of various datasets and feature selection algorithms, employing both 5-fold and 10-fold cross-validation techniques. The mean accuracy values, accompanied by their respective standard deviations, shed light on the performance of each combination. Notably, the results demonstrate that the utilization of feature selection algorithms yields higher accuracy rates compared to relying solely on the mRMR algorithm. Among the feature selection approaches, the mRMR+CSAHHO combination consistently stands out as the most effective, attaining remarkably high mean accuracy values ranging from 92.32% to a perfect 100% across different datasets. This compelling

**Table 4.3** Accuracies of the proposed algorithm with the mRMR, mRMR+CSA, and mRMR+HHO for the SVM classifier with 5-fold cross-validation and 10-fold cross-validation techniques.

| Datasets | mRMR | 5-fold cross-validation | | | 10-fold cross-validation | | |
|---|---|---|---|---|---|---|---|
| | | mRMR+CSA Mean(±STD) | mRMR+HHO Mean(±STD) | mRMR+ CSAHHO Mean(±STD) | mRMR+CSA Mean (±STD) | mRMR+HHO Mean(±STD) | mRMR+ CSAHHO Mean(±STD) |
| Colon | 83.2± 5.19 | 95.5 ±4.90 | 93.6 ± 3.80 | 97.7 ± 1.99 | 91.1 ± 3.97 | 95.5 ± 2.79 | 100 ± 0 |
| Acute Leukemia | 82.2 ± 6.29 | 83.5 ± 5.21 | 88.5 ± 3.65 | 91.0 ± 6.17 | 91.1 ± 3.76 | 93.4 ± 2.89 | 96.3 ± 3.15 |
| Prostate Tumor | 82.03 ± 4.11 | 91.71 ± 2.09 | 93.4 ± 1.4 | 95.3 ± 3.09 | 92.7 ± 4.76 | 94.7 ± 2.65 | 99.9 ± .01 |
| High Grade Glioma | 83.2 ± 4.77 | 84.71 ± 3.99 | 88.71 ± 3.19 | 92.32 ± 3.44 | 91.23 ± 4.02 | 92.6 ± 2.05 | 96.54 ± .06 |
| Lung Cancer II | 84.72 ± 5.98 | 92.53 ± 2.11 | 92.53 ± 2.11 | 96.52 ± 1.77 | 92.2 ± 4.45 | 94.2 ± 2.06 | 99.93 ± 11 |
| Leukemia 2 | 84.45 ± 3.99 | 94.54 ± 2.17 | 94.54 ± 2.17 | 97.42 ± 1.99 | 94.9 ± 0.8 | 96.1 ± 1.2 | 100 ± 0 |

evidence suggests that integrating feature selection techniques into the classification models significantly enhances their predictive capabilities, offering valuable insights into the underlying patterns of the data.

Figure 4.3 presents a comprehensive comparison of errors obtained from different analysis approaches applied to microarray cancer datasets. The primary focus is on evaluating the performance of the mRMR algorithm and its comparison with two popular cross-validation techniques: 5-fold cross-validation and 10-fold cross-validation. Additionally, the diagram also includes the performance of three distinct algorithms utilized for analysis. It is clear from the diagram that 10-fold validation has the least error with the SVM classifier.

The diagram presents a comprehensive comparison of errors obtained from different analysis approaches applied to microarray cancer datasets. The primary focus is on evaluating the performance of the mRMR algorithm and its comparison with two popular cross-validation techniques: 5-fold cross-validation and 10-fold cross-validation. Additionally, the diagram also includes the performance of three distinct algorithms utilized for analysis. It is clear from the diagram that 10-fold cross-validation has the least error with the SVM classifier.

The radar graph presented in this analysis showcases the variance observed in the three algorithms: mRMR+CSA, mRMR+HHO, and mRMR+CSAHHO. These algorithms were evaluated using six microarray cancer datasets. The radar curve illustrates the variance-based performance of each algorithm. In the graph, the magnitude of the area under the curve indicates the algorithm's performance level. A larger area under the curve indicates an inferior ability to accurately detect and classify different

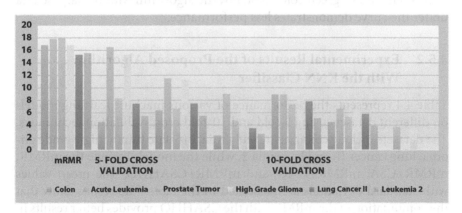

**Figure 4.3** Error comparison with the SVM classifier.

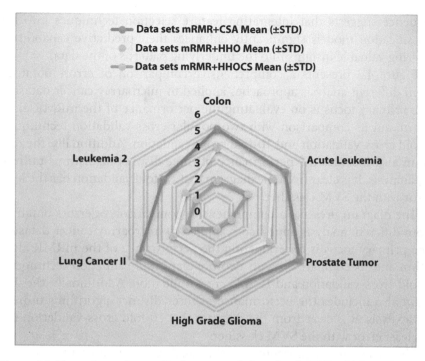

**Figure 4.4** The variance observed in the proposed algorithm (mRMR+CSAHHO) compared to the mRMR+CSA and mRMR+HHO algorithms with the SVM classifier.

classes. Figure 4.4 in the graph focuses on the variance achieved using the SVM classifier for all three algorithms. The mRMR+CSA algorithm is represented by the captivating blue color, while the mRMR+HHO algorithm is depicted in a vibrant orange shade. The mRMR+CSAHHO algorithm stands out with its green color. Notably, the algorithm with the largest area under the curve demonstrates less performance.

## 4.5.2   Experimental Results of the Proposed Algorithm With the KNN Classifier

Table 4.4 represents the performance of various machine learning models on different datasets using 5-fold and 10-fold cross-validation techniques. The datasets include colon, acute leukemia, prostate tumor, high-grade glioma, lung cancer II, and leukemia 2, while the models include the mRMR, mRMR+CSA, mRMR+HHO, and mRMR+CSAHHO. The mean values with standard deviations are presented in the table. The results show that the combination of the mRMR with the CSAHHO provides better results in

**Table 4.4** Accuracies of the proposed algorithm with the mRMR, mRMR+CSA, and mRMR+HHO for the KNN classifier with 5-fold cross-validation and 10-fold cross-validation techniques.

| Datasets | mRMR | 5-fold cross-validation | | | 10-fold cross-validation | | |
|---|---|---|---|---|---|---|---|
| | | mRMR+CSA Mean(±STD) | mRMR+HHO Mean(±STD) | mRMR+CSAHHO Mean(±STD) | mRMR+CSA Mean(±STD) | mRMR+HHO Mean(±STD) | mRMR+CSAHHO Mean(±STD) |
| Colon | 74.9 ± 5.31 | 95.5 ± 4.90 | 97.6 ± 2.3 | 98.7 ± 1.99 | 91.1 ± 3.97 | 95.2 ± 2.02 | 100 ± 1.0 |
| Acute leukemia | 77.2 ± 6.75 | 83.5 ± 5.21 | 87.4 ± 2.02 | 91.0 ± 6.17 | 91.1 ± 3.76 | 93.3 ± 1.15 | 96.3 ± 3.15 |
| Prostate tumor | 77.7 ± 4.56 | 91.71 ± 2.09 | 93.7 ± 1.02 | 95.3 ± 3.09 | 92.7 ± 2.76 | 96.2 ± 1.11 | 99.9 ± .01 |
| High-grade glioma | 78.4 ± 5.37 | 84.71 ± 3.99 | 87.81 ± 2.02 | 92.32 ± 3.44 | 91.23 ± 2.02 | 92.1 ± 1.71 | 96.54 ± .06 |
| Lung cancer II | 77.02 ± 8.09 | 92.53 ± 2.11 | 94.01 ± 2.02 | 96.52 ± 1.77 | 94.2 ± 1.45 | 97.2 ± 1.23 | 99.93 ± .11 |
| Leukemia 2 | 76.82 ± 4.56 | 94.54 ± 2.17 | 96.76 ± 1.59 | 97.42 ± 1.99 | 93.89 ± 0.8 | 94.4 ± 1.27 | 100 ± 0 |

most cases than using the mRMR alone or with other models. For instance, in the colon dataset, the combination of the mRMR with the CSAHHO achieves the highest accuracy of 97.6% with a standard deviation of 2.3%, while the mRMR alone achieves 74.9% with a standard deviation of 5.31%. Similarly, in the leukemia 2 dataset, the combination of the mRMR with the CSA achieves the highest accuracy of 96.76% with a standard deviation of 1.59%, while the mRMR alone achieves 76.82% with a standard deviation of 4.56%. Furthermore, the use of 10-fold cross-validation generally results in higher mean values than using 5-fold cross-validation. For instance, using 10-fold cross-validation, the combination of the mRMR and the CSAHHO in the lung cancer II dataset produces a mean accuracy of 97.2% with a standard deviation of 1.23%, but with 5-fold cross-validation, the accuracy is 92.53% with a standard deviation of 2.11%. The results show that the mRMR and the CSAHHO work better together than other models, and that using 10-fold cross-validation typically yields higher mean values than using 5-fold cross-validation.

Figure 4.5 shows a thorough comparison of the errors caused by various analytic techniques applied to microarray cancer datasets. The main objective is to evaluate and compare the performance of the mRMR algorithm with two commonly used cross-validation methods: 5-fold and 10-fold cross-validation. Figure 4.5 also demonstrates the performance of three different algorithms utilized in the analysis. Notably, the diagram reveals that the approach employing 10-fold cross-validation and a KNN classifier achieves the lowest error rate.

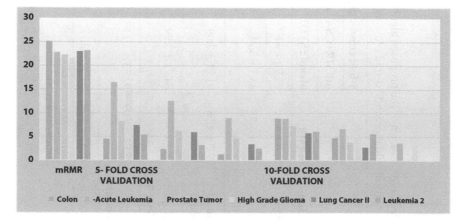

**Figure 4.5** Error comparison with the KNN classifier.

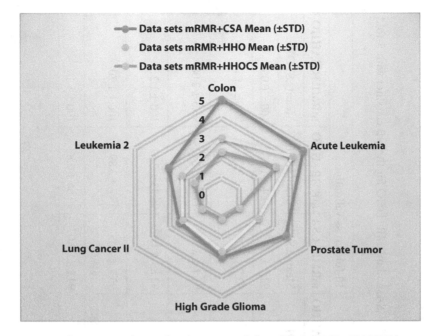

**Figure 4.6** The variance observed in the proposed algorithm (mRMR+CSAHHO) compared to the mRMR+CSA and mRMR+HHO algorithms with the KNN classifier.

Figure 4.6 illustrates the variability of the three algorithms utilizing the KNN classifier. The graph offers valuable insights into the performance and disparities among these algorithms. Specifically, the proposed algorithm using the KNN classifier demonstrates a smaller coverage area compared to the other algorithms, indicating less variance in the achieved results of classification performance.

### 4.5.3 Experimental Results of the Proposed Algorithm With the NB Classifier

Table 4.5 shows how various feature selection techniques and classification algorithms performed on diverse datasets. The datasets utilized in the study are represented by the first column, and the effectiveness of the mRMR feature selection approach is displayed in the second column. The performance of various combinations of the mRMR with the cuckoo search algorithm and Harris hawks optimization feature selection methods is shown in the next six columns. Two popular cross-validation methods, 5-fold and 10-fold cross-validation, are used to assess performance. Each column contains the mean and standard deviation for the accuracy of each

**Table 4.5** Accuracies of the proposed algorithm with the mRMR, mRMR+CSA, and mRMR+HHO for the NB classifier with 5-fold cross-validation and 10-fold cross-validation techniques.

| Datasets | mRMR | 5-fold cross-validation | | | 10-fold cross-validation | | |
|---|---|---|---|---|---|---|---|
| | | mRMR+CSA | mRMR+HHO | mRMR+CSAHHO | mRMR+CSA | mRMR+HHO | mRMR+CSAHHO |
| | mRMR | Mean(±STD) | Mean(±STD) | Mean(±STD) | Mean(±STD) | Mean(±STD) | Mean(±STD) |
| Colon | 88.4 ± 5.19 | 90.16 ± 2.02 | 93.8 ± 2.56 | 95.7 ± 1.97 | 92.7 ± 3.02 | 94.4 ± 1.17 | 100 ± 0.09 |
| Acute leukemia | 84.4 ± 5.22 | 84.16 ± 2.19 | 86.4 ± 6.34 | 89.3 ± 2.25 | 92.7 ± 3.01 | 95.3 ± 2.29 | 99.9± 1.01 |
| Prostate tumor | 88.3 ± 3.23 | 86.5 ± 1.76 | 88.4 ± 2.33 | 91 ± 2.88 | 91.1 ± 2.51 | 93.9 ± 3.34 | 96.3 ± 2.08 |
| High-grade glioma | 85.6 ± 5.22 | 85.31 ± 3.24 | 88.34 ± 3.76 | 90.37 ± 3.34 | 92.83 ± 4.32 | 96.33 ± 2.67 | 100 ± 1.2 |
| Lung cancer II | 90.72 ± 4.56 | 92.33 ± 2.33 | 94.45 ± 4.23 | 95.72 ± 1.22 | 95.7 ± 2.25 | 98.7 ± 3.89 | 100 ± 1.70 |
| Leukemia 2 | 90.38 ± 5.32 | 91.34 ± 2.11 | 94.56 ± 2.71 | 96.62 ± 1.7 | 94.71 ± 2.07 | 99.66 ± 2.87 | 100 ± 1.10 |

method. With regard to the colon dataset, the mRMR and CSAHHO combination obtains the maximum accuracy, with a 5-fold cross-validation accuracy of 93.8% and a 10-fold cross-validation accuracy of 100%. Similar to this, using 5-fold and 10-fold cross-validation, the combination of the mRMR and the CSAHHO yields the greatest accuracy for the prostate tumor dataset, with 88.4% and 96.3%, respectively. The combination of the mRMR and the CSAHHO yields the maximum accuracy for both 5-fold and 10-fold cross-validation for the datasets for acute leukemia and high-grade glioma. The best accuracy is obtained when the mRMR is combined with the HHO or CSA for the lung cancer II and leukemia 2 datasets, respectively. Overall, the findings imply that the mRMR and the CSAHHO can greatly enhance the performance of classification systems.

Figure 4.7 provides a comprehensive comparison of error rates obtained from different analysis methods applied to microarray cancer datasets. The primary emphasis is on assessing the performance of the mRMR algorithm in comparison to two commonly employed cross-validation techniques, 5-fold and 10-fold cross-validation. The diagram also presents the performance results of three distinct algorithms used in the analysis. Notably, it is clear from the diagram that the 10-fold cross-validation approach with the NB classifier demonstrates the lowest error rate.

Figure 4.8 portrays the variance of all three algorithms using the NB classifier. This depiction further highlights the distinct performance characteristics of each algorithm and helps in understanding its strengths and limitations. Overall, the radar graph and the numbers that go with it provide an appealing visual depiction of the variation found in the mRMR+CSA, mRMR+HHO, and mRMR+CSAHHO algorithms when applied

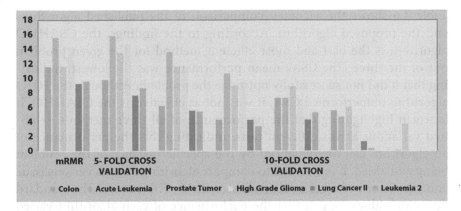

**Figure 4.7** Error comparison with the NB classifier.

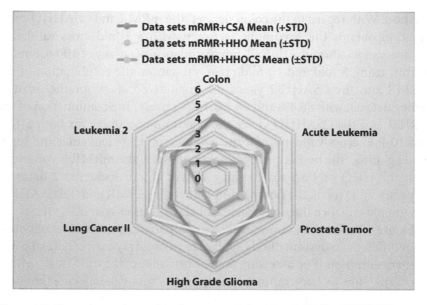

**Figure 4.8** The variance observed in the proposed algorithm (mRMR+CSAHHO) compared to the mRMR+CSA and mRMR+HHO algorithms with the SVM classifier.

to various classifiers. In order to enable successful detection and classification in cancer research and diagnosis, it is essential to have this information when choosing the best algorithm for certain cancer datasets.

### 4.5.4    Comparison of the Proposed Algorithm Compared to Other Recently Published and Popular Algorithms for Cancer Classification

Table 4.6 shows the accuracy comparison of the published algorithms and the proposed algorithm. According to the findings, the CSAHHO algorithm is the best and most efficient method for the given problem out of the three. The CSA's mean performance was the lowest, indicating that it did not successfully optimize the problem. Although the HHO algorithm outperformed CSA, it was not as effective as the CSAHHO. It is worth highlighting that the performance of all three methods exhibited variations across different tests, indicating that the performance of an algorithm can be influenced by the specific instance of the problem being addressed. It is essential to compare algorithms across various issue contexts in order to get a fuller view of their performance. The standard deviation values suggest that the performance of each algorithm varied

**Table 4.6** Comparison of the different published methods with the proposed method for cancer classification.

| Methods | Colon | Acute leukemia | Prostate tumor | High-grade glioma | Lung cancer II | Leukemia 2 |
|---------|-------|----------------|----------------|-------------------|----------------|------------|
| GWO + SVM [40] | 95.935% | _ | _ | 94.33% | _ | 94.33% |
| DL + DIP [41] | 96.33% | _ | _ | _ | 96.33% | _ |
| SCLB+ CLB [42] | 99.58% | _ | 89.32% | _ | 99.58% | _ |
| NN +CT [43] | _ | 97.63 | _ | _ | 93.3% | _ |
| ICA + ABC [44, 45] | 98.14% | 98.68% | 98.88% | 94.22% | 92.45% | 97.33% |
| miRNA [46] | _ | _ | _ | _ | 91.55% | _ |
| FHTWSVM [47] | _ | _ | 90.48% | _ | _ | 92.43% |
| CNN + ECA +VGG16 [48] | _ | 94.34% | _ | 96.33% | _ | 91.01% |
| Proposed method | 99.2% | 98.7% | 99% | 97.34% | 97.66% | 100% |

significantly across the different experiments. This indicates that the performance of an algorithm may be sensitive to changes in the problem instance or input parameters. Therefore, it is important to carefully tune the input parameters of an algorithm to ensure that it is able to effectively optimize the problem.

Overall, the results and comments demonstrate that the CSAHHO approach is the most successful and efficient for the specified task out of the three methods. To confirm the generalizability and scalability of these algorithms to other issues and contexts, additional research and experimentation are necessary.

## 4.6   Conclusion

The study investigated the effectiveness of three optimization methods for identifying and classifying cancer features. The findings revealed that, for the given problem, the CSAHHO algorithm demonstrated superior efficiency and effectiveness compared to the other two algorithms. However, the study highlighted the need for further experimentation and evaluation on different cancer datasets and scenarios to verify the generalizability and scalability of the suggested algorithm. The findings emphasize the importance of carefully tuning algorithm input parameters and evaluating algorithms across multiple problem instances to obtain a comprehensive understanding of their performance. The work gives knowledge for more research in this area and aids in the development of hybrid optimization algorithms for cancer feature selection and classification.

The generalizability and scalability of the suggested approach might be established through additional testing and evaluation on various cancer datasets in the future directions of this study. The employment of additional hybrid optimization algorithms or machine learning techniques applied to the selection and classification of cancer feature sets can offer additional benefits. In order to enhance the precision and efficiency of the categorization procedure, this can involve the incorporation of deep learning models or ensemble learning techniques. Researchers could also look into how the suggested approach might be used in sectors other than cancer feature selection and classification. Finally, the development of user-friendly software tools for implementing the proposed algorithm could make it more accessible to researchers and practitioners in the medical community.

## References

1. Tefferi, A. *et al.*, The 2008 World Health Organization classification system for myeloproliferative neoplasms: Order out of chaos. *Cancer*, 115, 17, 3842–3847, 2009, doi: 10.1002/cncr.24440.
2. Kourou, K. *et al.*, Machine learning applications in cancer prognosis and prediction. *Comput. Struct. Biotechnol. J.*, 13, 8–17, 2015, doi: 10.1016/j.csbj.2014.11.005.
3. Nakariyakul, S., A hybrid gene selection algorithm based on interaction information for microarray-based cancer classification. *PLoS One*, 14, 2, e0212333, 2019, doi: 10.1371/journal.pone.0212333.

4. Nanglia, P. *et al.*, A hybrid algorithm for lung cancer classification using SVM and Neural Networks. *ICT Express*, 7, 3, 335–341, 2021, doi: 10.1016/j. icte.2020.06.007.

5. Sahu, B., Mohanty, S., Rout, S., A hybrid approach for breast cancer classification and diagnosis. *EAI Endorsed Trans. Scalable Inf. Syst.*, 6, e2, 2018.

6. Motieghader, H. *et al.*, A hybrid gene selection algorithm for microarray cancer classification using genetic algorithm and learning automata. *Inform. Med. Unlocked*, 9, 246–254, 2017, doi: 10.1016/j.imu.2017.10.004.

7. Shunmugapriya, P. and Kanmani, S., A hybrid algorithm using ant and bee colony optimization for feature selection and classification (AC-ABC Hybrid). *Swarm Evol. Comput.*, 36, 27–36, 2017, doi: 10.1016/j.swevo.2017.04.002.

8. Jansi Rani, M.J. and Devaraj, D., Two-stage hybrid gene selection using mutual information and genetic algorithm for cancer data classification. *J. Med. Syst.*, 43, 8, 235, 2019, doi: 10.1007/s10916-019-1372-8.

9. Elyasigomari, V. *et al.*, Development of a two-stage gene selection method that incorporates a novel hybrid approach using the cuckoo optimization algorithm and harmony search for cancer classification. *J. Biomed. Inform.*, 67, 11–20, 2017, doi: 10.1016/j.jbi.2017.01.016.

10. Jain, I. *et al.*, Correlation feature selection based improved-Binary Particle Swarm Optimization for gene selection and cancer classification. *Appl. Soft Comput.*, 62, 203–215, 2018, doi: 10.1016/j.asoc.2017.09.038.

11. Shahbeig, S. *et al.*, A fuzzy multi-objective hybrid TLBO-PSO approach to select the associated genes with breast cancer. *Signal Process.*, 131, 58–65, 2017, doi: 10.1016/j.sigpro.2016.07.035.

12. Lu, H. *et al.*, A hybrid feature selection algorithm for gene expression data classification. *Neurocomputing*, 256, 56–62, 2017, doi: 10.1016/j. neucom.2016.07.080.

13. Naeem, S. *et al.*, Machine-learning based hybrid-feature analysis for liver cancer classification using fused (MR and CT) images. *Appl. Sci.*, 10, 9, 2020, doi: 10.3390/app10093134.

14. Kharrat, A. and Neji, M., Feature selection based on hybrid optimization for magnetic resonance imaging brain tumor classification and segmentation. *Appl. Med. Inform.*, 41, 9–23, 2019, Available at: https://ami.info.umfcluj.ro/index.php/AMI/article/view/648.

15. Zheng, Y. *et al.*, A novel hybrid algorithm for feature selection based on whale optimization algorithm. *IEEE Access*, 7, 14908–14923, 2019, doi: 10.1109/ACCESS.2018.2879848.

16. Stephan, P. *et al.*, A hybrid artificial bee colony with whale optimization algorithm for improved breast cancer diagnosis. *Neural Comput. Appl.*, 33, 20, 13667–13691, 2021, doi: 10.1007/s00521-021-05997-6.

17. Khamparia, A. *et al.*, Diagnosis of breast cancer based on modern mammography using hybrid transfer learning. *Multidimens. Syst. Signal Process.*, 32, 2, 747–765, 2021, doi: 10.1007/s11045-020-00756-7.

18. Shukla, A.K. *et al.*, A two-stage gene selection method for biomarker discovery from microarray data for cancer classification. *Chemom. Intell. Lab. Syst.*, 183, 47–58, 2018, doi: 10.1016/j.chemolab.2018.10.009.

19. Aziz, R.M., Application of nature inspired soft computing techniques for gene selection: A novel frame work for classification of cancer. *Soft Comput.*, 26, 22, 12179–12196, 2022, doi: 10.1007/s00500-022-07032-9.

20. Kilicarslan, S. *et al.*, Diagnosis and classification of cancer using hybrid model based on ReliefF and convolutional neural network. *Med. Hypotheses*, 137, 109577, 2020, doi: 10.1016/j.mehy.2020.109577.

21. Melekoodappattu, J.G. and Subbian, P.S., Automated breast cancer detection using hybrid extreme learning machine classifier. *J. Ambient Intell. Hum. Comput.*, 14, 5489–5498, 2023, https://doi.org/10.1007/s12652-020-02359-3.

22. Keerthana, D. *et al.*, Hybrid convolutional neural networks with SVM classifier for classification of skin cancer. *Biomed. Eng. Adv.*, 5, 2023, doi: 10.1016/j.bea.2022.100069.

23. Dara, S. and Tumma, P., Feature extraction by using deep learning: A survey. *Second Int. Conf. Electron. Commun. Aerosp. Technol.*, vol. 2018, 2018, doi: 10.1109/ICECA.2018.8474912.

24. Fister, I. *et al.*, Cuckoo search: A brief literature review. *Stud. Comput. Intell.*, 516, 49–62, 2014, doi: 10.1007/978-3-319-02141-6_3.

25. Kalita, K. *et al.*, Optimizing frequencies of skew composite laminates with metaheuristic algorithms. *Eng. Comput.*, 36, 2, 741–761, 2020, doi: 10.1007/s00366-019-00728-x.

26. Kalita, K. *et al.*, A comparative study on the metaheuristic-based optimization of skew composite laminates. *Eng. Comput. Springer*, 38, 4, 3549–3566, 2022, doi: 10.1007/s00366-021-01401-y.

27. Alabool, H.M. *et al.*, Harris hawks optimization: A comprehensive review of recent variants and applications, in: *Neural Comput. & Applic.*, vol. 33, no. 15, pp. 8939–8980, Springer, London, 2021, doi:10.1007/s00521-021-05720-5.

28. Heidari, A.A. *et al.*, Harris hawks optimization: Algorithm and applications. *Future Gener. Comput. Syst.*, 97, 849–872, 2019, doi: 10.1016/j.future.2019.02.028.

29. Shukla, S. and Naganna, S., A review on K-means data clustering approach. *Int. J. Inf. Comput. Technol.*, 4, 17, 1847–1860, 2014.

30. Priyadarshini, J. *et al.*, Analyzing physics-inspired metaheuristic algorithms in feature selection with K-nearest-neighbor. *Appl. Sci.*, 13, 2, 906, 2023, doi: 10.3390/app13020906.

31. Ganesh, N. *et al.*, Efficient feature selection using weighted superposition attraction optimization algorithm. *Appl. Sci.*, 13, 5, 3223, 2023, doi: 10.3390/app13053223.

32. Reddy, G.T. *et al.*, Analysis of dimensionality reduction techniques on big data. *IEEE Access*, 8, 54776–54788, 2020, doi: 10.1109/ACCESS.2020.2980942.

33. Bhattacharya, S. *et al.*, A comparative analysis on prediction performance of regression models during machining of composite materials. *Mater. (Basel)*, 14, 21, 6689, 2021, doi: 10.3390/ma14216689.

34. Gayathri, R. *et al.*, A comparative analysis of machine learning models in prediction of mortar compressive strength. *Processes*, 10, 7, 1387, 2022, doi: 10.3390/pr10071387.

35. Narayanan, G. *et al.*, PSO-tuned support vector machine metamodels for assessment of turbulent flows in pipe bends. *Eng. Comput.*, 37, 3, 981–1001, 2019, doi: 10.1108/EC-05-2019-0244.

36. Aziz, R.M., Application of nature inspired soft computing techniques for gene selection: A novel frame work for classification of cancer. *Soft Comput.*, 26, 22, 12179–12196, 2022, doi: 10.1007/s00500-022-07032-9.

37. Lv, J. *et al.*, A multi-objective heuristic algorithm for gene expression microarray data classification. *Expert Syst. Appl.*, 59, 13–19, 2016, doi: 10.1016/j.eswa.2016.04.020.

38. Alshamlan, H. *et al.*, mRMR-ABC: A hybrid gene selection algorithm for cancer classification using microarray gene expression profiling. *Biomed. Res. Int.*, 2015, 604910, 2015, doi: 10.1155/2015/604910.

39. Mohamed, N.S. *et al.*, Metaheuristic approach for an enhanced mRMR filter method for classification using drug response microarray data. *Expert Syst. Appl.*, 90, 224–231, 2017, doi: 10.1016/j.eswa.2017.08.026.

40. AbdElNabi, M.L.R. *et al.*, Breast and colon cancer classification from gene expression profiles using data mining techniques. *Symmetry*, 12, 3, 408, 2020, doi: 10.3390/sym12030408.

41. Masud, M. *et al.*, A machine learning approach to diagnosing lung and colon cancer using a deep learning-based classification framework. *Sensors (Basel)*, 21, 3, 1–21, 2021, doi: 10.3390/s21030748.

42. Ali, M. and Ali, R., Multi-input dual-stream capsule network for improved lung and colon cancer classification. *Diagnostics (Basel)*, 11, 8, 1–18, 2021, doi: 10.3390/diagnostics11081485.

43. Kuruvilla, J. and Gunavathi, K., Lung cancer classification using neural networks for CT images. *Comput. Methods Programs Biomed.*, 113, 1, 202–209, 2014, doi: 10.1016/j.cmpb.2013.10.011.

44. Aziz, R. *et al.*, A fuzzy based feature selection from independent component subspace for machine learning classification of microarray data. *Genomics Data*, 8, 4–15, 2016, doi: 10.1016/j.gdata.2016.02.012.

45. Aziz, R. *et al.*, A novel approach for dimension reduction of microarray. *Comput. Biol. Chem.*, 71, 161–169, 2017, doi: 10.1016/j.compbiolchem.2017.10.009.

46. Yanaihara, N. *et al.*, Unique microRNA molecular profiles in lung cancer diagnosis and prognosis. *Cancer Cell*, 9, 3, 189–198, 2006, doi: 10.1016/j.ccr.2006.01.025.

47. Hua, D. *et al.*, Tumor classification of gene expression data by fuzzy hybrid twin SVM. *Chin. J. Electron.*, 31, 1, 99–106, 2022.

48. Zakir Ullah, M. *et al.*, An attention-based convolutional neural network for acute lymphoblastic leukemia classification. *Appl. Sci.*, 11, 22, 10662, 2021, doi: 10.3390/app112210662.
49. Peng, H., Long, F., Ding, C., Feature selection based on mutual information criteria of max-dependency, max-relevance, and min-redundancy. *IEEE Trans. Pattern Anal. Mach. Intell.*, 27, 8, 1226–1238, 2005.

# 5

# Anomaly Identification in Surveillance Video Using Regressive Bidirectional LSTM with Hyperparameter Optimization

Rajendran Shankar[1]* and Narayanan Ganesh[2]

[1]*Department of Computer Science and Engineering, Koneru Lakshmaiah Education Foundation, Vaddeswaram, India*
[2]*School of Computer Science & Engineering, Vellore Institute of Technology, Chennai, India*

## Abstract

Urban planners and academics are influenced by the idea of smart cities to develop sustainable, modern, and reliable infrastructure that offers their citizens a respectable standard of living. To meet this demand, there have been video monitoring devices installed to improve public security and welfare. Despite scientific advancements, it is difficult and labor-intensive to identify odd events in surveillance video systems. In this research, we concentrate on the improvement of anomaly detection in intelligent video surveillance using regressive bidirectional Long Short-Term Memory (LSTM) (RBLSTM) with hyperparameter optimization (HO). The suggested framework is tested on a real-time dataset, the ShanghaiTech Campus dataset, and it outperforms state-of-the-art techniques in terms of performance. It is important to take advantage of higher-quality features from accessible videos. This work uses the Video Swin Transformer model to extract features. As a consequence, anomaly detection in video surveillance applications provides reliable outcomes for real-time situations. In this study, an abnormality was correctly identified in videos with a 98.5% accuracy rate. Future research might explore further experiments by investigating other methods to reduce the noise present in the positive bag.

*Keywords*: Regressive bidirectional LSTM (RBLSTM), hyperparameter optimization (HO), video anomaly detection, Video Swin, ShanghaiTech

*Corresponding author*: shankarrajendran75@kluniversity.in

Kanak Kalita, Narayanan Ganesh and S. Balamurugan (eds.) Metaheuristics for Machine Learning: Algorithms and Applications, (135–148) © 2024 Scrivener Publishing LLC

## 5.1    Introduction

The use of video anomaly detection in surveillance systems has received a lot of interest. Even if the amount of installing monitoring devices has decreased dramatically in recent years, aberrant activities like fighting, abuse, and theft still need to be detected by humans. The development of efficient video anomaly detection algorithms is necessary due to the increased expense of human labor and the loss of productive time [1]. Anomaly identification is challenging because anomalies are ill-defined and annotated data are not readily available. Protection of ourselves and one's property is more vital nowadays. The real-time video surveillance serves a beneficial purpose. As a result of these demands, cameras are installed at every turn, and video surveillance systems can comprehend the situation and recognize unusual activity right away [2]. The primary component recognizes the activity and automatically alerts the operator or users when an unexpected occurrence occurs. When it comes to managing personal safety and security as well as public safety, video surveillance works more effectively than conventional approaches. To reduce the burden of an observer, as well as build an autonomous surveillance device to replace observer-oriented services provided by humans. Cameras are used to gather information on various events that indicate the behavior of anomalies in a surveillance-enforced environment during the anomaly identification process. The system's functionality conducts feature extraction on the gathered data, processes it, and then converts the generated features into various inputs for the designated algorithm [3]. Contextual, local, and communal anomalies are all possible. Data instances that are examined against a specific context connected with the data instance are referred to as contextual anomalies. Single data examples that vary from others are referred to as point anomalies. Intelligent video surveillance systems detect suspicious activity and sound alarms without human involvement [4]. Data are gathered by visual sensors in the surveillance environment throughout the detecting phase. The next step is feature extraction and preprocessing of these raw visual data. Video surveillance anomaly detection is a delay-sensitive application that needs minimal latency [5].

In this study, we aim to provide readers with a comprehensive overview of various anomaly detection strategies and viewpoints. We will also discuss how different surveillance targets are selected based on the usage of the device. Previous evaluations of anomaly detection methods have varied in terms of surveillance targets, and we will consider recent methods for anomaly detection. A key contribution of this study is the introduction of regressive bidirectional LSTM (RBLSTM) with hyperparameter optimization (HO) for anomaly detection in intelligent video surveillance. Additionally, we will address the challenges and prospects of anomaly detection in video surveillance. Notably, this study is the first to discuss how anomaly detection in video surveillance has converged.

The following are the scientific contributions of this research article:

1. The research that is being presented attempts to establish connections between the various issue formulations and offered solutions for anomaly identification.
2. It provides a comprehensive classification of anomaly detection algorithms based on the aims and techniques of monitoring.
3. Anomaly detection methods are discussed in the application domain, surveillance targets, learning strategies, and modeling approaches.
4. A more recent transformer-based feature extraction approach called Video Swin Transformer is utilized to enhance comprehension of the videos.
5. The suggested model's impacts on the open-source ShanghaiTech dataset are investigated via a comparison to existing state-of-the-art methodologies.

The remaining sections of the article are organized as follows: Section 5.2 reviews the literature on anomaly detection, while Section 5.3 introduces the proposed approach. In Section 5.4, we present the results of our experimental analysis, and Section 5.5 concludes the article with our observations.

## 5.2    Literature Survey

To identify actions in sporting events, researchers developed an attention-based LSTM. To enhance the spatial characteristics, convolution block attention was used [6]. To find abnormalities in complicated situations, they suggested an ensemble of deep models. A human position estimate model that recognizes the human joints is integrated into the initial stage. The second phase involves treating the discovered joints as features and providing them with a densely linked complete CNN for anomaly detection [7]. They introduced an unsupervised method for finding anomalies in films utilizing time-varying sparse coding, online query signals, and sparse reconstruction skills developed from a learned event-specific terminology. It has remained difficult to acquire the capacity to spot an anomaly promptly, which has drawn the attention of various academics [8]. The researchers created a deep auto-encoder based on clustering to effectively extract data from routine occurrences. To learn spatial–temporal feature regularity, two modules are employed, with the first module's spatial auto-encoder taking care of the last individual video frame. In contrast, the second module's temporal auto-encoder works and generates the RGB difference between the frames. Additionally, abnormalities in videos are found using generative models [9]. The researchers suggested a tube extraction method that makes use of coordinates to create an abnormality regression model. Before transferring the data to the regression model, the medium pooling layer mixes the temporal aspects of the ideal flow with the spatial variables from the inception block [10]. The researchers created a method for spotting irregularities with limited supervision and a supervised system for action classification with noisy labels. Because the anomalous occurrences were unexpected, the novelty consisted of merely keeping the anomaly video labels loud. In addition, a graph CNN was trained to clean up these noisy labels, and an action classifier was used to categorize the actions [11].

Following this context, the researchers proposed the creation of anomaly detection in intelligent video surveillance using RBLSTM with HO, which covers both short- and long-range temporal dependencies and requires less computational power than alternative approaches. The suggested approach enhances the performance of the model overall by extracting features using a more efficient transformer-based model.

## 5.3  Proposed Methodology

The suggested approach assumes that although clips taken from anomaly videos would contain at least one anomaly, clips taken from regular videos would only contain normal clips. A normalization procedure is used for preprocessing in stage 1. Stage 2 of the Video Swin model uses the extracted features from the clips. Stage 3 involves applying RBLSTM and HO to the characteristics to cover relevant long- and short-range temporal relationships. The final step involves performance analysis by employing optimization to find anomalies. Figure 5.1 depicts the suggested model in this article.

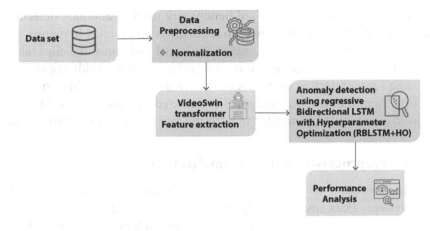

**Figure 5.1** Schematic architecture of our proposed system.

## 5.3.1  Dataset

The ShanghaiTech Campus dataset [12] is a large-scale video anomaly detection dataset used in this article. It comprises videos captured by street surveillance cameras with a fixed perspective. The dataset includes 337 videos from 13 different settings, of which 80 are abnormal and 257 are

**Figure 5.2** Normal and abnormal clips from the ShanghaiTech dataset.

normal. This dataset is a standard benchmark used in anomaly detection tasks and contains data that are both anomalous and typical in nature.

Figure 5.2 displays several samples of normal and abnormal clips taken from the dataset. The dataset was reorganized into a weakly supervised training set by selecting examples of abnormalities testing films and converting them into training images. This ensured that each of the 14 background clips would be included in both the testing set and the training set.

## 5.3.2   Preprocessing Using Normalization

The identification of anomalies is crucial in an intelligent transportation system. Data undergo early processing to prepare information for either primary processing or further analysis. When several procedures are required to prepare data for the user during the first or preliminary processing phase, the term "data normalization" may be employed. Data normalization refers to the process of improving, standardizing, and preserving the integrity of data. The process reduces the need for storage space by removing any redundant or duplicate data from the database. Normalization can be a scaling technique, a mapping approach, or a preprocessing step. It can be useful for making forecasts or predictions whenever a new range can be inferred from an old range. As there are various ways to anticipate or make predictions, we took measures to standardize the data during preprocessing. Equation 5.1 is applied to the data as part of the normalization procedure.

$$P_{nor} = \frac{P - P_{min}}{P_{max} - P_{min}} \tag{5.1}$$

where $P_{nor}$ = Normalized value
$P_{max}$ = Maximum value and
$P_{min}$ = Minimum value.

## 5.3.3   Feature Extraction Using Video Swin Transformer

The Video Swin Transformer model is utilized in this work to extract features. When using a pretrained model, we can extract higher-quality features. In the case of images, standard transformer models compute self-attention for all components, but this operation can be computationally expensive. The Swin Transformer addresses this issue by dividing images into windows and computing self-attention only within the current window. The window is then shifted across the images to obtain the self-attention value for all image collections in a more time-efficient manner.

To begin the process of feature extraction, the videos must first be split into individual frames (of size C × N, for example). The collection of these frames, denoted by the letter S, is the video that will be used for feature extraction, with each image containing RGB channels. This provides us with the following formula for determining the input dimension: M × H × S × C × N, where M is the batch size and H is the number of channels.

### 5.3.4   Anomaly Detection

The suggested RBLSTM with HO model is used for anomaly detection. In this model, normal video clips are represented by minimum-magnitude features, while anomaly video clips are represented by maximum-magnitude features. The suggested method is based on the assumption that abnormal clips have a higher mean feature magnitude than typical clips.

#### 5.3.4.1   *Regressive Bidirectional LSTM*

The suggested approach carries out the task of predicting a dependent variable (target) based on the provided independent variable(s). Therefore, this regressive approach identifies a linear connection between a dependent variable and other provided independent variables. Unlike a standard LSTM, an RBLSTM's output relies on both the next and preceding frames in the sequence. For this study, we utilized an RBLSTM with two cells per layer, one for the ahead pass and one for the reverse pass. The RBLSTM receives the characteristics extracted by Video Swin in the form of chunks to categorize the condition supplied as either normal or abnormal for an abnormality detection conclusion. The input to the RBLSTM at a time t is composed of the first section of the thousand features from the first frame of the video, followed by the second section of the following feature at a time t+1, and so on. Algorithm 1 represents the proposed RBLSTM approach.

---

**Algorithm 1: RBLSTM**

---

Procedure anomaly_dectector (data)

Model, detector<-CREATE ()

$N_n$, $V_n$, $T_n$, < – SPLIT (data)

For n epochs and batch_size do

Model train ($N_n$, $V_n$)

End for

N_prediction$_n$ <-model. predict ($N_n$)

N_error$_n$<-compute the loss function

Thresholds<-detector.SET_THERSHOLD as given in Equation (5.2)

$$2\frac{1}{K}\sum_{n=1}^{k}N - Nerror_n \qquad (5.2)$$

Detector.APPLY (thresholds)

For every $T_n$ do

T_prediction$_n$ <-model. predict ($T_n$)

T_eroor$_n$<-compute the loss function

If (T_eroor$_n$<(thresholds) then

$T_n$ is a normal point

Else

$A_n$<-$T_n$ is anomalous

Return [$T_n$]

Stop for

Stop procedure

---

### 5.3.4.2   *Hyperparameter Optimization*

Optimizing hyperparameters to enhance algorithm performance is crucial, since almost all machine learning (ML) methods include them [13, 14]. With the help of these hyperparameters, performance is optimized, requiring less work from the user and leading to a quicker, easier solution. The success of machine learning strongly depends on humans choosing the right hyperparameters. This is a difficult and time-consuming operation that becomes much more crucial when it must be performed by ML nonexperts rather than professionals, which occurs fairly often. The process of finding the ideal combination of hyperparameter values to obtain the best performance on the data in the shortest possible time is called hyperparameter optimization. It may provide you with hyperparameter optimized settings that increase the predicted accuracy of your model [15]. The hyperparameter optimization process is represented by Algorithm 2, which may be used to make predictions once the model has been trained. A test point must have all of its hash values generated before it can be checked. The precomputed counts in the model, which indicate the characteristics of the training data distribution, are used to build an estimate.

---

**Algorithm 2: Hyperparameter Optimization**

---

Input: p← Test point,
hasher← Hasher of the trained model,
*estPerHash*← Estimator dictionary,
*threshold*← Estimator threshold,
Output: Boolean value indicating whether *p* is an anomaly
*hashes* ←*hasher.HASH(p)*;
*estimator* ←0;
For every *h* ϵ *hashes* do
*estimator*←*estimator* + *estPerHash* [*h*];
Stop
Output: *estimator* < *threshold*

---

## 5.4   Result and Discussion

The dataset from ShanghaiTech Campus is utilized in this study for analysis. Video Swin serves as the backbone model for feature extraction. Comparison and result evaluation provide a full assessment of the proposed RBLSTM with HO technique. When compared to other methodologies such as the graph convolutional network (GCN) [16], margin learning embedded prediction (MLEP) [17], and 3-dimensional convolutional networks (3D ConvNets) [18], the suggested methodology proves powerful and effective in identifying anomalies in video surveillance. Accuracy, precision, recall, and error rate are performance metrics.

Equation 5.3 used to calculate accuracy is defined as the proportion of all forecasts to the corrected predictions.

$$Accuracy = \frac{(tn+tp)}{(tp+fp+tn+fn)} \tag{5.3}$$

where *tn* is true negative, *tp* is true positive, *fn* is false negative, and *fp* is false positive.

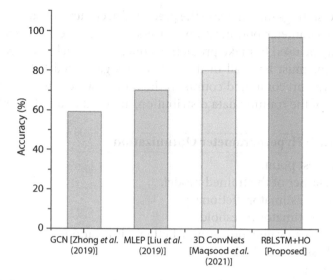

**Figure 5.3** Accuracy comparison between the suggested and current techniques.

Figure 5.3 displays the accuracy of the proposed system, along with the accuracy prediction of existing systems. The suggested method is denoted as well. The GCN has achieved 74%, the MLEP has acquired 66%, and the 3D ConvNets has reached 85%. In contrast, the suggested method achieves 98.5% accuracy. This demonstrates that the proposed approach is more effective than the existing ones.

Precision can be calculated using Equation 5.4 below.

$$Precision = \frac{tp}{tp + fp} \tag{5.4}$$

Figure 5.4 illustrates the precision of the proposed system as well as the precision of current systems' consumption predictions. The GCN achieves 60%, the MLEP achieves 71%, the 3D ConvNets achieves 81%, and the suggested system achieves 98% precision. This demonstrates that the proposed approach is more effective than the current ones.

As seen here in Equation 5.5, we can calculate the recall as follows:

$$Recall = \frac{tp}{tp + fn} \tag{5.5}$$

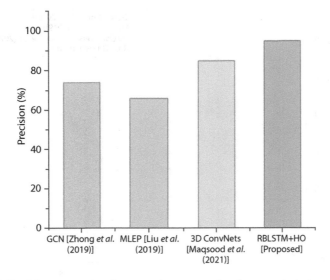

**Figure 5.4** Precision comparison between the suggested and current techniques.

Figure 5.5 displays the recall of the proposed system as well as the recall of the consumption estimates from existing systems. The suggested system achieves 90% recall, while the GCN achieves 74%, the MLEP achieves 83%, and the 3D ConvNets achieves 62%. This proves that the suggested technique is more efficient than the current ones.

The error rate is the ratio of invalid data units to all other data units delivered.

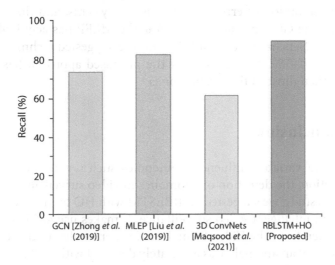

**Figure 5.5** Recall comparison between the suggested and current techniques.

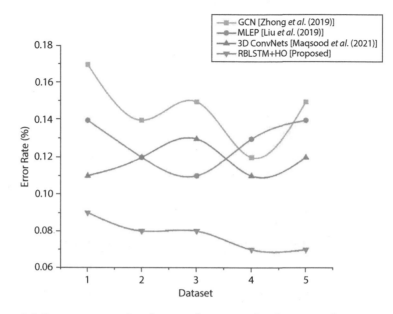

**Figure 5.6** Error rate comparison between the suggested and current techniques.

$$Error = \left( \frac{Estimatd\ Number - Actual\ Number}{Actual\ Number} \right) \times 100 \qquad (5.6)$$

Figure 5.6 illustrates the error rate of the proposed system, the prediction of consumption of error rate in existing systems, and the suggested technique. The GCN has attained 0.15%, the MLEP has acquired 0.14%, the 3D ConvNets has reached 0.12%, and the suggested technique has an error rate of 0.07%. This shows that the proposed approach has a lower error rate than those of the existing ones.

## 5.5 Conclusion

Due to several variables influencing outcomes, such as video noise, outliers, and resolution, the detection of anomalies in video surveillance is a tough task. In this study, we suggested an RBLSTM with HO to improve anomaly detection in intelligent video surveillance. It makes use of higher-quality features taken from the Video Swin Transformer model. In this investigation, a video of an anomaly was accurately detected with a 98.5% accuracy rate, 98% precision, 90% recall, and 0.07% error rate. According to experimental results that show the importance of anomaly detection, locating anomalies in the frame helps to provide outstanding results throughout extensive video surveillance, and this method is highly robust. Due to the rare incidence of anomalous occurrences, inconsistent behavior of various types of anomalies, and an uneven availability of data for normal and abnormal settings, anomaly identification in videos is a difficult challenge. In the future, further tests may be conducted by experimenting with various methods to reduce the noise present in the positive bag.

# References

1. Franklin, R.J. *et al.*, Anomaly detection in videos for video surveillance applications using neural networks, in: *Fourth International Conference on Inventive Systems and Control. (ICISC)*, 2020, doi: 10.1109/ICISC47916.2020.9171212.
2. Zhu, S. *et al.*, Video anomaly detection for smart surveillance, in: *Computer Vision: A Reference Guide*, pp. 1–8, Springer International Publishing, Cham, 2020, doi: 10.1007/978-3-030-03243-2_845-1.
3. Nasaruddin, N. *et al.*, Deep anomaly detection through visual attention in surveillance videos. *J. Big Data*, 7, 1, 1–17, 2020, doi: 10.1186/s40537-020-00365-y.
4. Tang, Y. *et al.*, Integrating prediction and reconstruction for anomaly detection. *Pattern Recognit. Lett.*, 129, 123–130, 2020, doi: 10.1016/j.patrec.2019.11.024.
5. Pranav, M. and Zhenggang, L., A day on campus-an anomaly detection dataset for events in a single camera, in: *Proc. Asian Conference on Computer Vision*, 2020.
6. Ullah, M. *et al.*, Attention-based LSTM network for action recognition in sports. *J. Electron. Imaging*, 2021, 302–301, 2021, doi: 10.2352/ISSN.2470-1173.2021.6.IRIACV-302.
7. Riaz, H. *et al.*, Anomalous human action detection using a cascade of deep learning models, in: *9th European Workshop on Visual Information Processing (EUVIP)*, 2021, doi: 10.1109/EUVIP50544.2021.9484062.
8. Wu, C., Shao, S., Tunc, C., Satam, P., Hariri, S., An explainable and efficient deep learning framework for video anomaly detection. *Clust. Comput.*, 25, 2715–2737, 2021.
9. Chang, Y. *et al.*, Clustering-driven deep autoencoder for video anomaly detection, in: *Computer Vision-ECCV, 16th European Conference, Proceedings, Part XV*, pp. 329–345, 2020, doi: 10.1007/978-3-030-58555-6_20.
10. Landi, F. *et al.*, Anomaly locality in video surveillance, arXiv preprint arXiv:1901.10364, 2019.

11. Madan, N. *et al.*, Temporal cues from socially unacceptable trajectories for anomaly detection, in: *Proc. IEEE/CVF International Conference on Computer Vision*, pp. 2150–2158, 2021, doi: 10.1109/ICCVW54120.2021.00244.
12. Deshpande, K. *et al.*, Anomaly detection in surveillance videos using transformer-based attention model, 2022, arXiv Preprint ArXiv:2206.01524, doi: 10.1007/978-981-99-1648-1_17.
13. Ganesh, N. *et al.*, Efficient feature selection using weighted superposition attraction optimization algorithm. *Appl. Sci.*, 13, 5, 3223, 2023, doi: 10.3390/app13053223.
14. Priyadarshini, J. *et al.*, Analyzing physics-inspired metaheuristic algorithms in feature selection with K-nearest-neighbor. *Appl. Sci.*, 13, 2, 906, 2023, doi: 10.3390/app13020906.
15. Shaik, K. *et al.*, Big data analytics framework using squirrel search optimized gradient boosted decision tree for heart disease diagnosis. *Appl. Sci.*, 13, 9, 5236, 2023, doi: 10.3390/app13095236.
16. Zhong, J.-X. *et al.*, Graph convolutional label noise cleaner: Train a plug-and-play action classifier for anomaly detection, in: *Proc. IEEE/CVF Conference on Computer Vision and Pattern Recognition*, pp. 1237–1246, 2019, doi: 10.1109/CVPR.2019.00133.
17. Liu, W. *et al.*, Margin learning embedded prediction for video anomaly detection with A few anomalies, in: *IJCAI*, pp. 3023–3030, 2019, doi: 10.24963/ijcai.2019/419.
18. Maqsood, R. *et al.*, Anomaly recognition from surveillance videos using 3D convolution neural network. *Multimedia Tools Appl.*, 80, 12, 18693–18716, 2021, doi: 10.1007/s11042-021-10570-3.

# 6

# Ensemble Machine Learning-Based Botnet Attack Detection for IoT Applications

Suchithra M.

*Department of Computing Technologies, School of Computing, SRM Institute of Science and Technology, Kattankulathur, Chennai, India*

## Abstract

The Internet of Things (IoT) systems are currently the subject of a rising prevalence of attacks as a result of their fast development and widespread adoption. It has been claimed that attacks using botnets account for the majority of those in IoT networks. Because the majority of IoT systems possess the memory and processing power necessary for effective security methods, there are still several security vulnerabilities in these systems. Additionally, attackers are capable of circumventing many of the present rule-based detection algorithms. Even though the machine learning (ML)-driven method can identify the variations of the various types of attacks, periodically special new types of attacks can be initiated. As a result, this paper suggests a novel ML technique termed random tree-adaptive artificial neural network (RT-ANN) in detecting botnet attacks. Initially, we collect the raw data samples and these samples are normalized. Principal component analysis (PCA) is used to retrieve key aspects of the RT-ANN. Our proposed RT-ANN method's performance is analyzed, and comparative analysis is also provided. The experimental results demonstrate that the proposed method achieves the highest detection rate in the botnet attack detection.

*Keywords*: Internet of Things (IoT), machine learning (ML), botnet attacks, principal component analysis (PCA), random tree-adaptive artificial neural network (RT-ANN)

*Email*: suchithm@srmist.edu.in

Kanak Kalita, Narayanan Ganesh and S. Balamurugan (eds.) Metaheuristics for Machine Learning: Algorithms and Applications, (149–162) © 2024 Scrivener Publishing LLC

## 6.1 Introduction

The fast development of Internet of Things (IoT) devices in recent years has improved the convenience of our everyday routines. IoT devices averaged one assault every 2 minutes [1]. The IoT collects, processes, and analyzes vast volumes of data from a variety of heterogeneous IoT devices to seamlessly link millions of smart objects and devices. The IoT is one of the top 10 key technology developments identified by Gartner in 2020. According to this forecast, in 2023, there will be 20 times as many smart devices as traditional IT equipment. It is anticipated that the IoT will be used more widely across a variety of industries, including utilities, healthcare, government, physical security, and automobiles. However, the Internet of Things infrastructure is being built quickly at the expense of more assaults and security vulnerabilities. According to Symantec, an IoT device gets attacked every 2 minutes [2]. The IoT is one of the networking industry's newest concepts. It may be characterized as the interconnection of objects with limited computing resources. It allows for the transmission and reception of data via the Internet without the need for computer-to-computer or person-to-person communication. The networked IP-enabled objects are referred to as things (both physical and virtual). Along with the regular IoT, it is important to discuss resource-constrained IoT devices. Although these gadgets use IoT applications, they are battery-operated, compact, low-power gadgets with a variety of design trade-offs. They also have restricted computational and storage capacities. Simply put, resource-constrained devices are sensors on endpoints that are utilized for a certain application. These gadgets have limited storage and processing power, restricted energy owing to energy-vulnerable batteries, and other resource limitations. Additionally, they are linked via weak radio circumstances, low-power lossy communications, and without human involvement [3]. The proliferation of IoT devices in recent years has brought forth new dangers like botnet assaults. Such assaults may be organized and seem to compromise the target devices. A botnet refers to an unauthorized remote control of a host. Attackers are in charge of hacked IoT devices, using them to carry out nefarious deeds. Botnets may cause significant harm in the real world, as shown in the 2016 Mirai attack that impacted approximately 1,000 closed-circuit television (CCTV) cameras [4]. A botnet is a group of Internet-connected computers that have been infiltrated and are now being remotely managed by an attacker using bots, a kind of malicious software. Malicious software is often used by an attacker. Among many other hazards, botnets will benefit the most from IoT security weaknesses.

Botnets are networks made up of nodes that have been infected with malware that turns them into attacking bots that follow orders from a botmaster. The Internet of Things provides a great setting for botnets for two main reasons. First, the absence of security mechanisms in IoT devices makes virus transmission and installation easier. Second, the sheer number of linked devices that are anticipated in the next year will enable huge attacks, providing unprecedented quantities of susceptible resources to attackers [5]. In this article, we propose a random tree-adaptive artificial neural network (RT-ANN) for detecting botnet attacks.

The organizational structure of the paper can be understood by referring to the following outline. Section 6.2 provides a thorough analysis of relevant work. In Section 6.3, we outline the formulation of the proposed work. Section 6.4 presents and discusses the results. Finally, in Section 6.5, we offer the conclusions and recommendations for further research.

## 6.2    Literature Survey

Sriram *et al.* [6] proposed a botnet detection mechanism based on network traffic flows and deep learning (DL). The platform uses a DL model to capture network traffic flows, convert them into connection records, and identify attacks originating from compromised IoT devices. Popoola *et al.* [7] presented the federated deep learning (FDL) strategy for preventing data privacy leaks in IoT edge devices by detecting zero-day botnet attacks. This approach uses an ideal deep neural network (DNN) architecture to classify network traffic. Al-Duwairi *et al.* [8] proposed an IoT botnet DDoS attack detection and mitigation system based on Security Information and Event Management. Several IoT companies offer a wide range of heterogeneous IoT solutions, each implementing their own network and communication protocol. Hussain *et al.* [9] provided a comprehensive set of characteristics to more effectively identify botnet attacks, regardless of the underlying dataset. The experimental findings showed that the norms and principles feature set effectively supports machine algorithms to better identify various forms of botnet attacks. Zagrouba and Alhajri [10] proposed ML strategies with low-power consumption for identifying IoT botnet attacks, utilizing random forest as an ML-based detection method and detailing IoT typical assaults with their countermeasures. Hikal and Elgayar [11] developed a lightweight anomaly-based machine learning intrusion detection system based on the use of an ensemble data preparation step in advance. Al-Sarem *et al.* [12] offered a methodology for feature selection based on aggregate mutual information and ML techniques to improve the detection of botnet attacks.

This research analyzed actual traffic data from nine commercial IoT devices to analyze the N-BaIoT benchmark dataset to identify different botnet attack types. The experimental findings demonstrated that, when a binary dataset was employed, the mutual information filter-based approach produced the greatest score.

McDermott *et al.* [13] suggested that a bidirectional strategy lengthens processing times and adds cost to each epoch, but eventually turns out to be a more effective progressive model. Alissa *et al.* [14] suggested machine learning techniques for categorizing binary classes using the freely accessible dataset UNSW-NB15. As a result, cybercriminals are always searching for fresh ways to identify and take advantage of security gaps. Vishwakarma and Jain [15] offered a honeypot-based methodology that uses machine learning methods to identify malware. Abu Khurma *et al.* [16] proposed a wrapper feature selection model by hybridizing the salp swarm algorithm and ant lion optimization. The findings indicate that by employing these pertinent subsets of characteristics, the ant lion optimization achieved the greatest outcomes in terms of the metrics under study. Vinayakumar *et al.* [17] proposed a botnet detection system based on a two-level deep learning framework for semantically discriminating botnets and legitimate behaviors at the application layer of the domain name system services. Nõmm and Bahşi [18] created models for unsupervised learning that are very accurate and have reduced feature set lengths, allowing for a reduction in the amount of CPU power needed.

## 6.3   Proposed System

In the following section, we discuss in detail an enhanced model for predicting botnet attacks and explain the proposed method of the random tree-adaptive artificial neural network. Figure 6.1 illustrates the proposed methodology. Initially, raw data samples are collected and normalized. The dataset is then prepared, and data processing techniques, such as normalization and principal component analysis (PCA), are used to extract the key features for the RT-ANN model.

### 6.3.1   Dataset

The studies discussed in this section utilized the N-BaIoT dataset, which was obtained by executing hazardous IoT malware such as Mirai and BASHLITE. The dataset comprises a total of 849,233 instances, including

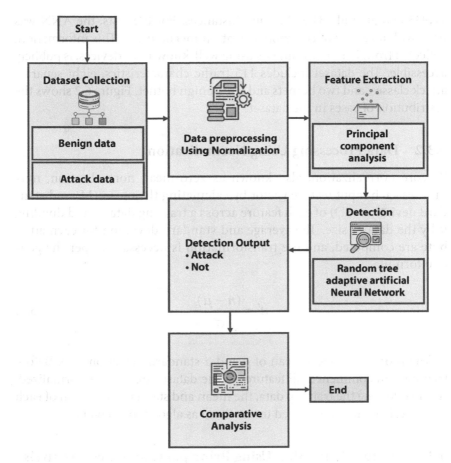

**Figure 6.1** The proposed methodology.

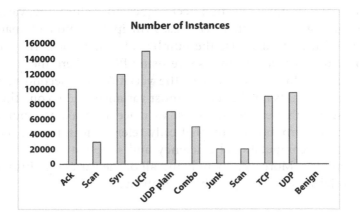

**Figure 6.2** The dataset's distribution.

17,935 benign and 831,298 assault instances. For the tests, the ANN was used with a variety of common activation mechanisms. This information, collected from IoT environments using well-known IoT devices, is publicly accessible. The dataset includes 115 traffic characteristics, eight separate attack classes, and two botnets and one benign botnet. Figure 6.2 shows the distribution of cases in the dataset.

## 6.3.2    Data Processing Using Normalization

Z-score normalization, also known as zero-mean normalization, normalizes each input feature vector by calculating the mean (M) and standard deviation (SD) of each feature across a training dataset and dividing it by the dataset size. The average and standard deviation for each attribute are computed, and the transformation is necessary as per the general formula.

$$n' = \frac{(n - \mu)}{\sigma} \tag{6.1}$$

The property n has a mean of $\mu$ and a standard deviation of $\sigma$. Before training can commence, all features of the dataset are z-score normalized. After collecting the training data, the mean and standard deviation of each characteristic should be saved to use them as algorithm weights.

## 6.3.3    Feature Extraction Using Principal Component Analysis

To enhance our model's performance, we employed dimensionality reduction and feature selection techniques to reduce the variability while retaining the important features. Principal component analysis is one method used to decrease the number of dimensions. The data are transformed into a new feature space using PCA, where the first coordinate accounts for the majority of the variation, the second principal component accounts for the second most variance, and so on. The traits in this research that exhibit the most variance are used as input by the classifiers. This process ensures that only relevant features are selected, improving the computational efficiency and simplicity of the machine learning models. Moreover, by utilizing all of the variables, this method can potentially reduce any possible overfitting.

### 6.3.4    Random Tree-Adaptive Artificial Neural Network

The random tree algorithm is comparable to the random forest approach and shares many of its advantages, as it uses some decision trees. It can effectively manage data with high-dimensional features without the need for feature selection, and it has a strong classification impact and high accuracy. The execution process can be parallelized to achieve efficiency. Unlike the random forest method, which generates training samples via bootstrap sampling in the integrated learning approach, the extreme random tree strategy employs all of the original data for each decision tree. Moreover, when the extreme random tree divides at a node, the splitting node is chosen at random, and the ideal splitting threshold or feature is not used. Figure 6.3 illustrates the architecture of the ANN.

The artificial neural network is a fundamental building block of the neural network technique. The paradigm is useful for teaching vector-valued functions. The components, which are also known as neurons, operate in parallel and are interconnected. The layer is a subgroup that deals with the components that are linked together. The hidden, output, and input layers are essentially the layers in the neural network. Although the corresponding weights are present in each connecting connection, they must be adjusted during the backward calculation stages to have the best weight values.

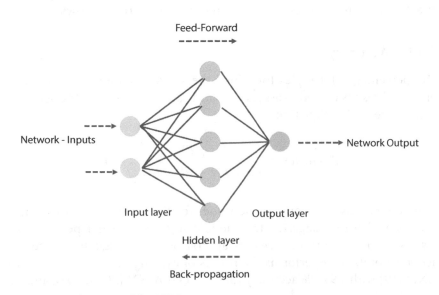

**Figure 6.3** Architecture of the ANN.

$$l(x) = \frac{1}{1 + a^{-x}} \tag{6.2}$$

$$l(x) = \frac{sinsinh(x)}{coscosh(x)} = \frac{a^x - a^{x-x}}{a^x + a^{-x}} \tag{6.3}$$

$$l(x) = (0, x) = \{x, x \geq 0, x < 0 \tag{6.4}$$

Therefore, the activation function assumes a crucial role in obtaining these ideal weight vectors. Equations 6.1–6.3 show some well-known activations, such as the sigmoid, ReLU, and tanh functions.

## 6.4   Results and Discussion

This study explores the use of ensemble ML-based botnet attack detection for IoT applications. Raw data samples are collected and normalized, and principal component analysis is used to retrieve the key aspects of the RT-ANN. The performance of our proposed RT-ANN method is analyzed, and a comparative analysis is provided. Accuracy, recall, precision, and F-measure metrics are used to test the system's ability to identify botnet attacks. The equations used to define these metrics are as follows:

### 6.4.1   Accuracy

The percentage of samples for which the suggested approach accurately predicted results is used to assess how accurate the system is. The accuracy is calculated using Equation 6.5.

$$Accuracy = \frac{TP + TN}{TP + TN + FP + FN} \times 100 \tag{6.5}$$

Figure 6.4 displays comparable values for the accuracy metrics, and it is evident that the suggested technique can generate better performance results than the current research approaches. The suggested method's accuracy of 97% outperforms the results of existing methods, such as the CNN [19] with a 91.6% accuracy rate, the LGBA-NN [20] at 90%, and the

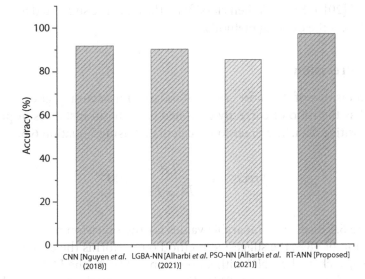

**Figure 6.4** Results of accuracy.

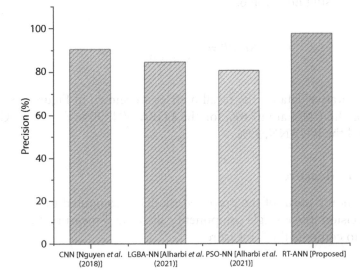

**Figure 6.5** Results of precision.

PSO-NN [20] at 85.2%. When classifying the data, the suggested technique outperforms the existing methods.

## 6.4.2   Precision

Precision is one of the most crucial standards for accuracy, and it is well-defined as the ratio of correctly classified cases to all instances of predictively positive data. The precision is calculated using Equation 6.6.

$$precision = \frac{TP}{TP + FP} \times 100 \qquad (6.6)$$

Figure 6.5 displays comparable values for the precision measures. With a precision of 98%, the suggested method outperforms the currently used methods, such as the CNN with a precision of 90.9%, the LGBA-NN with 85%, and the PSO-NN with 81%. The proposed method achieved better data categorization precision than other currently used methods.

## 6.4.3   Recall

Recall is the potential of a model to identify each important sample within a data collection. It is statistically defined as the percentage of true positives (TPs) divided by the sum of TPs and false negatives (FNs). The recall is calculated using Equation 6.7.

$$Recall = \frac{FN}{FN + TP} \times 100 \qquad (6.7)$$

Comparative data for the recall metrics are shown in Figure 6.6. Recall rates for the CNN are 97.6%; for the LGBA-NN, 90%; for the PSO-NN, 85%; and the RT-ANN, 99%.

## 6.4.4   F-Measure

The harmonic mean of the proposed model is computed to merge recall and precision into a single component called the F-measure. Equation 6.8 is used to compute the F-measure.

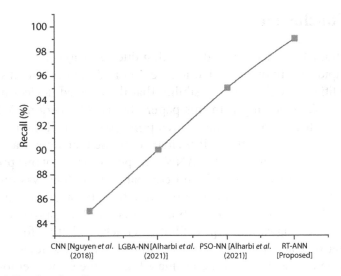

**Figure 6.6** Results of recall.

$$F - Measure = \frac{(precision) \times (recall) \times 2}{precision + recall} \times 100 \qquad (6.8)$$

In Figure 6.7, the RT-ANN scored 98% on the F-measure, followed by the CNN (scored 94.1%), LGBA-NN (86%), and PSO-NN (86.23%).

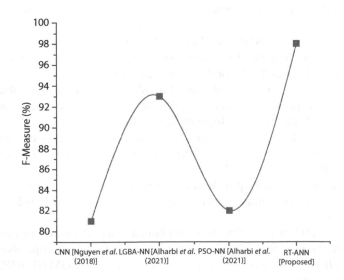

**Figure 6.7** Results of the F-measure.

## 6.5   Conclusion

The IoT botnet attacks can be devastating due to various factors, including the rapid growth of connected IoT devices and their potential security vulnerabilities, as well as the possibility that the affected devices may not display any signs of danger. In this paper, the use of emerging ML techniques for detecting botnet attacks was proposed. We collected raw data samples and normalized them. Principal component analysis was used to extract the key features of the RT-ANN. The performance of our proposed RT-ANN method was analyzed, and comparative analysis was provided. The results of the experiments demonstrate that the suggested approach has the highest detection rate for botnet attacks. This approach may be capable of detecting various types of botnet attacks and other forms of disruptive network activity. To confirm the findings, future studies using the complete dataset will need to be evaluated using the same methodology. Additionally, to evaluate the performance of the algorithms with other botnet attacks, this experiment can potentially be expanded to include more datasets, such as the Bot-IoT dataset and the CTU-13, which are more current.

## References

1. Soe, Y.N. *et al.*, Machine learning-based IoT-botnet attack detection with sequential architecture. *Sensors (Basel)*, 20, 16, 4372, 2020, doi: 10.3390/s20164372.
2. Alkahtani, H. and Aldhyani, T.H.H., Botnet attack detection by using the CNN-LSTM model for the Internet of Things applications. *Secur. Commun. Netw.*, 2021, 1–23, 2021, doi: 10.1155/2021/3806459.
3. Abu Al-Haija, Q. and Al-Dala'ien, M.A.-M., ELBA-IoT: An ensemble learning model for botnet attack detection in IoT networks. *J. Sens. Actuator Netw.*, 11, 1, 18, 2022, doi: 10.3390/jsan11010018.
4. Alqahtani, M. *et al.*, IoT botnet attack detection is based on optimized extreme gradient boosting and feature selection. *Sensors (Basel)*, 20, 21, 6336, 2020, doi: 10.3390/s20216336.
5. Rethinavalli, S. and Gopinath, R., Botnet attack detection in the Internet of Things using optimization techniques. *Int. J. Electr. Eng. Technol.*, 11, 412–420, 2020.
6. Sriram, S. *et al.*, Network flow-based IoT botnet attack detection using deep learning, in: *IEEE Conference on Computer Communications Workshops (INFOCOM WKSHPS)*, IEEE Infocom, 2020, doi: 10.1109/ INFOCOMWKSHPS50562. 2020.9162668.

7. Popoola, S.I., *et al.*, Federated deep learning for zero-day botnet attack detection in IoT-edge devices. *IEEE Internet Things J.*, 9, 5, 3930–3944, 2021, doi: 10.1109/JIOT.2021.3100755.

8. Al-Duwairi, B. *et al.*, SIEM-based detection and mitigation of IoT-botnet DDoS attacks. *Int. J. Electr. Comput. Eng.*, 10, 2, 2182, 2020, doi: 10.11591/ijece.v10i2.pp2182-2191.

9. Hussain, F. *et al.*, Towards universal features set for IoT botnet attack detection, in: *23rd International Multitopic Conference (INMIC)*, IEEE, 2020, doi: 10.1109/INMIC50486.2020.9318106.

10. Zagrouba, R. and Alhajri, R., Machine learning-based attacks detection and countermeasures in IoT. *Int. J. Commun. Netw. Inf. Secur.*, 13, 2, 158–167, 2021, doi: 10.17762/ijcnis.v13i2.4943.

11. Hikal, N.A. and Elgayar, M.M., Enhancing IoT botnets attack detection using machine learning-IDS and ensemble data preprocessing technique, in: *The Internet Things-Appl. Future Proc. ITAF*, vol. 2020, 2019, doi: 10.1007/978-981-15-3075-3_6.

12. Al-Sarem, M. *et al.*, An aggregated mutual information-based feature selection with machine learning methods for enhancing IoT botnet attack detection. *Sensors (Basel)*, 22, 1, 185, 2021, doi: 10.3390/s22010185.

13. McDermott, C.D. *et al.*, Botnet detection in the Internet of Things using deep learning approaches, in: *International Joint Conference on Neural Networks (IJCNN)*, vol. 2018, 2018, doi: 10.1109/IJCNN.2018.8489489.

14. Alissa, K. *et al.*, Botnet attack detection in IoT using machine learning. *Comput. Intell. Neurosci.*, 2022, 4515642, 2022, doi: 10.1155/2022/4515642.

15. Vishwakarma, R. and Jain, A.K., A honeypot with a machine learning-based detection framework for defending IoT-based botnet DDoS attacks, in: *3rd International Conference on Trends in Electronics and Informatics (ICOEI)*, vol. 2019, 2019, doi: 10.1109/ICOEI.2019.8862720.

16. Abu Khurma, R. *et al.*, IoT botnet detection using salp swarm and antlion hybrid optimization model. *Symmetry*, 13, 8, 1377, 2021, doi: 10.3390/sym13081377.

17. Vinayakumar, R. *et al.*, A visualized botnet detection system based on deep learning for the Internet of Things networks of smart cities. *IEEE Trans. Ind. Appl.*, 56, 4, 4436–4456, 2020, doi: 10.1109/TIA.2020.2971952.

18. Nõmm, S. and Bahşi, H., Unsupervised anomaly-based botnet detection in IoT networks. *17th IEEE International Conference on Machine Learning and Applications (ICMLA)*, vol. 2018, 2018, doi: 10.1109/ICMLA.2018.00171.

19. Nguyen, H.T. *et al.*, IoT botnet detection approach based on PSI graph and DGCNN classifier, in: *IEEE International Conference on Information Communication and Signal Processing (ICICSP)*, vol. 2018, 2018, doi: 10.1109/ICICSP.2018.8549713.

20. Alharbi, A. *et al.*, Botnet attack detection using local global best bat algorithm for the industrial internet of things. *Electronics*, 10, 11, 1341, 2021, doi: 10.3390/electronics10111341.

# 7

# Machine Learning-Based Intrusion Detection System with Tuned Spider Monkey Optimization for Wireless Sensor Networks

Ilavendhan Anandaraj[1]* and Kaviarasan Ramu[2]

[1]*School of Computer Science and Engineering, Vellore Institute of Technology, Chennai, India*
[2]*Department of Computer Science and Engineering, RGM College of Engineering and Technology, Nandyal, India*

## Abstract

An intrusion detection system is used to look into the problem that occurs in a wireless sensor network (WSN) or system. Intrusion detection is software or a piece of hardware that looks for suspicious activity on a system or network. As computers become more connected to each other, intrusion detection becomes more important for network security. Different types of intrusion detection systems (IDSs) have been made to protect wireless sensor networks with the help of machine learning and statistical methods. Accuracy is the most important factor in how well an IDS works. The accuracy of intrusion detection needs to be improved to cut down on false alarms and raise the rate of detection. The main job of an IDS is to look at huge amounts of network traffic data. To solve this problem, a well-organized way to classify intrusion is needed. This issue is taken into account in this research. In this article, we suggest machine learning techniques such as the support vector machine (SVM) with the tuned spider monkey optimization (TSMO) for wireless sensor networks. The NSL-KDD knowledge discovery dataset is used to measure how well an intrusion detection system works. The results show that the suggested model works better than the methods that are already in use. The suggested model is assessed on a number of performance criteria, and it is compared to other models to figure out how well it works overall.

*Corresponding author*: ilavendhan.a@vit.ac.in

Kanak Kalita, Narayanan Ganesh and S. Balamurugan (eds.) Metaheuristics for Machine Learning: Algorithms and Applications, (163–178) © 2024 Scrivener Publishing LLC

*Keywords*: Intrusion detection, support vector machine (SVM), spider monkey optimization (SMO), wireless sensor networks, machine learning

## 7.1 Introduction

The fundamental structure of a wireless sensor network (WSN) consists of sensor nodes. These nodes are often dispersed thickly to facilitate data processing, data sensing, transmission, and computation. WSNs consist of a variety of tasks, operations, and capacities. WSNs may be deployed in parks, highways, battlefields, certain machines, commercial structures, and even on the human body [1]. Distributed, infrastructure-free, failure, extensible, and dynamical are all characteristics of wireless sensor networks. Multiple security flaws exist in WSNs, which may reduce their efficiency. Despite providing secure data transmission through access control, strong authentication, and secure network algorithms, these methods are unable to guarantee the timely delivery of messages. In plenty of other words, these safeguards function to prevent malicious outsiders from accessing the network but fall short when faced with malicious insiders. Data privacy, identification, and data integrity are all goals. These methods protect sensitive data from prying eyes during an external assault. When an insider attacks a sensor system, a node inside the network begins acting maliciously without first attempting to get access to the data in the messages it has received. Computer and wireless sensor network intrusions may be identified with the help of an intrusion detection system (IDS). There are a few main methods to categorize IDSs, the most prevalent of which are misuse-based and anomaly-based. Misuse-based intrusion detection systems are effective at spotting common attacks like a snort. When compared to other IDSs, this one generates less false positives. As it does not modify any of the predefined instructions in its database, it cannot identify novel threats. Anomaly-based intrusion detection systems first create a baseline of normal behavior, then identify and flag any noteworthy departures from that baseline as potential security threats. There is a significant false alarm rate with this IDS; however, it can identify both known and unknown assaults. False positives are reduced by the use of a number of machine learning (ML) methods [2].

### 7.1.1 Intrusion Detection System

The term intrusion poses one of the most significant threats to online security based on the assumption that a single error or incursion may quickly take over or destroy data from a computer or a system's architecture. System security flaws can cause system harm and result in massive economic losses and actual hardware operations, leading to inaccurate data in the cyber digital war. To avoid failures, an intrusion detection system and error identification architecture are required [3].

In a matter of minutes, data stored on computers or wireless sensor networks can be accessed or lost if an attack occurs, making infiltration one of the most pressing issues in network safety. Intruders can cause damage to system hardware. Various IDSs are used to combat intrusions; however, accuracy is a key concern. Detection rate and false alarm rate are critical for accuracy analysis. To reduce false alarms and improve the detection rate, intrusion detection must be enhanced.

## 7.1.2  Machine Learning

Analytical models can be automatically built with the assistance of machine learning, a method of data analysis. Artificial intelligence (AI) operates on the premise that computers can learn to solve problems, make decisions, and identify patterns with little human intervention. The two main types of ML are supervised and unsupervised learning. Training algorithms often require labeled instances, such as input and desired output. Unsupervised learning is used to train new instances in the absence of such labels. The primary objectives of unsupervised learning are to (1) detect patterns in the data and (2) learn more about the data. Semi-supervised learning and reinforcement learning are two other strategies utilized.

Semi-supervised learning employs less labeled data and vast volumes of unlabeled data for training purposes. Reinforcement learning adopts a trial-and-error approach to determine which activities offer the greatest rewards. The methods of categorization, regression, and prediction are used. In this learning approach, agent, environment, and actions are the three key components. The goal is for the agent to select activities that maximize the predicted payoff. By using a sound strategy, the agent may achieve the objective much faster [4]. Therefore, in this research, the support vector machine (SVM) with the tuned spider monkey optimization (TSMO) is used. These algorithms can handle classification. Additionally, normalization and feature reduction are used to conduct a comparative analysis.

This work is divided into five sections, starting with the introduction. The second section describes related works. Additionally, the methodology was outlined in section 7.3. Performance evaluations were presented in section 7.4. In conclusion, section 7.5 concludes the article.

## 7.2    Literature Review

A digital test bed with a star topology and hosts and servers connected to the OpenFlow OVS-switch mimics the actual network environment. The signature-based Snort IDS monitors and detects attacks by mirroring server traffic. The risk assessment demonstrates that the Snort IDS sufficiently protects the network topology against threats, except for a few that require mitigation. A flow-based IDS model is created for architecture-scaled threat detection. The flow-based outlier detection using machine learning defeats the signature-based IDS [5]. Verma and Ranga [6] proposed ML classification techniques that are used to secure the Internet of Things (IoT) against DoS attacks. Classifiers that enhance anomaly-based IDSs are thoroughly studied. Classifiers are evaluated using popular metrics and validation techniques. CIDDS-001, UNSW-NB15, and NSL-KDD datasets are used to benchmark classifiers. Friedman and Nemenyi tests compare classifiers quantitatively. Raspberry Pi tests classifier response time on IoT frameworks. The primary focus of the study is on the latest most authoritative literature available on the subject of machine learning techniques and their implementation in the IoT and the IDS for the purpose of protecting computer networks. Therefore, the aim of the study is to conduct a comprehensive literature review of current publications that address the intersection of the IoT and ML in the IDS for computer networks [7]. The IDSs have been using deep learning (DL), along with other new approaches, to improve their effectiveness in safeguarding computer networks and hosts. Lansky et al. [8] proposed a comprehensive study and categorization of DL-based intrusion detection techniques. It begins with a presentation of the fundamental ideas of IDS designs and the different DL techniques. Then, it groups the designs according to the specific DL techniques they employ. It explains how the use of deep learning networks can enhance the accuracy of intrusion detection. The expansion of cybersecurity research projects, such as those focusing on intrusion detection and prevention systems, is of critical importance. The use of an intrusion detection system, often known as an IDS, is an efficient method of guarding against harmful assaults. During the course of research conducted by Alrowaily et al. [9], the CICIDS2017 intrusion detection dataset was used in a variety of tests carried out on seven different machine learning algorithms. The most effective method of preventive control against assaults originating from IoT devices is the use of ML and DL techniques, as Asharf et al. [10] provided an overview of intrusion detection techniques and a detailed assessment of the technologies, protocols, design, and dangers connected to IoT systems that arise from compromised IoT devices. That study also includes an evaluation of several machine learning and deep learning-based strategies that may be used to spot Internet of Things devices affected by intrusions. Rahman *et al.* [11] proposed two approaches, semi-distributed and distributed, that combine high-performing feature extraction and selection with the possibility of fog-edge synchronized analytics to overcome the limitations of the centralized IDS for devices with limited resources. To divide up the work, they each create their simultaneous ML algorithms for a split intrusion dataset. On the semi-distributed side, parallel methods are used for feature choices on both the edge and fog sides, and then a single multilayer perceptron is used for categorization. In the distributed manner, feature extraction and multilayer perceptron categorization are carried out independently by the parallel systems, and then the results are aggregated by a coordinating edge or fog. Sarker *et al.* [12] described an intrusion detection tree machine learning-based security model that first ranks security mechanisms by relevance and then builds a tree-based generalized intrusion detection algorithm based on the chosen critical features. The model predicts unseen test cases accurately and reduces computation costs by lowering feature dimensionality. Dang [13] analyzed the existing research by explicating the choices made by IDSs constructed in earlier research. Users' confidence in using the system will increase if they have a stronger grasp of the IDS, while programmers may depend on the explanation to tweak the system. Based on the model's interpretation, the experimental findings indicate that they may greatly lower the computing power requirements of the IDS. Idrissi *et al.* [14] analyzed well-known security risks in accordance with the Cisco IoT reference model architecture to examine the current state of the art in IoT security threats and vulnerabilities. Existing studies in the subject of IoT security are also reviewed, with a focus on those that use DL methods to detect intrusions. DL techniques are on the rise and are becoming more important in many sectors, including cybersecurity. Sethi *et al.* [15] presented a deep reinforcement learning-based adaptive cloud IDS framework that overcomes the restrictions mentioned above while performing accurate determination and fine-grained categorization of novel and sophisticated assaults. They conducted thorough testing using the benchmark UNSW-NB15 dataset, which demonstrates higher accuracy and lower False Positive Rate (FPR) when matched to state-of-the-art IDSs. Network entities are susceptible to serious assaults due to a lack of security measures. An effective security framework for dealing with threats and detecting assaults is required to solve that. To address the massive volume of intrusion data categorization difficulties and enhance detection accuracy by lowering false alarm rates, Ethala and Kumarappan [16] proposed a hybrid optimization technique that combines the spider monkey optimization and hierarchical particle swarm optimization. The random forest classifier was used to classify assaults from the NSL-KDD and UNSW-NB 15 datasets after identifying the most optimal values. Wang [17] used the NSL-KDD dataset to analyze the effectiveness of several attack techniques against deep learning-based intrusion detection. It is experimentally shown that neural networks used by IDSs are vulnerable in certain ways. The function of various characteristics in producing hostile data is investigated, and they analyze the practicality and viability of the assault strategies in light of their results.

## 7.3  Proposed Methodology

### 7.3.1  Problem Statement

The detection accuracy also decreases, and the number of false alarm reports of network intrusion rises as a result of the massive amounts of data. This is a significant problem if the system is attacked by something it has never seen before. Improving accuracy while reducing false positives is a top priority. The SVM with the TSMO is proposed to tackle the aforementioned problems.

### 7.3.2  Methodology

The investigation used the NSL-KDD dataset, and data preparation was conducted to remove undesirable data from the dataset. In the SVM and the TSMO, the characteristics from which the leader selects whether to split or merge are discussed, resulting in the selection of the optimal feature value. Additionally, the TSMO hierarchically arranges the particles based on their optimal function and categorizes the attacks using the SVM. The flowchart of the SVM-TSMO is illustrated in Figure 7.1.

### 7.3.3  Data Collection

The NSL-KDD dataset is built on the KDD Cup 99 datasets, with duplicate and redundant data removed. The NSL-KDD dataset contains 41 labeled features, such as assault kinds. It is suggested as a solution to the problems with the KDD'99 datasets. The training and testing sets both provide

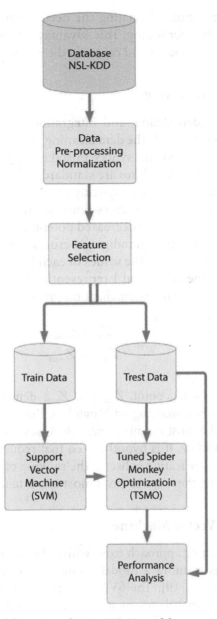

**Figure 7.1** Flowchart of the proposed SVM-TSMO model.

enough data to be useful, eliminating the need to randomly pick a small subset of the collection for testing. This advantage enables results from different studies to be compared and contrasted consistently [16].

### 7.3.4   Data Preprocessing

Data cleansing, standardization, and integration are among the preprocessing techniques employed. The data cleaning process includes removing empty fields, duplicate records, syntax mistakes, and missing codes. The datasets' data cleansing procedures are standardized to facilitate data analysis, and the cleaned data may be quickly retrieved for study. To accomplish normalization, new data vectors must be created. One of the main benefits of normalizing data is a decreased potential for data inconsistency. The Min-Max normalization paradigm is crucial when it comes to integrating and normalizing data. The values of each feature range from 0 to 1, with 0 representing the lowest and 1 representing the maximum.

Equation 7.1 expresses the normalization process.

$$Z_{norm} = \frac{Z_r - Z_{min}}{Z_{min} - Z_{max}} \tag{7.1}$$

where $Z_r$ represents a data point, $Z_{min}$ and $Z_{max}$ denote the minimum and maximum values when working with batches. Recursive feature elimination (RFE) ranks the most essential characteristics and returns their relative relevance as a value. It is hypothesized that reducing redundant data would result in smaller feature subsets. The ranking of characteristics may be derived by sorting the features from most important to least important.

### 7.3.5   Support Vector Machine

The supervised learning approach from which the support vector machine is derived involves training a model using data from a wide range of sources and topics [18, 19]. The SVM is capable of generating a hyperplane or multiple hyperplanes in a high-dimensional space. The ideal hyperplane is the one that effectively partitions the input data into distinct categories. A nonlinear classifier employs a variety of kernel functions to evaluate the distances between hyperplanes. The primary objective of kernel functions, such as linear, polynomial, radial basis, and stochastic, is to maximize the distance between hyperplanes. The growing interest in the SVMs has resulted in the development and exploration of various notable

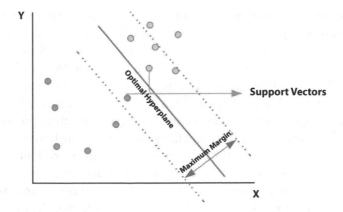

**Figure 7.2** The support vector machine.

applications. The SVM plays a significant role in image analysis and pattern recognition. Figure 7.2 illustrates the SVM basic diagram.

In most cases, the primary aspect of a classification task involves splitting data into two distinct groups: the training datasets and the testing datasets. Within the context of this class, labels will be referred to as target variables, while attributes will be understood as features or observed variables.

## 7.3.6   Tuned Spider Monkey Optimization

The TSMO is a swarm intelligence-based system that consists of a cluster of social media (SM) whose foraging activity inspires them. The decision to fission or join together is based on the number of monkeys in one group. The algorithm depends on the social structure of a set of characteristics determined by the leader, who decides whether to pool resources or move in separate directions in the quest for food. The global leader is in charge of all groups, while the local leaders are in charge of their respective groups. One idea is that different parts of the brain have different control over different aspects of the mind's thought processes, and the similarities between these operations and the monkey brain are well recognized. A fission-fusion society is a community observed in ethology where animals undergo constant transformations. They are split into smaller groups during the day, which have the fission status, and mixed back together at night with the fusion status. Spider monkeys provide a good example of this kind of civilization. In this community, female monkeys are viewed as leaders over their male counterparts, while male monkeys are at a lower status (i.e., they are not dominating) despite their greater activity.

This society's customs are based on the same social arrangement as that of a spider monkey, which allows for a unique blend of old and new. Several research studies have been conducted on the TSMO technique. These efforts show that the TSMO performs well in exploration and exploitation, but there are still certain details to consider in order to achieve optimal performance. Mini-groups of 40 or 50 partners are formed inside the larger female-governed monkey communities, with locating the food supply being a top priority for these smaller groupings. If one female-led group does not achieve its goal, another female-led subgroup will attempt, and so on, until the mission is accomplished. In an effort to keep up with the times, several changes have been made, such as analyzing search volumes and selecting the most relevant results. The TSMO approach is segmented and built on population repetitive methodology, with each stage detailed below. Figure 7.3 shows the proposed model block diagram.

Phase 1: Initialization
One starting point involves finding N completely random answers. The spider monkey population, m, is divided into n equal halves. Then, a local leader is appointed to each group, with a global leader overseeing all groups.

$$J_{rm} = J_{\min m} + I(0,1) \times (J_{\max m} - J_{\min m}) \tag{7.2}$$

where $J_{\min m}$ and $J_{\max m}$ are limits of $J_r$ in the *mth* vector. $I(0,1)$ is an arbitrary number (0, 1).

Phase 2: Local Leader
At this stage, the SMs will be aware of what their local leader and their nearby neighbor know, and they will update their location as a result. The following are the steps involved:

$$J_{new\,rm} = J_{rm} + I(0,1) \times (AA_{gm} - J_{rm}) + I(-1,1) \times (J_{im} - J_{rm}) \tag{7.3}$$

Phase 3: Global Leader
During this phase, the SMs have another opportunity to update their positions using fitness and reach the global optimum. They can draw inspiration from their perseverance, their neighbors, and their global leaders. The updating behavior at this stage is more precisely described by the following equation:

$$J_{new\,mr} = J_{rm} + I(0,1) \times (KA_r - J_{rm}) + I(-1,1) \times (J_{im} - J_{rm}) \tag{7.4}$$

Phase 4: Local Leader Learning
Since the global optimum has already been identified, the method determines the leader of the local subgroups and the local optimal solutions. This step involves determining whether or not local leaders have updated themselves by assessing the threshold's number.

Phase 5: Global Leader Learning
The phase's name alone suggests that the global leader is present within the pack. It also verifies whether the leader has updated its position to a specific limit, allowing for an increase in activity.

Phase 6: Local Leader Decision
When this happens, the social media managers in the group will upgrade the platform entirely either by following the instructions of the global leader or by initializing randomly based on the perturbation rate. This will happen regardless of whether the local leaders have already been updated to a certain threshold or not.

$$J_{new\,rm} = J_{rm} + I(0,1) \times (KA_r - J_{r\,m}) + I(-1,1) \times (J_{im} - AA_{gm}) \quad (7.5)$$

Phase 7: Global Leader Decision
During this phase, the group undergoes both fission and fusion, particularly regarding the concept of a limit global leader, which suggests that global leaders do not need to meet a specific threshold to be considered as such.

## 7.4    Result and Discussion

After constructing the SVM-TSMO model, it is important to adjust its parameters to meet the prediction requirements. The key elements to consider include precision, accuracy, recall, and F1-measure [20, 21].

### 7.4.1    Accuracy

The accuracy of the recommended intrusion detection scheme is a measure of how effectively it detects intrusions. Figure 7.3 shows a comparison between the accuracy of the suggested model and the current model, indicating that the suggested system is more precise than the current one.

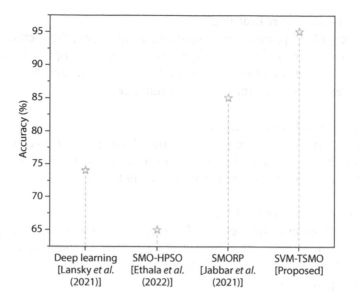

**Figure 7.3** Accuracy of the existing and proposed methods.

$$Accuracy = \frac{(TP + TN)}{(TP + TN + FP + FN)} \qquad (7.6)$$

### 7.4.2 Precision

Precision, also known as positive predictive value, is the proportion of relevant concepts among the recoverable occurrences. It serves as a benchmark for quality and represents the average likelihood of recovery. In comparison to existing methods, the proposed research is much more precise. Figure 7.4 provides a comparison between the precision of the recommended and existing methods.

$$Precision = \frac{TP}{TP + FP} \qquad (7.7)$$

### 7.4.3 Recall

Recall, also known as sensitivity or true positive rate, represents the number of instances that were searched for and recovered. The proposed approach

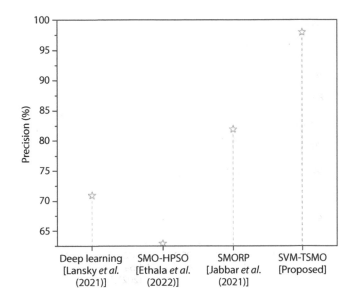

**Figure 7.4** Precision of the existing and proposed methods.

has the highest recall rate when compared to conventional approaches. Figure 7.5 provides a comparison between the suggested method and the existing one in terms of recall.

$$Recall = \frac{TP}{TP + FN} \tag{7.8}$$

### 7.4.4  F1 Score

The F1-measure is a unified metric that considers both the frequency and amplitude of a system's clarity and memory harmonic means. Its primary purpose is to evaluate the relative merits of two approaches, with higher F1 scores indicating a more efficient system. In comparison to the old approach, the proposed approach has a better F1 score. Figure 7.6 presents a comparison of the F1-measure for both new and old approaches.

$$F1 - measure = \frac{2 * Precision * Recall}{Precision + Recall} \tag{7.9}$$

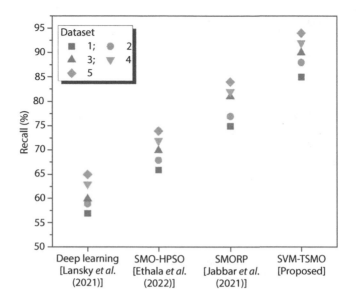

**Figure 7.5** Recall % of the existing and proposed methods.

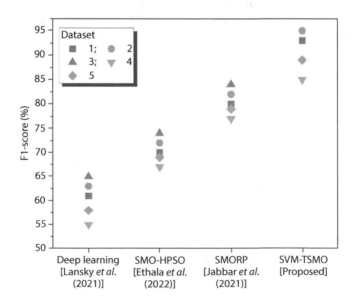

**Figure 7.6** F1-measure of the existing and proposed methods.

## 7.5    Conclusion

Staying up to date with the latest security developments involves both detecting and preventing intrusions. Given that most activities rely heavily on networks and information systems, both intrusion detection and prevention are crucial. Various methodologies have been used to develop intrusion detection systems, with ML algorithms like the SVM with the TSMO playing a crucial role. The comparison results between the recommended approach and the other three techniques demonstrate that the suggested method performs much better in terms of intrusion detection according to the same criteria.

## References

1. Jabbar, A.H. and Alshawi, I.S., Spider monkey optimization routing protocol for wireless sensor networks. *Int. J. Electr. Comput. Eng.*, 11, 3, 2432–2442, 2021, doi: 10.11591/ijece.v11i3.pp2432-2442, (2088-8708).
2. Halimaa, A. and Sundarakantham, K., Machine learning based intrusion detection system, in: *3rd International Conference on Trends in Electronics and Informatics (ICOEI)*, vol. 2019, 2019, doi: 10.1109/ICOEI.2019.8862784.
3. Azizan, A.H. *et al.*, A machine learning approach for improving the performance of network intrusion detection systems. *Ann. Emerg. Technol. Comput.*, 5, 5, 201–208, 2021, doi: 10.33166/AETiC.2021.05.025.
4. Disha, R.A. and Waheed, S., Performance analysis of machine learning models for intrusion detection system using Gini Impurity-based Weighted Random Forest (GIWRF) feature selection technique. *Cybersecurity*, 5, 1, 1, 2022, doi: 10.1186/s42400-021-00103-8.
5. Abubakar, A. and Pranggono, B., Machine learning based intrusion detection system for software defined networks, in: *Seventh International Conference on Emerging Security Technologies (EST)*, 2017, doi: 10.1109/EST.2017.8090413.
6. Verma, A. and Ranga, V., Machine learning based intrusion detection systems for IoT applications. *Wirel. Pers. Commun.*, 111, 4, 2287–2310, 2020, doi: 10.1007/s11277-019-06986-8.
7. Da Costa, K.A.P. *et al.*, Internet of Things: A survey on machine learning-based intrusion detection approaches. *Comput. Netw.*, 151, 147–157, 2019, doi: 10.1016/j.comnet.2019.01.023.
8. Lansky, J. *et al.*, Deep learning-based intrusion detection systems: A systematic review. *IEEE Access*, 9, 101574–101599, 2021, doi: 10.1109/ACCESS.2021.3097247.
9. Alrowaily, M. *et al.*, Effectiveness of machine learning based intrusion detection systems, in: *Security, Privacy, and Anonymity in Computation, Communication,*

*and Storage, Proceedings: 12th International Conference*, SpaCCS 2019, Atlanta, GA, USA, July 14-17, 2019, 2019, doi: 10.1007/978-3-030-24907-6_21.

10. Asharf, J. *et al.*, A review of intrusion detection systems using machine and deep learning in internet of things: Challenges, solutions and future directions. *Electronics*, 9, 7, 1177, 2020, doi: 10.3390/electronics9071177.

11. Rahman, M.A. *et al.*, Scalable machine learning-based intrusion detection system for IoT-enabled smart cities. *Sustain. Cities Soc.*, 61, 102324, 2020, doi: 10.1016/j.scs.2020.102324.

12. Sarker, I.H. *et al.*, Intrudtree: A machine learning based cyber security intrusion detection model. *Symmetry*, 12, 5, 754, 2020, doi: 10.3390/sym12050754.

13. Dang, Q.-V., Understanding the decision of machine learning based intrusion detection systems, in: *Future Data and Security Engineering*, pp. 379–396, 2020, doi: 10.1007/978-3-030-63924-2_22.

14. Idrissi, I. *et al.*, IoT security with deep learning-based intrusion detection systems: A systematic literature review, in: *Fourth International Conference on Intelligent Computing in Data Sciences (ICDS)*, vol. 2020, 2020, doi: 10.1109/ICDS50568.2020.9268713.

15. Sethi, K. *et al.*, Deep reinforcement learning based intrusion detection system for cloud infrastructure, in: *International Conference on Communication Systems & NetworkS (COMSNETS)*, vol. 2020, 2020, doi: 10.1109/COMSNETS48256.2020.9027452.

16. Ethala, S. and Kumarappan, A., A hybrid spider monkey and hierarchical particle swarm optimization approach for intrusion detection on Internet of Things. *Sensors (Basel)*, 22, 21, 8566, 2022, doi: 10.3390/s22218566.

17. Wang, Z., Deep learning-based intrusion detection with adversaries. *IEEE Access*, 6, 38367–38384, 2018, doi: 10.1109/ACCESS.2018.2854599.

18. Kumar, G. *et al.*, MLEsIDSs: Machine learning-based ensembles for intrusion detection systems-a review. *J. Supercomput.*, 76, 11, 8938–8971, 2020, doi: 10.1007/s11227-020-03196-z.

19. Narayanan, G. *et al.*, PSO-tuned support vector machine metamodels for assessment of turbulent flows in pipe bends. *Eng. Comput.*, 37, 3, 981–1001, 2019, doi: 10.1108/EC-05-2019-0244.

20. Bhattacharya, S. *et al.*, A comparative analysis on prediction performance of regression models during machining of composite materials. *Materials (Basel)*, 14, 21, 6689, 2021, doi: 10.3390/ma14216689.

21. Shaik, K. *et al.*, Big data analytics framework using squirrel search optimized gradient boosted decision tree for heart disease diagnosis. *Appl. Sci.*, 13, 9, 5236, 2023, doi: 10.3390/app13095236.

# 8

# Security Enhancement in IoMT-Assisted Smart Healthcare System Using the Machine Learning Approach

Jayalakshmi Sambandan[1]*, Bharanidharan Gurumurthy[2]
and Syed Jamalullah R.[3]

*[1]Department of Master of Computer Applications, MEASI Institute
of Information Technology, Royapettah, Chennai, India
[2]Department of BCA, The New College, Chennai, India
[3]Department of Computer Science and Engineering, Sathyabama Institute of
Science and Technology, Chennai, India*

## Abstract

The Internet of Medical Things (IoMT) is an emerging area that offers numerous valuable benefits to patients and healthcare providers in the identification and management of various illnesses. Despite its advantages, security remains a concern. IoMT devices contain a vast amount of clinical data, including personal information such as names, addresses, and medical histories, making data privacy and security challenging to maintain. The IoMT is highly susceptible to security breaches due to inexperienced users' weak security practices and the prevalence of various intermediate attacks that may compromise sensitive medical data. To address these concerns, we propose utilizing the support vector machine with multilayer particle swarm optimization (SVM-MPSO) to enhance the IoMT data security. In the experimental analysis, the suggested techniques outperform the current system. The proposed method can be evaluated using a variety of criteria, including accuracy, precision, security, and sensitivity. The findings demonstrate that the recommended approach enhances security measures.

*Keywords:* Internet of Medical Things, security and privacy, machine learning, optimization, smart healthcare system

*Corresponding author*: jayalakshmi.s@measiit.edu.in

Kanak Kalita, Narayanan Ganesh and S. Balamurugan (eds.) Metaheuristics for Machine Learning: Algorithms and Applications, (179–194) © 2024 Scrivener Publishing LLC

## 8.1 Introduction

The Internet of Medical Things (IoMT) has emerged as the new technique for handling patient health data. It primarily serves a variety of purposes in homes, hospitals, and body sensors. The IoMT environment is made up of a vast array of medical equipment, sensors, and other things. Additionally, these effective technologies have the capacity to cover a specific body surface. The medical business can simply manage medical identification, where the practitioner assists in the early identification of illnesses and effective diagnosis, thanks to the IoMT system's quick development [1]. Even while IoMT applications have been growing steadily over the last several years, security and privacy remain major issues. Given that the health data stored through the IoMT architecture comprises many pieces of medical information, its management is essential. The illustrative nature of the IoMT network makes it vulnerable to a variety of assaults that may severely impact its efficiency. As a result, it loses all the crucial information. When medical equipment or sensors are not properly authorized or authenticated, when users do not understand the need of data encryption, when device interfaces are not properly protected, etc., the whole system is put at risk. For an IoMT system to be useful, it must include authentication procedures to keep patient information safe and private [2]. IoMT-smart healthcare-based systems are shown in Figure 8.1.

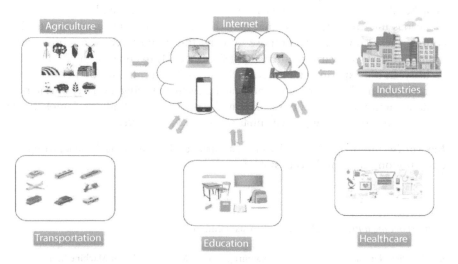

**Figure 8.1** The IoMT-smart healthcare system.

The economy has benefited immensely from smart healthcare systems (SHSs), which are now an indispensable part of it. Telehealth, smart medication, and local and remote monitoring of medical resources are just a few examples of how the IoMT is essential to the growth of SHSs. The degree to which a patient follows their doctor's advise and modifies their behavior in response to therapy is important for the success of the process. The IoMT refers to the network of sensor-enabled healthcare equipment that is linked to one another. By reducing the number of needless hospital visits, the IoMT has the potential to lessen the burden on healthcare facilities. Additionally, it offers a secure data transfer environment for the exchange of private medical data across various medical sectors. The practical uses of the IoMT have improved people's quality of life. Rapid development in issues related to the safety, privacy, and trustworthiness of the IoMT has occured in recent times. Recently, the research community has been paying increasing attention to security, privacy, and trust [3]. Data security involves taking precautions during data storage and transfer to protect the data's veracity, accuracy, and completeness. In addition, it guarantees that only authorized individuals have access to the data and may make any necessary changes. When developing an SHS, it is also important to keep privacy protection (PP) in mind. When information is sent via an unsecured route, its severity and sensitivity are taken into consideration. There are both subject matter and environment constraints in PP. Content privacy

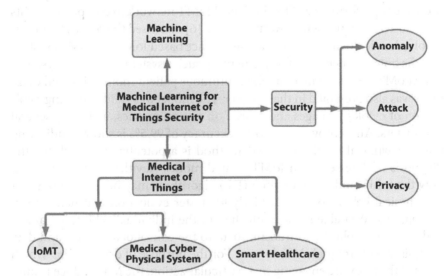

**Figure 8.2** A systematic diagram of security enhancement in the IoMT using machine learning.

prevents sensitive medical data from being leaked, but protecting patients' identities may be challenging because an assailant may readily determine the health state of a patient by learning the identity of the treating doctor. Contextual privacy must also be protected. The concept of "contextual privacy" pertains to the safeguarding of the communication's background details. Multiple asymmetric and symmetric encryption techniques are utilized in the IoMT-enabled SHS to protect user data [4]. Figure 8.2 shows the systematic block of security enhancement in the healthcare system.

The rest of the paper will be presented below. In section 8.2, we will examine the existing works. The theory behind the suggested procedures is detailed in section 8.3. In section 8.4, we will discuss the metrics we used and the outcomes we obtained. The last section of the report will summarize the findings.

## 8.2   Literature Review

Ahmed *et al.* [5] presented an overview of several federated learning (FL) architectures and future IoMT-based FL architectural techniques. Furthermore, they explored how physical layer security may be used for the efficient protection of data privacy in the FL-based IoMT. They discussed current research in this field and important research problems associated with Physical Layer Security (PLS)-assisted FL in the IoMT. In addition, they demonstrated a case study indicating that clustering IoMT devices improves the secrecy performance of the FL-based IoMT network in comparison to its non-clustering equivalent. Awotunde *et al.* [6] discussed the research hurdles involved in deploying an artificial intelligence based IoMT (AIIoMT) system and the potential benefits of implementing such a system in medical systems. An AIIoMT-based architecture for continuous patient monitoring and diagnosis was also presented in that chapter. The model was validated using a collection of cytology images and scored on several metrics, including several parameters. An improved diagnostic accuracy of 99.5% is shown, indicating that the artificial intelligence (AI) method is a potential approach for the diagnosis of illnesses in an IoMT-related model. Kavitha *et al.* [7] showed how the IoMT and deep learning (DL) algorithms may be used to observe the physical behaviors of the elderly for faster evaluation and better therapy options. Wearable sensors attached to the individual's chest, left ankle, and right arm collect and transmit data to the consolidated cloud and data analysis layer through IoMT devices. For the purpose of determining which parts of the body are engaging in a particular action, the MapReduce framework is put to good use in tandem with a complex-valued deep Convolution Neural Network (CNN) with an improved political optimizer, a classifier that boasts both increased flexibility and superior performance relative to its contemporaries. Rehman *et al.* [8] examined the literature on the intersection of blockchain technology and federated learning in the medical field in depth. The aim of that research is to build a blockchain-based IDS-enabled healthcare 5.0 system that can monitor patients with the help of sensors and provide physicians with the data they need to make periodic diagnoses and treatments based on the predicted course of the disease.

The results of this study show that the suggested system is a successful optimization of the method for healthcare monitoring. The framework relies on edge computing for its design, which protects user privacy using hybrid encryption methods and lightens the burden on the main server as a bonus. Security is further strengthened by using differential privacy based on Laplacian noise on the common characteristics, ensuring that the transmitted data remain private even in the face of an adversary. The experimental findings on benchmark datasets reveal that the variation in key system performance metrics is not proportional to the change in the volume of gradients communicated and the proportion of people involved [9]. Machine learning has been effectively used for the resolution of a wide range of networking issues, including routing, traffic engineering, resource allocation, and security. There has been a recent uptick in the use of ML-based approaches for enhancing several Internet of Things (IoT) applications. While research on big data analytics and ML is abundant, research on the development of ML-based methodologies for big data analysis in the IoT healthcare industry is lacking. Li *et al.* [10] provided an in-depth look at how machine learning may be used to analyze large amounts of healthcare data. Abbas *et al.* [11] proposed a blockchain-assisted secure data management architecture for health information based on the IoMT to facilitate the safe transfer of patient data and improve the scalability and accessibility of the healthcare system. The suggested blockchain-assisted secured data management framework (BSDMF) allows for the safe transfer of information between local and remote servers, such as those located in the cloud and those located on a user's local network, for the sake of medical treatment. To provide secure data management and data transfer across connected nodes, the IoMT-related security architecture makes use of blockchain technology. Artificial intelligence is a new and dynamic concept that will revolutionize IoMT-related applications and innovations.

The use of AI in IoMT-based diagnostics and monitoring may speed up the process and reduce the workload involved. Thus, the scope of use for IoMT-related systems that may use AI is explored in that section. Several outstanding potential and research problems brought about by AI-enabled IoMT are also discussed in that chapter. In addition to decreasing the workload on healthcare systems by shortening the assessment time required for traditional approach detection methods, that technology has also been employed to achieve reasonably accurate identification accuracy. Human intervention in healthcare will be reduced as a result of the continuing use of AI using IoMT-based techniques, which will greatly enhance healthcare monitoring, diagnosis, analysis, forecasting, and the creation of drugs and vaccines [12]. Concerns about patient privacy are heightened by IoMT's lax security measures regarding sensitive data. Fresh information sent out by the sensor node is not guaranteed to be genuine. For this reason, a blockchain-based system is essential. A healthcare professional would be able to get access to a patient's medical data using a more secure authentication-based method regardless of the network connection used. Al-Otaibi [13] offered a novel method of safe authentication that makes use of machine learning. In that study, they use K-nearest neighbor and ML through smart contracts to detect and authenticate dynamic temporal attacks in an IoMT setting (KNN-MLSC). It increases safety for both doctors and patients, decreases waiting time, and protects personal information in health records.

## 8.3 Proposed Methodology

There is a need to boost the safety of IoMT applications in healthcare settings. As a result, we recommend protecting the data using a support vector machine and multilayer particle swarm optimization (SVM-MPSO). The suggested method is described in great depth below. The steps of the suggested technique are displayed in Figure 8.3.

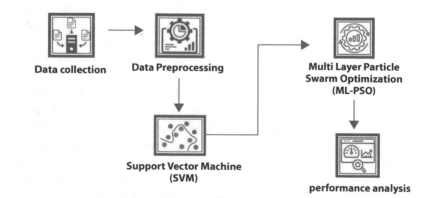

**Figure 8.3** Diagrammatic representation of the proposed method.

### 8.3.1  Data Collection

The Information Security Centre of Excellence 2012 dataset was used to run the experiments and estimate how well the proposed way of finding anomalies worked. The whole set of data includes nearly 1.5 million network traffic packets with 20 features that cover 7 days of activity on the network. There are more details about the dataset that can be found. A random part of the original dataset has been taken out. The training data consists of 30,814 "regular" lines and 15,375 "attack" links. There are 13,154 regular links and 6,580 more attack lines in the testing data [14].

### 8.3.2  Data Preprocessing

A new dataset with 14 characteristics was constructed from the specified dataset's original format. Since the vast majority of packets included nothing, we removed the payload feature, which included the packet itself. In its stead, we implemented a duration feature that combines the functionality of the previously separate start time and end time fields. For the purpose of eliminating the bias of higher-valued features, the attributes were scaled between [0,1] using the Min-Max approach during the data normalization step, with the corresponding math looking like this:

$$Z' = \frac{z - \min(z)}{\max(z) - \min(z)} \tag{8.1}$$

Categorical characteristics are not accepted by most classifiers; hence, the data mapping approach was employed to convert them to numerical values.

### 8.3.3  Support Vector Machine

A supervised machine learning classification method, the SVM algorithm finds the greatest separation hyperplane across classes to distinguish between positive and negative samples. Since the kernel controls the form of the separating hyperplane, multiple kernels may be employed as part of the SVM approach depending on the nature of the dataset. When the data can be separated along a straight line, a linear kernel may be used to describe the hyperplane as a linear equation. However, other kernels are required when the data are not linearly separable. The Gaussian kernel is one example of a suitable kernel that can be used in this case. This kernel transforms the input data into a greater feature space [15].

$$l(y) = u^D \Phi(y) + p \tag{8.2}$$

The basic goal of the SVM model is to choose the hyperplane that optimally divides classes and maximizes the lowest distance between any two data points (margin). In this sense, all boundary points are support vectors. Figure 8.4 shows a simplified representation of the basic variant of this system, the linear SVM model.

The optimal hyperplane equation is found below.

$$margin = \frac{\arg min\, d(Y)}{Y \in T} = \frac{\arg min}{Y \in T} \frac{|Y.U + p|}{\sqrt{\sum_{j=1}^{t} u_j^2}} \tag{8.3}$$

where

Y: is the normal vector of the decision hyperplane

Data point $i$ is denoted by the symbol $Yi$.

$xi$: classifies data point $i$ as belonging to either the positive or negative set

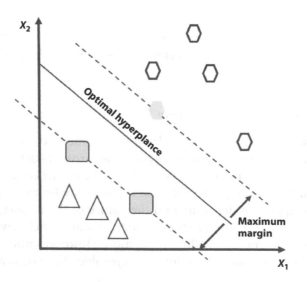

**Figure 8.4** The linear SVM model.

The formula for the classifier is as follows: $f(yi) = sign\,UTyi + p$
The formula $xi = UTyi + p$ describes the functional margin of $xi$.

---

**Algorithm:** Support vector machine algorithm

---

N←choice of input features
Sv←the support vector
ft ← characteristic of support vector machines
out ←The Results of the Decision Function
for $j$ ← 1 ti M do
$$L = 0;$$
for $i$ ← 1 *to* Sv do
$$dist = 0$$
for $r$ ← 1 to ft do
$g$ ← Sv [$i$]mul l(r)
GG ← M[i] mull d(r)
$t$ ← g sub gg
dist ← $t2$
end
$r$ ← $-x$ mul dist
LL ← e mul r
L ← LL add LL
end
out ← L mul p
end

---

For classification purposes, the Multi Support Vector Machine (MSVM) creates a hyperplane in a high-dimensional feature space to divide the data into two groups. The search for the best hyperplane fulfills the classification requirement and employs a tailored method to achieve a nearly ideal level of margin separation. In the theory of learning, the margin scale is an illustration of the capacity to generalize to very large settings, and the maximum generalization power of the SVM is required for the largest margin scale.

## 8.3.4   Multilayer Particle Swarm Optimization

The MLPSO algorithm is a method of SI global random search that simulates the swarming and migrating behavior of feeding insects. The usual strategy toward each part of the swarm aggregation method is to guard every piece of information, accomplish each information rate in the nearby area, and change the information center regardless of where they are going in the case of MPSO. The multilayer particle swarm optimization, commonly known as the MLPSO, locates a particle in the search space that best addresses each optimization challenge. The fitness value of each particle is determined by the optimum function, and the distance traveled by each particle is determined by its velocity. Particles follow the optimum particle, which leads the way, and move across the subspace. Figure 8.5 depicts the flow diagram for the most fundamental form of the MLPSO algorithm. The MLPSO is integrated with a specified analytical model to increase the level of security of the data transfer process. As a result, the various types of assaults that are currently active inside the system are uncovered. The iteration values are determined by a set of population matrices, in which each individual is assigned a particular set of fitness values ranging from 0.5 to 1 because the MLPSO is being used. The variation in these two values generates a binary matrix that yields two optimal values for individuals represented by the variables p and g. The optimal values, indicated above, shift between 10 and 100 with each new iteration, with a step variation of 20 between each number. After identifying the optimal value location for low-security elements, the associated rapidity rates are measured as the output of the MLPSO. This is done when the speed of the search space is boosted with security measures.

The phrase $b_{best}$ [j], also known as the individual extremum, is used to refer to the position that particle j has determined to be the best possible option [16]. The global ideal point that was found by the comprehensive particle swarm search is denoted by the abbreviation $s_{best}$ [j]. The following set of random values is used to update the locations and velocities of the particles in accordance with Equation 8.4 so that the next generation may be generated correctly.

$$iter(j+1) = iter(j).z + c_i.Rand_j.(b_{best}(j) * s_{best}(j) - z_j) \qquad (8.4)$$

$$z_j(iter+1) = z_j(iter) + h_j(iter+1) \qquad (8.5)$$

where $iter$ denotes the $j-th$ generational iteration, $Rand_j$ denotes ranges of random integers between 0 and 1 that are dispersed equally, $z_j$ denotes the particle's unique velocity value, and h denotes the inertia weight that established the particle's speed before the present speed and acts as a hybrid of the global search algorithm and the local search capability.

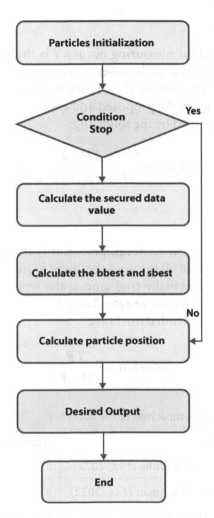

**Figure 8.5** The MLPSO algorithm flowchart.

Convergence and accuracy for the MLPSO approach both increase with decreasing inertia weight. In order to improve the MLPSO algorithm's precision, the inertia weight factor may be computed.

## 8.3.5  Performance Evaluation

Several performance criteria, such as accuracy, precision, sensitivity, security, and specificity, are evaluated to find out how well the proposed method works.

### 8.3.5.1   Accuracy

The standard method for measuring accuracy is the weighted arithmetic mean, which is also known as the inverse precision of the precision value. Accuracy measures the precise classification of secured data. Table 8.1 illustrates the accuracy of the proposed and existing methods.

Accuracy is determined by the following:

$$Accuracy = \frac{TP + TN}{TP + TN + FP + FN} \tag{8.6}$$

### 8.3.5.2   Precision

In the field of information retrieval, precision is the number of relevant observation results out of all the ones that were found. It is the percentage of documents that are actually true among the reported to be true, also known as the positive predictive rate. Table 8.2 presents the precision of the existing and recommended methods.

$$Precision = \frac{TP}{TP + FP} \tag{8.7}$$

**Table 8.1**  Comparison of the accuracy.

| Methods | Accuracy (%) |
|---|---|
| Deep CNN (Kavitha *et al.*, 2022) | 91 |
| Blockchain (Rehman *et al.*, 2022) | 85 |
| KNN (Al-Otaibi, 2022) | 73 |
| SVM-MLPSO (Proposed) | 98 |

**Table 8.2**  Comparison of the precision.

| Methods | Precision (%) |
|---|---|
| Deep CNN (Kavitha *et al.*, 2022) | 83 |
| Blockchain (Rehman *et al.*, 2022) | 75 |
| KNN (Al-Otaibi, 2022) | 85 |
| SVM-MLPSO (Proposed) | 97.5 |

### 8.3.5.3 Sensitivity

Sensitivity is the ratio of true positives to the sum of true positives and false negatives, which determines how well a test can detect positive instances. It is calculated as the positive classification of secured data and can also be referred to as true positive or false negative. Table 8.3 presents the sensitivity of the old and new strategies.

The sensitivity is computed by using the following:

$$True\ Positive\ Rate = \frac{TP}{TP + FN} \qquad (8.8)$$

### 8.3.5.4 Specificity

Specificity measures the negative classification of secured data when the actual condition is not present. It is expressed as a false positive or true negative rate. Table 8.4 presents the specificity of the existing and proposed methods.

Table 8.3 Comparison of the sensitivity.

| Methods | Sensitivity (%) |
|---|---|
| Deep CNN (Kavitha et al., 2022) | 70 |
| Blockchain (Rehman et al., 2022) | 87 |
| KNN (Al-Otaibi, 2022) | 79 |
| SVM-MLPSO (Proposed) | 96 |

Table 8.4 Comparison of the specificity.

| Methods | Specificity (%) |
|---|---|
| Deep CNN (Kavitha et al., 2022) | 70 |
| Blockchain (Rehman et al., 2022) | 80 |
| KNN (Al-Otaibi, 2022) | 85 |
| SVM-MLPSO (Proposed) | 95 |

**Table 8.5** Comparison of the security.

| Methods | Security (%) |
|---|---|
| Deep CNN (Kavitha *et al.*, 2022) | 85 |
| Blockchain (Rehman *et al.*, 2022) | 73 |
| KNN (Al-Otaibi, 2022) | 90 |
| SVM-MLPSO (Proposed) | 97.6 |

It is determined by the following:

$$Specificity = \frac{TN}{TN + FP} \tag{8.9}$$

### 8.3.5.5 Security

A security metric is a set of interconnected dimensions (measured against a standard) that allows the measurement of the degree of protection against potential harm or loss from malicious attacks. Table 8.5 illustrates the security comparison between the current and proposed techniques.

## 8.4 Conclusion

The SVM-MLPSO methods are used in this research to protect the data. While the suggested technique offers excellent security characteristics for IoMT applications, some of its shortcomings become apparent when it is used in actual situations. The particle swarm optimization approach yields more accurate results as compared to other methods. The required charts demonstrate that without utilizing any feature extraction techniques, the accuracy of the suggested strategy employing the MLPSO improves to 99%. In contrast to the observed values in the current approach, the suggested method offers 98% accuracy, which is substantially greater. Additionally, the MLPSO iteration values provide optimum outcomes that raise the prediction and quantifiable score throughout the process. The suggested study employing the MLPSO may be expanded in the future to include a variety of cloud computing platforms, which will further enrich the complete dataset with high-security characteristics. The expansion is also made feasible by taking into account the distinction between internal and external assaults in situations where all users may send and receive various pieces of data using a machine learning method.

# References

1. Khatiwada, P. and Yang, B., An overview on security and privacy of data in IoMT devices: Performance metrics, merits, demerits, and challenges, in: *pHealth*, vol. 2022, pp. 126–136, 2022, doi:10.3233/SHTI220970.

2. Khan, I.A. *et al.*, XSRU-IoMT: Explainable simple recurrent units for threat detection in Internet of Medical Things networks. *Future Gener. Comput. Syst.*, 127, 181–193, 2022, doi: 10.1016/j.future.2021.09.010.

3. Vaiyapuri, T., Binbusayyis, A., Varadarajan, V., Security, privacy and trust in IoMT enabled smart healthcare system: A systematic review of current and future trends. *Int. J. Adv. Comput. Sci. Appl. (IJACSA)*, 12, 2, 1–7, 2021, http://dx.doi.org/10.14569/IJACSA.2021.0120291.

4. Mawgoud, A.A. *et al.*, A secure authentication technique in internet of medical things through machine learning, arXiv Preprint ArXiv:1912.12143, 2019.

5. Ahmed, J. *et al.*, On the physical layer security of federated learning based IoMT networks. *IEEE J. Biomed. Health Inform.*, 27, 2, 691–697, 2023, doi: 10.1109/JBHI.2022.3173947.

6. Awotunde, J.B., Folorunso, S.O., Ajagbe, S.A., Garg, J., Ajamu, G.J., AiIoMT: IoMT-based system-enabled artificial intelligence for enhanced smart healthcare systems. In *Machine Learning for Critical Internet of Medical Things*, F. Al-Turjman, A. Nayyar (eds.), Springer, Cham, USA, 2022, https://doi.org/10.1007/978-3-030-80928-7_10

7. Kavitha, D. *et al.*, An efficient IoMT based health monitoring using complex valued deep CNN and political optimizer. *Trans. Emerg. Telecommun. Technol.*, 33, 12, e4610, 2022, doi: 10.1002/ett.4610.

8. Rehman, A. *et al.*, A secure healthcare 5.0 system based on blockchain technology entangled with federated learning technique. *Comput. Biol. Med.*, 150, 106019, 2022, doi: 10.1016/j.compbiomed.2022.106019.

9. Nair, A.K. *et al.*, Privacy preserving Federated Learning framework for IoMT based big data analysis using edge computing. *Comput. Stand. Interfaces*, 86, 103720, 2023, doi: 10.1016/j.csi.2023.103720.

10. Li, W. *et al.*, A comprehensive survey on machine learning-based big data analytics for IoT-enabled smart healthcare system. *Mob. Netw. Appl.*, 26, 1, 234–252, 2021, doi: 10.1007/s11036-020-01700-6.

11. Abbas, A. *et al.*, Blockchain-assisted secured data management framework for health information analysis based on Internet of Medical Things. *Pers. Ubiquitous Comput.*, 1–14, 2021, doi: 10.1007/s00779-021-01583-8.

12. Awotunde, J.B., Chakraborty, C., AbdulRaheem, M., Jimoh, R.G., Oladipo, I.D., Bhoi, A.K., Chapter 1 - Internet of medical things for enhanced smart healthcare systems, in: *Intelligent Data-Centric Systems, Implementation of Smart Healthcare Systems Using AI, IoT, and Blockchain*, C. Chakraborty, S. Kumar Pani, A.A. Mohd, X. Qin (eds.), pp. 1–28, Academic Press, USA, 2023, https://doi.org/10.1016/B978-0-323-91916-6.00009-6.

13. Al-Otaibi, Y.D., K-nearest neighbour-based smart contract for internet of medical things security using blockchain. *Comput. Electr. Eng.*, 101, 108129, 2022, doi: 10.1016/j.compeleceng.2022.108129.

14. Injadat, M. *et al.*, Bayesian optimization with machine learning algorithms towards anomaly detection, in: *IEEE Global Communications Conference (GLOBECOM)*, vol. 2018, 2018, doi: 10.1109/GLOCOM.2018.8647714.

15. Narayanan, G. *et al.*, PSO-tuned support vector machine metamodels for assessment of turbulent flows in pipe bends. *Eng. Comput.*, 37, 3, 981–1001, 2019, doi: 10.1108/EC-05-2019-0244.

16. Shankar, R. *et al.*, Hybridized particle swarm-gravitational search algorithm for process optimization. *Processes*, 10, 3, 616, 2022, doi: 10.3390/pr10030616.

**9**

# Building Sustainable Communication: A Game-Theoretic Approach in 5G and 6G Cellular Networks

**Puppala Ramya\*, Tulasidhar Mulakaluri, Chebrolu Yasmina, Pandi Bindu Madhavi and Vijay Guru Balaji K. S.**

*Department of Computer Science and Engineering, Koneru Lakshmaiah Education Foundation, Vaddeswaram, Guntur, India*

*Abstract*

High data volume is added to the currently used digital technologies as a result of cellular networks' technical development. These new digital technologies must maintain trade-offs between clients and service providers, which present issues in terms of quality of service (QoS). Real-time, audio, visual, and text data types, each of which has specific needs, are handled by cellular service providers in an effort to satisfy the demands of end customers. There were many potential incentive-based algorithms to achieve an effective QoS. The mobile network operator and access points are not guaranteed a fair share of the profits under these programs, however. Furthermore, these schemes are unable to guarantee an equitable channel distribution during crowning time and do not offer the end user efficient QoS. In order to offload the method of decision-making in a diverse network, we present a motivation-based strategy employing game theory and a two-stage Stackelberg technique for integrated data. Our suggested design models an individual mobile base station and many built-in access points in a congested urban region. Here is competition among access sites for incentives when traffic is unloaded at this station, which gives financial incentives depending on the sorts of traffic. To simulate and evaluate a real-world event, a mathematical game is developed. By comparing the findings with those from other models, the experimental technique is used to verify the numerical results.

*\*Corresponding author*: mothy274@kluniversity.in

Kanak Kalita, Narayanan Ganesh and S. Balamurugan (eds.) Metaheuristics for Machine Learning: Algorithms and Applications, (195–214) © 2024 Scrivener Publishing LLC

*Keywords*: Cellular networks, digital technologies, game theory, Stackelberg approach, Nash equilibrium

## 9.1   Introduction

Due to the growing need for fifth-generation (5G) wireless networks to have more coverage and capacity, ultra-dense networks (UDNs) have been used to address some of the most critical issues. In order to overcome the basic impasses of beyond, the deployment of UDNs on a very wide scale has been envisioned [1]. The sixth-generation (6G) wireless networks will bring several orders of magnitude greater improvements than current technology. However, it is generally acknowledged to be a formidable challenge to use a mathematical tool to optimize the system performance under the strict radio resource constraints [2]. Current UDNs typically do system-level performance optimization by relying on numerical simulations, which are often time-consuming and have proven increasingly challenging in the setting of 6G with exceptionally high density [3]. Therefore, it is crucial to create a practical mathematical model for optimizing the 6G UDNs. In this work, we present difficulties and problems that must be carefully taken into account while implementing UDNs in a practical setting. In order to improve the performance of UDNs, we review effective mathematical approaches including game theory and real-time optimization [4]. Additionally, emerging technologies that can be used in UDNs are also covered. While some of them are already being investigated, others are anticipated to improve UDN performance to meet 6G requirements. Some of them have already been used in UDNs with high efficiency. The combined optimum technique of real-time optimization and game theory (ROG), which is a powerful tool to handle the optimization issues of large-scale UDNs with minimal complexity, is important, and we present it for the first time [5]. Then, we go over two methods for utilizing ROG in UDNs. Finally, a few ROG case studies are provided to show how to use ROG to address issues with various applications in UDNs.

## 9.2   Related Works

The research [6] examined physical layer security issues on device-to-device (D2D) communications in light of various attack scenarios. The hierarchical and diverse interactions between authorized users and active intruders in 5G Internet of Things (IoT) networks are described using game theory, and then several scalable machine learning techniques are suggested to find situations of equilibrium between various agents. The study [7] presented historical discussion of the many concepts used to reduce or eliminate the interference issue in 5G communication systems. It has also been suggested where future research should go. The study [8] provided a brand-new gamification framework using utilizing geometric modeling and evaluate cache-enabled small cell base stations (SBSs) with the shared framework for regional 5G open platforms. The study [9] provided thorough analysis of the area of wireless communication resource distribution. The survey starts out by providing a general resource distribution summary issue in current linked wireless network papers on the assessment of resource distribution strategies. The article [10] provided a reduced-constraints method for finding solutions for two non-convex mixed-integer problems with combined allocation of power and channel assignment that are not ideal nonlinear programming (MINLP). The research [11] examined the issue of the offloading choice-making systems engineering for the intelligent secure mobile edge computing (MEC) system with a unmanned aerial vehicle (UAV) eavesdropper, where the eavesdropper may be hearing the safe computational job from the user to the computational access point (CAP). The research [12] suggested an adaptive VR architecture that enables high-quality wireless VR in mobile edge computing-enabled wireless networks. Tasks related to instant VR rendering may be adaptively offloaded to MEC servers, and these servers' cache-related abilities allow further performance enhancement.

## 9.3  Methodology

Due of its portability, wireless cellular networks are widely used, and cellular communication is presently the most populated sector. The amount of data traffic through cellular networks has dramatically expanded along with technical advancement. Mobile network operators (MNOs) implement 4/5G LTE, which offers the quickest cellular connection, to accommodate customers and their data needs. Although network service providers are implementing the most recent technology, the constant volume of motionless traffic reduces their output by impacting throughput, reaction time, and other quality of service (QoS) parameters. Costly technologies have been shown to be far less able to satisfy end user needs. The traffic flow is increasingly crowded, and the response is becoming worse every day due to end users' growing data needs and the increased bandwidth being used for a variety of activities through networks, particularly cellular networks. Customers are given services at a QoS-level via the

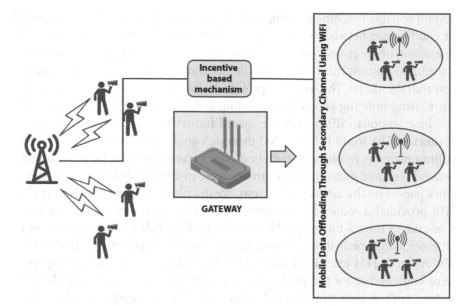

**Figure 9.1** IDO based on a game model.

suggested incentive-based strategy. Figure 9.1 depicts a densely populated area where the majority of residents use smart devices, such as phones and tablets, for example various Internet access. Due to the overuse of data services, the quality of service was degraded, and many new customers were allowed. Particularly during peak hours, a very packed atmosphere was created; nevertheless, things were different during off-peak hours. The demand for video streaming, which uses a lot of bandwidth, was strong during peak hours. In order to experience the situation actually, an example of an unbalanced network simulation made up of a mobile base station (MBS) and a few access points (APs) was created taking these aspects into account and unloading while implanting through Wi-Fi was implemented as the solution to the issue.

MBS has a greater coverage area, but APs within its range with lesser coverage areas have nonoverlapping zones of coverage. For this offloading process in this network that is diverse, we take into account one MBS and many APs in order to simulate it accurately.

$$M_{MBS} = E_{MBS} - \sum_{r=1}^{m} E_{AP} \tag{9.1}$$

where

MBS coverage area equals AMBS, while AP coverage area equals AAP.

The MBS area without an offload option

The following formulae may be used to calculate the physical areas of the areas mentioned above.

$$E_{MBS} = \pi k_n^2 \tag{9.2}$$

$$E_{AP} = \pi k_e^2 \tag{9.3}$$

The 5G and 6G communication models are shown in the above graphic. Every user is online and working on downloading and uploading tasks. We use the integrated data offloading (IDO) using a game concept to prevent the congestion problem.

Adding these numbers to Equation 9.1, we acquire the MBS coverage area, which no AP is able to access. In Equation 9.1, $M_{MBS}$ depicts the portion of the MBS without offloading circumstance, $E_{MBS}$ reflects the region that MBS covers, $E_{AP}$ displays the region that APs cover. The following categories are used to distinguish distinct traffic kinds:

$$DD = \{K, C, E, D\} \tag{9.4}$$

For Equation 9.4, DD shows different forms of traffic, K reflects current information, C is used for video, E for sound, whereas the set of APs is provided by represents text data

$$B = \{EB_1, EB_2, EB_3, \ldots EB_m\} \tag{9.5}$$

P denotes a team of players, and EB indicates the entry point in Equation 9.5 from 1 to m [2]. For each AP, the different sorts of data are represented by the Cartesian product of the two sets previously indicated:

$$E_B D_D = \{(EB_{1_K}), (EB_{1_C}), (EB_{1_E}), (EB_{1_D}), (EB_{2_K}), (EB_{2_C}), (EB_{2_E}), (EB_{1_D}), \ldots\ldots\} \tag{9.6}$$

In Equation 9.6 [1], $E_B D_D$ demonstrates how in an unloading scenario, various types of traffic are offloaded by the access point, including real, audio, video, and text the total traffic per
*EB*, is given as:

$$EB_{yf} = \sum_{r \in DD}^{m} EB_y D_l \qquad (9.7)$$

In Equation 9.6 [1], $E_B D_D$ demonstrates in an unloading scenario the entry point.offloads many traffic kinds, including text, audio, video, and real. The total of function f's components, where any specific EB when this relationship is taken into account, the total traffic per
EB, which is stated to be:

$$f_m = \sum_{r=1}^{m} f_r \qquad (9.8)$$

In Equation 9.7, $f_m$ reveals the entire amount of traffic. Among these, the traffic that a cellular network offloads includes the following:

$$f_m = f_m - \sum_{r=1}^{m} EB_{rf} \qquad (9.9)$$

In Equation 9.7, the variable $f_m$ stands for traffic that a mobile phone network has offloaded, where $f_m$ displays the location of the download and $EB_{rf}$ demonstrates the discharge posture. Our simulation is built based on a game-theoretic process that aims to achieve the highest offloading EBs; however, a traffic-wise offloading mechanism will be used to control offloading percentage during peak and off-peak hours. For this, the present rate of EB is considered to be its time, which is symbolized by Ka, in which the subscript makes a distinction EB. Utilizing this immediate rate, we are able to display the throughput of certain EB as follows:

$$K_r EB_{rf} \leq K_l Thro \qquad (9.10)$$

In Equation 9.10, $K_r$ demonstrates the immediate pace of $EB$, where Thro stands for throughput. The sum of the two nodes represents the heterogonous network's entire amount.

$$Throughput(thr) = Throughput_{MBS} + Throughput_{EBs} \quad (9.11)$$

In Equation 9.11, $Throughput_{MBS}$ shows the throughput of MBS, and $Throughput_{EBs}$ represents throughput of $EBs$ autonomous decision-making from a variety of methods is used to study the construction of real-world models and how they interact. Three things are involved: players, strategy, and payout. It defines how players react and make decisions, as well as how they adopt different positions and work together. The payoff function is given by the following:

$$B_r \sum_{n \in DD} \beta_m \frac{f_m}{\sum_{r \in b} f_r} - \sigma_{rm} f_{rm} \quad (9.12)$$

The various functions are represented by the variables in Equation 9.12: $B_r$ is the payoff function in action, $\beta_m$ displays the reward being given, and $\sigma_{rm}$ highlights the price paid for the incentive that was provided. The payback function is intended to assess how well the model based on spurs provided by MBS and the volume that was by offloading EBs performs. When AP competes against its rival to increase its revenue, the game is said to be noncooperative. The following items are included in the game set.

$$Game(S) = \{Bf, G_r, B_r\} \quad (9.13)$$

In Equation 9.13, $r \in B, S$ exemplifies the game, $Bf$ symbolizes MBS participants in the game, and $EBs$ and $G_r$ represent a group of strategies that players can use to obtain the highest payout, and $Br$ is the reward or a scoring mechanism that depicts the players' earnings.

In Equation 9.14 [5], $f_r$ demonstrates the existence of a quadrilateral space for traffic load. Q, R, S, T are subspaces. To indicate a particular instance data load, the ordered pair below is used:

$$f_r = (f_O, l_K, f_G, f_D) \quad (9.14)$$

where $l_O = \{r_1, r_2, \ldots, r_o\}, l_K = \{r_1, r_2, \ldots, r_k\}, l_G = \{r_1, r_2, \ldots, r_g\}, and \ l_D = \{r_1, r_2, \ldots, r_d\}$

### 9.3.1   Nash Equilibrium

In the case of the aforementioned game set, Nash equilibrium exists if, for each $r \in B, B_r\left(f_r, f_{-r}\right) \geq B_r\left(f_r, f_{-r}\right)$ aimed at wholly $f_r \geq 0$, somewhere, $B_r\left(f_r, f_{-r}\right)$ continues to be the next bid for the r participant, presuming that the results of the extra troupes' tenders $f - r$ [6]. $B_r$ is concave in $f_r$, while $G_r$ in the specified spaces is convex.

$$G = \left\{\left(G_r : f_r\right) \mid r \in B \wedge 0 \leq f_r \leq K_r\right\} \tag{9.15}$$

Data are offloaded using a kind-based method that takes into account a clearly determined importance; for example, video data may stream with a higher priority than text data. We remove the second-order derivative pertaining to km after confirming its wrap and seeing that Utlm continues to l. The following equation makes a leading derivative assumption:

$$\frac{\partial B_r}{\partial f_r} = \sum_{n \in DD} \beta_m \left[\frac{\sum_{n \in b \wedge n \neq r} f_n}{\sum_{r \in b} f_r^2}\right] - \sigma_{rm} \tag{9.16}$$

The partial derivative rule is used by Equation 9.16 [7] to demonstrate its concavity. The element $\partial$ demonstrates partial derivative, $\beta_m$ displays the reward provided for Wi-Fi, $f_n$ demonstrates redirected traffic, and $\sigma_{rm}$ displays the amount spent on that unloading traffic.

Regarding the second derivative for $f_n$, we have the following:

$$\frac{\partial^2 B_r}{\partial^2 f_r} = -2\left[\sum_{n \in DD} \beta_m \left[\frac{\sum_{n \in b \wedge n \neq r} f_n}{\sum_{r \in b} f_r^3}\right]\right] \tag{9.17}$$

The second-order derivative in Equation 9.15 [8] displays a negative multiplier, and it turns out that in each instance, the outcome will be unfavorable, demonstrating that $B_r$ is a concave function. Um is concave, as may be seen in $f_n$, while the $G_r$ is convex; thus, in the game, the Nash equilibrium is present. In Equation 9.15, the variables have previously been explained.

### 9.3.2   Unique Nash Equilibrium

The game contains a Nash equilibrium, as has been shown before vector $f_n$. To prove its originality, to ensure consistency, the Best Response function $K$ must be given, which requires understanding. Scalability is one of the three prerequisites, positivity, and monotonicity. Here, $R(f_n)$ depicts the Best Response feature.

The optimum result for the ideal reaction would be for all traffic downloaded by any *EB* is limited to the EB's full capability. In any case, the former would not be as good and could not match the later. This limitation may thus be mathematically represented as indicated below [9]:

$$\sigma_r \sum_{n \neq r} f_n < \beta \Rightarrow K(f_r) > 0 \tag{9.18}$$

The variables in Equation 9.18 are $\sigma_r$, the unloading fee, which provides a driving incentive, and $K(f_r)$, which depicts the Best Response feature. The aforementioned connection meets the game's positive attributes. The immediate rate of AP, which includes the component specified in Equation 9.15, would be approached by the Best Response function in order to increase revenue. Adding to the Best Response relation is the following:

$$0 \leq \sqrt{\frac{\beta \sum_{n \neq r} f_n}{\sigma_r}} - \sum_{n \neq r} f_n < K_r \tag{9.19}$$

Equation 9.19 demonstrates [10], a monotonic growth; nevertheless, to demonstrate its scalability, we take into account the following scenario:

$$\alpha K_r(f) = \alpha \left[ \sqrt{\frac{\beta \sum_{e \neq p} f_e}{\sigma_r}} - \sum_{e \neq p} f_e \right] \tag{9.20}$$

$$K_r(\propto f) = \sqrt{\frac{\beta\alpha \sum_{e\neq p} f_e}{\sigma_r}} - \alpha \sum_{n\neq r} f_e = \sqrt{\alpha} \left[ \sqrt{\sqrt{\frac{\beta\alpha \sum_{e\neq p} f_e}{\sigma_r}} - \sum_{e\neq p} f_e} \right]$$

(9.21)

In Equations 9.20 and 9.21, the variables $K_r(\alpha l)$ show the Best Respone function for the cost paid for offloading. $f_e$ shows the offloaded traffic. Combining Equations 9.17 and 9.18 and simplifying them, we obtain $\alpha - \sqrt{\alpha}$ as change parameter, which is always greater than 0; therefore, using the Best Response feature is also scalable. By satisfying all three criteria, it is ensured that the Best Response function is a standard function and satisfies the Nash equation.

### 9.3.3   Total Unique Equilibrium

The game's traffic type set's overall unique equilibrium may be calculated as [10] $l_n^* = \sum_{r\in DD} f_{n(r)}$, where

$$f_{e(p)} = \left[ \frac{\beta_p(M-1)}{\sum_{e(p)\in b} \sigma_{e(p)}} \times \left[ 1 - \frac{(M-1)\sigma_p}{\sum_{e(p)\in b} \sigma_{e(p)}} \times \right] \right]_0^{K_{e(p)}}$$

(9.22)

where $f_n^*$ for which the Best Response value exists $f$ in cases when $\beta$ is dependent on meeting both of the requirements in Equations 9.18 and 9.19, and going over either side will cause it to approach the limitations. This brings about the game's complete unique balance.

The MBS return may be calculated as follows:

$$B_{MBS(r)} = \left(\delta - \beta_r\right) \sum_{n \in b} f_{e(r)} \tag{9.23}$$

where $r \in DD, \delta$ is unit spectrum made clear of congestion using $EBs$ for offloading, and $\beta$ is a financial inducement for r-type traffic. The MBS will optimize its usefulness in this competitive game by optimizing the $\beta$ incentive in its broadest sense. Equation 9.16 is substituted, and the highest utility benefit is as follows:

$$B_{MBS(r)} = \beta_r \left(\delta - \beta_r\right) \left[ \frac{(M-1)}{\sum_{e(p) \in B}^{m} \sigma_{e(p)}} \times \sum_{e(p) \in B} \left(1 - \frac{(N-1)\sigma_{e(p)}}{\sum_{e(p) \in B}^{m} \sigma_{e(p)}}\right) \right] \tag{9.24}$$

Subject to $\beta \leq \beta^{max}$.

The utilitarian feature of the MBS is convex in shape because it can be maximized. Equity and justice must be offloaded in between $EBs$. The logarithmic goal will be accomplished. The MBS utility may be calculated in several ways as [11]:

$$B_{MBS(DD)} = \delta \sum_{e \in b}^{m} \log\left(f_{e(p)}\right) - \left(\sum_{p \in DD} \beta_p\right) \sum_{e \in b} f_{e(p)} = \delta \log\left(\prod_{e(p) \in B} f_{e(p)}\right) - \sum_{e \in DD} \beta_p \sum_{e \in b}^{m} f_{e(p)} \tag{9.25}$$

Substituting Equation 9.16, we obtain:

$$= \delta \log\left(\sum_{r \in DD} \beta_r\right)^N \left(\prod_{e(r) \in B} \left[ \frac{(N-1)}{\sum_{e(p) \in B} \sigma_{e(p)}} \times \left[1 - \frac{(N-1)\sigma_r}{\sum_{e(p) \in B} \sigma_{e(p)}}\right] \right]\right) -$$
$$\left(\sum_{r \in DD} \beta_r\right)^2 \left[ \frac{(N-1)}{\sum_{e(p) \in B} \sigma_{e(p)}} \times \left[1 - \frac{(N-1)\sigma_p}{\sum_{e(p) \in B} \sigma_{e(p)}}\right] \right] \tag{9.26}$$

By replacing $\Gamma$ and $\varphi$, we obtain:

$$= \delta log \left( \sum_{p \in DD} \beta_r \right)^N \Gamma . \left( \sum_{p \in DD} \beta_p \right)^2 \varphi \qquad (9.27)$$

The inference implies that the app's MBS feature is concave. The right first-order status is related to determine the overall economic advantage.

$$\left( \sum_{p \in DD} \beta_p \right)^* = \left[ \sqrt{\frac{\delta N}{2 \varphi}} \right]_{r \varepsilon DD}^{(\Sigma \beta_p)^{max}} \qquad (9.28)$$

Considering the problem's Lagrangian with consideration $\lambda$ being a Lagrange multiplie [12], the outcome is as follows:

$$F \left( \sum_{p \in DD} \beta_p, \lambda \right) = \delta log \left( \sum_{p \in DD} \beta_r \right)^N \Gamma . \left( \sum_{p \in DD} \beta_p \right)^2 \varphi + \lambda \left( \sum_{p \in DD} \beta_p \right) - \left( \sum_{p \in DD} \beta_p \right)^{max}$$

$$(9.29)$$

The dual function 0 is the topic of the maximum state of the aforementioned equation, which may be solved via sub-gradient retrieval of the Lagrange multiplier as shown below:

$$\lambda(g+1) = \left[ \lambda(g) + r(g) \left( \sum_{p \in DD} \beta_p(g) \right) - \left( \sum_{p \in DD} \beta_p(g) \right)^{max} \right]^+$$

$$(9.30)$$

wherever $r(g)$ is a step-by-step size in repetition s. The step size is always positive of the form, $[X]+ = max\{0, X\}$ total economic stimulation $\beta^*$ can be acquired using Karush–Kuhn–Tucker (KKT), given that the first-order derivative of the Lagrangian function of $\beta_r$ with respect to $\beta$ is 0. The whole financial gain solution has been simplified as follows [13]:

$$\left( \sum_{p \in DD} \beta_p \right)^* = \left[ \frac{\lambda + \sqrt{\lambda^2 + 8 \delta N \varphi}}{4 \varphi} \right] \qquad (9.31)$$

According to the demand-based traffic categorization, the suggested strategy in independent games rewards to the secondary participants. Using comprehensive data offloading, which is based on the philosophy of Stackelberg, it will enhance QoS to prevent the congestion problem. The Stackelberg model, a noncooperative game theory model, is what we have used to address the congestion problem faced by mobile consumers. Nash equilibrium in the Stackelberg model was established by the point where the Best Response intersects functions from each player. The MBS information is the input of the algorithm, which efficiently provides the greatest output reward and offloading to benefit the cellular network. The spectrum, the unit electricity cost, and the proper kind of incentives are all represented by different symbols. Temporary variables like fm are added, and lm is utilized as AP's condition, in order to condense more complex equations with recurring components. Numerous calculations are carried out, including those for total cost, individual costs, economic incentives, progressive balance, proportional fairness, and others. MBS then determines the net profit gain before making a decision. To calculate optimum rewards and traffic conditions, which are often utilized in various forms, two functions are needed: ideal incentives and cutoff information.

## 9.4    Result

The data flow rate offloading each unit of time is represented by the offload ratio. We collect data in chunks of 10 MB and measure time in seconds. Our model's first accomplishment is maximized offload, which has a significant impact on the other elements shown in the data. According to the graph in Figure 9.2, offloading begins as soon as at least one AP is deployed and grows as additional APs are added. The suggested approach successfully offloaded 70 MB/s of data onto 20 APs in seven units. As seen in Figures 9.2 and 9.3, this demonstrates a sufficient improvement over the models that are already in use. Based on the incentive structure each model offers, the lines are distinguished. Comparatively speaking, our model did well.

Overload traffic causes a drop in QoS, which causes network congestion. Five picocells have been found to be adequate to manage range value 2 congestion; whereas IMDO and IFPC models perform the same function with 12 and 17 picocells, correspondingly. This is because our model proposes a plan for resolving the problem that results in maximal offloading and special integrated Wi-Fi management. This demonstrates that, in contrast to previous models, our approach improved the management of congestion, as illustrated in Figure 9.3. The suggested model's output is

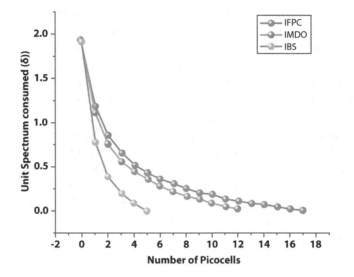

**Figure 9.2** Spectrum use ratio.

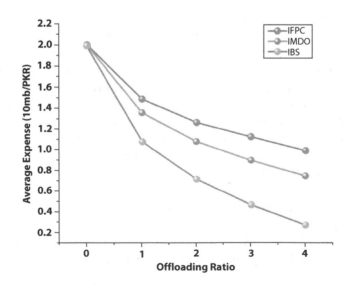

**Figure 9.3** Offload ratio.

superior to those of the other models. The method of making decisions in a diverse network has been improved by our idea of a motivation-based system based on a two-stage process and game theory Stackelberg technique for integrated data offloading. To mimic our suggested system, an individual mobile base station, a few cross-platform access points in a populated urban area are used. Access points face rivalry against one another to gain rewards for unloading traffic at this station, which gives financial incentives depending on the sorts of traffic. Through simulation, a game using math is derived by examination of real-world situations. The quantity of data that is sent from a source to a destination in a certain period of time is known as throughput. While seconds are the unit of time and the amount of data is expressed in bytes, throughput is their benchmark and is frequently expressed as a percentage. The graph displays throughput results in relation to the chosen spectrum. The utilized spectrum is between 0 and 2, and its effect on each of all three models' throughput is investigated. Spectrum 0 indicates no throughput, whereas spectrum 1 indicates improved throughput. Congestion causes throughput to decrease; however, when congestion is reduced by the models, throughput is increased. According to Figure 9.2's spectrum value 2, the suggested model achieves 100% throughput, whereas the other two models only manage 48% and 62%, respectively.

Based on the different traffic kinds, we determine the best incentives using the Stackelberg-based game model. The main player will provide the secondary player the ideal incentive, and the supporting character will unload optimally based on the ideal incentive. The throughput graph demonstrates that we have great offloading throughput. The suggested technique shown in Figure 9.4 has demonstrated the absolute outcome.

The term "response delay" refers to the length of time required for data to switch between host and a client. The lag is seen in the graph as shown measured in milliseconds on the y-axis, and the range is used to assess the reaction using the data's x-axis as the load on the spectrum increases. However, despite its impact, the increase in load for each of the three models lowered the spectrum's burden. Overall, IMDO fared the best in this outcome, although as can be seen in Figure 9.5, our model advanced more quickly.

IDO is used in the suggested approach to address the congestion problem. According to the kind of traffic, it will move movement from the major auxiliary channel to the main channel, reducing the delay and reducing the likelihood of congestion. The spectrum was under increasing demand, which decreased offloading latency and cleared the channels of congestion. Since it will make use of an independent game paradigm to

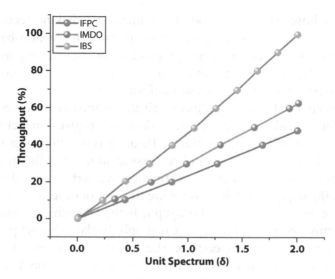

**Figure 9.4** Throughput analysis.

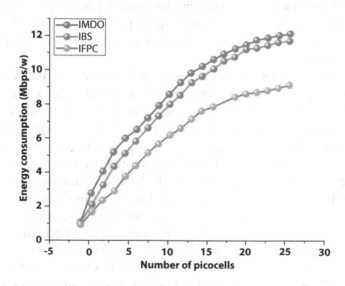

**Figure 9.5** Response delay analysis.

equally channelize both users' use, IMDO fared the best overall. Figure 9.5 displays the fair outcomes of our approach.

Energy use is thought to have a significant impact on the QoS of mobile devices. Modern wireless communication systems concentrate on reducing their energy needs. In consideration of the growing number of picocells,

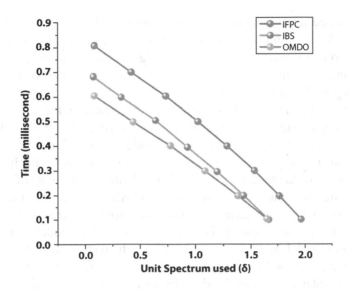

**Figure 9.6** Energy consumption analysis.

the use of energy is measured offloading megabytes per watt. The greatest performance came from the IMDO model, albeit with a little change; the suggested model displayed its results. The suggested plan is superior, but it is not perfect because of the integrated design, which requires extensive sublevel administration. Figure 9.6 illustrates that the outcome is excellent when compared to alternative approaches.

## 9.5    Conclusion

The usage of data-hungry services has greatly increased network traffic as a result of the widespread adoption of the newest smart gadgets and fast Internet connections. Mobile network operators must respond to the scenario by meeting the substantial requirements, the volume, scope, and superior QoS to secure the longevity of their connection with users and to profit in a more sophisticated manner. All providers can afford mobile data offloading, which improves QoS by lightening the strain on the network. Offloading data off the cellular network, many technologies are utilized, including Wi-Fi, mobile networks using WiMAX, femtocells, opportunistic communication, and IP. Internet offloading, however, is common among them since it is cost-effective for both service suppliers and customers. In order to test the linkage of Wi-Fi employing cellular networks to offload, we developed many scenarios and investigated offloading through Wi-Fi may be a choice. Our major goal was to use the Stackelberg technique to get the most offloading over Wi-Fi. We investigated the Stackelberg approach's effects on the commercial market. A model for a game with two levels has been presented. In the first stage, the MBS gives the APs economic stimulation depending on the kinds of traffic they utilize, and in the second phase, the APs take advantage of these impulses by releasing other forms of traffic. To analyze our efforts, a mathematical model is created and put through simulation and experimentation. In order to investigate the impact of incentives on offloading, we presented simulations for a range of incentive levels using the simulation program MATLAB. The performance of the QoS parameter was also examined and contrasted with that of the current model. The trials demonstrated showing the suggested model outperforms the current model, and the proposed approach enabled Nash equilibria to be reached using the Best Response potential function. The suggested traffic type-based game also attained a fully unique equilibrium. The suggested traffic type-based game is deemed to be objectively better in all significant structures and operations as a result of these numerical results. Our methodology achieves maximum offloading and increased throughput based on the best incentives. In such a two-way offloading procedure, privateness and security is a contentious subject for investigation, and research into numerous base stations and many connected APs with criteria for efficiency and delivery disparities is the unresolved problem that needs more study.

# References

1. Buffa, S. *et al.*, 5th generation district heating and cooling systems: A review of existing cases in Europe. *Renew. Sustain. Energy Rev.*, 104, 504–522, 2019, doi: 10.1016/j.rser.2018.12.059.
2. Stergiou, C.L. *et al.*, IoT-based big data secure management in the fog over a 6G wireless network. *IEEE Internet Things J.*, 8, 7, 5164–5171, 2020, doi: 10.1109/JIOT.2020.3033131.
3. Youn, J.Y. *et al.*, High-density proximity mapping reveals the subcellular organization of mRNA-associated granules and bodies. *Mol. Cell*, 69, 3, 517–532.e11, 2018, doi: 10.1016/j.molcel.2017.12.020.
4. Chen, S. *et al.*, A survey on user-centric cell-free massive MIMO systems. *Digit. Commun. Netw.*, 8, 5, 695–719, 2022, doi: 10.1016/j.dcan.2021.12.005.
5. Enkavi, G. *et al.*, Multiscale simulations of biological membranes: The challenge to understand biological phenomena in a living substance. *Chem. Rev.*, 119, 9, 5607–5774, 2019, doi: 10.1021/acs.chemrev.8b00538.

6. Luo, Y. *et al.*, Secure and reliable D2D communications with active attackers: A game-theoretic perspective and machine learning approaches, in: *Machine Learning and Intelligent Communications, Proc. 5: 5th International Conference, MLICOM 2020*, Shenzhen, China, September 26-27, 2020, Springer International Publishing, pp. 519–533, 2021, doi: 10.1007/978-3-030-66785-6_55.

7. Sarma, S.S. and Hazra, R., Interference mitigation methods for D2D communication in 5G network, in: *Cognitive Informatics and Soft Computing: Proceeding of CISC*, Springer, Singapore, pp. 521–530, 2020, doi:10.1007/978-981-15-1451-7_54.

8. Sanguanpuak, T. *et al.*, Radio resource sharing and edge caching with latency constraint for local 5G operator: Geometric programming meets Stackelberg game. *IEEE Trans. Mob. Comput.*, 20, 2, 707–721, 2019, doi: 10.1109/TMC.2019.2948630.

9. Liang, H. and Zhang, W., A survey and taxonomy of resource allocation methods in wireless networks. *J. Commun. Inf. Netw.*, 6, 4, 372–384, 2021, doi: 10.23919/JCIN.2021.9663102.

10. Hashad, O. *et al.*, Resources allocation in underlay device-to-device communications networks: A reduced-constraints approach. *IEEE Access*, 8, 228891–228904, 2020, doi: 10.1109/ACCESS.2020.3046417.

11. Lai, S. *et al.*, Intelligent secure mobile edge computing for beyond 5G wireless networks. *Phys. Commun.*, 45, 101283, 2021, doi: 10.1016/j.phycom.2021.101283.

12. Cite Guo, F., Yu, F.R., Zhang, H., Ji, H., Leung, V.C., Li, X., An adaptive wireless virtual reality framework in future wireless networks: A distributed learning approach. *IEEE Trans. Veh. Technol.*, 69, 8, 8514–8528, 2020.

13. Kadam, S., Bhargao, K.S., Kasbekar, G.S., Node cardinality estimation in a heterogeneous wireless network deployed over a large region using a mobile base station. *J. Network Comput. Appl.*, 221, 103779, 2024.

# 10

# Autonomous Vehicle Optimization: Striking a Balance Between Cost-Effectiveness and Sustainability

Vamsidhar Talasila[1]*, Sagi Venkata Lakshmi Narasimharaju[1],
Neeli Veda Vyshnavi[1], Saketh Naga Sreenivas Kondaveeti[1],
Garimella Surya Siva Teja[1] and Kiran Kumar Kaveti[2]

*[1]Department of Computer Science and Engineering, Koneru Lakshmaiah Education Foundation, Vaddeswaram, Guntur, India*
*[2]Department of Computer Science and Engineering, Vignan's Foundation for Science Technology and Research Deemed to be University, Vadlamudi, Guntur, India*

## Abstract

Transportation, energy use, and the environment are all projected to be significantly impacted by the mainstream deployment of autonomous vehicles (AVs). Even though AVs promise to minimize collisions, traffic, and pollution, they also spark questions about their affordability, sustainability, and societal effects. In this study, we offer a methodology for AV optimization that strikes a compromise between performance that is both cost-effective and sustainable. The suggested strategy minimizes trade-offs in sustainability and cost-effective effectiveness via offering adaptability, redundant operation, and adaptive capabilities for handling the logistic cluster. Analyses of the logistic network showed a 23% reduction in emissions of carbon dioxide by using the AV technique combined with consolidation facilities using actual information through interactions with experts in the food business. Due to the use of autonomous cars in the supply chain, the trip did not require any rest stops, which reduced the cost of the entire logistical network. Legislation and infrastructural concerns, however, impede the practical application of the established distribution strategy, delaying the development of a cost-effective supply chain.

*Corresponding author*: talasila.vamsi@kluniversity.in

Kanak Kalita, Narayanan Ganesh and S. Balamurugan (eds.) Metaheuristics for Machine Learning: Algorithms and Applications, (215–234) © 2024 Scrivener Publishing LLC

*Keywords*: Autonomous vehicles (AVs), cost-effective performance, sustainability, emissions

## 10.1  Introduction

Transportation is one of the sectors that is being severely impacted as the globe pushes toward more sustainable practices. Finding solutions for decreasing these emissions is essential for reaching sustainability goals because the transportation sector contributes significantly to greenhouse gas emissions. Utilizing autonomous vehicles (AVs), which are designed to strike a balance between sustainable performance and cost-effectiveness, is one way to address this issue. The term "autonomous vehicle" refers to a class of self-driving vehicles that can navigate and perform tasks on roads without a driver's input by using sensors, cameras, and sophisticated algorithms [1]. Being electrically powered, requiring less maintenance, and being able to maximize routes and speeds to save fuel consumption, AVs have the potential to significantly reduce the environmental impact of the transportation sector. But AVs must strike a balance between sustainability and cost-effective performance if they are to be a real solution to the sustainability issue facing the transportation sector. As a result, AVs must be adjusted to strike a balance between efficiency and long-term viability, which can be accomplished via several techniques [2].

Route optimization is one approach to AV performance and sustainability optimization for cost-effectiveness. AVs can customize their routes to use less fuel and emit fewer greenhouse gases by analyzing the current information on traffic, weather, and road conditions. Due to the decreased trip time and distance, AVs are now more cost-effective. Optimization can also lead to cost savings. Energy-efficient driving is another technique for AV performance and sustainability optimization. To maximize energy economy, AVs can be configured to accelerate and decelerate at the best possible rates and speeds. By doing this, AVs can increase the performance and longevity of the vehicle while lowering the consumption of fuel and carbon emissions [3].

The battery management systems of AVs can also be used to optimize them for sustainability. The longevity of the battery can be increased and the battery's need for regular charging decreased by having AVs keep track of the battery's level of charge and rate of discharge. AVs become more cost-effective because of this optimization, which also lowers their carbon footprint and maintenance expenses [4]. Vehicle-to-vehicle communication is an additional way that AVs might strike a balance between cost-effective performance and sustainability. AVs can adjust their speed and routes to save on fuel and cut down on carbon emissions by interacting with other vehicles on the road. Additionally, this communication can assist AVs in avoiding traffic jams, which can significantly cut down on fuel use and carbon emissions [5]. The production and disposal processes for AVs can also be improved for sustainability. To lessen their carbon footprint, AV producers should employ environmentally friendly resources and manufacturing techniques, such as recycling garbage and reducing waste. Similar to AVs, AVs may be made to be simple to disassemble and recycle, minimizing the negative environmental effects of their disposal [6]. A crucial answer to the sustainability issue facing the transportation sector is the employment of autonomous cars that are designed for cost-effective performance and sustainability. AVs may balance performance and sustainability through optimization of routes, energy-effective driving, charge administration, communication between vehicles, and environmentally friendly production and disposal methods. To achieve a more sustainable future, it will be crucial to optimize AVs for sustainability as the globe moves toward more sustainable practices [7].

Through information sharing, automated and connected cars (CAVs) have a great potential to increase traffic safety and efficiency. This study deals with the issue of longitudinal coordination between two strings of automobiles at highway on-ramps. For cars entering from the ramp and coming from the mainline, a rule-based adjusting algorithm is suggested to achieve a close-to-ideal merging sequence [8]. For the realization of an entirely autonomous system (vehicle and charger), wireless charging technology is a great fit for self-driving electric vehicles. This article presents a planned optimization study for a pilot concept of in-route mobile charging infrastructure servicing corrected-route immediately shared automated electric shuttles (SAESs) in Greenville, South Carolina, USA. The formulation of a single-objective nonlinear combined integers system planning optimization problem was presented. The whole induction-charged SAES system is represented by a detailed cost model that takes into account the costs of the installation, traction battery, power electronics, and road construction [9]. By enhancing travel mobility, autonomous vehicles are opening up new possibilities for the management and operation of transportation options in cities. They suggest using AVs in this study to address the first-mile (FM) problem, which entails getting people from their houses to metro stations. A fleet operator dispatches AVs and sets up rideshare in a rolling horizons framework once passengers submit their travel requests in advance. One AV is assigned to fulfill several requests following the vehicle's capacity, its maximum trip time, and its accessibility restrictions [10].

As more and more massive Internet applications are employed, energy costs in data center networks have skyrocketed. The interaction latency between two automobiles and vehicles and the controller in technology-defined vehicular networks (SDVNs) will sharply increase as the number of vehicles rises. To reduce latency, additional controllers are needed to offer communication services. High energy expenses are a result of more controllers. As a result, the issue of controller placement (CPP), or the quantity and positioning of controllers, needs to be addressed [11]. The DC nano grid with efficient energy management has recently received a lot of interest. In the future decades, it is anticipated that the DC nano grid could improve energy effectiveness and lessen carbon footprint due to its propensity to incorporate developing power electronics burdens, such as solar energy and electric vehicles (EVs), as well as renewable energy sources. In this study, a leadership structure based on a smart charging point is introduced that might be utilized to develop a small, inexpensive, and straightforward energy administration system for a nano grid [12]. Enhancing energy efficiency has been acknowledged as a successful strategy for promoting energy conservation, reducing emissions, and realizing sustainable development. Numerous and dispersed methods of enhancing energy efficiency toward environmentally friendly production are inadequate in terms of overall approaches and system integration. Following a thorough review of academic literature, 166 research papers specifically focused on enhancing energy performance are examined. To understand the pattern of energy use and implement efficient energy-saving measures, a thorough examination and analysis of energy surveillance, assessment, optimization, and benchmarking are conducted [13]. Autonomous vehicles need real-time performance to reach their present position in time for decision-making, while real-time localization is crucial for AVs to achieve safe, effective driving. There has not been a review paper that compares the real-time performance of various localization approaches using a variety of hardware systems and programming languages or that examines the connections between localization methodologies, real-time performance, and correctness. As a result, this study examines the most recent localization methods and evaluates how well they function in AV applications. This paper first proposes an equivalent comparison method based on the localization method operations capability (LAOC) to evaluate and analyze in depth the links between methodologies, computational difficulty, and accuracy after evaluating the relative computational cost of several localization approaches [14]. The development and implementation of automated and connected cars (CAVs) must include testing and assessment, but there is no organized structure for creating testing scenario libraries.

A broad architecture for the testing scenario library generation (TSLG) issue with various operating design domains (ODDs), CAV models, as well as performance metrics is what this paper intends to give. The evaluation scenario library is described as a crucial collection of situations that can be used for CAV testing, given an ODD [15]. For systems that assist drivers to be effective, traffic participants must be detected. The bulk of pedestrian fatalities that could have been avoided happened at night, according to data on traffic safety. Sensors like cameras may malfunction at night due to a lack of light [16]. The performance of several industries and enterprises, including the transportation industry, is being improved—thanks to the rapid pace of artificial intelligence (AI) development. The improvements brought forward by AI include extremely sophisticated computational techniques that resemble how the human brain functions [17]. Researchers introduce L3-Net, a new starting-to-learn-based LiDAR localization system with centimeter-level localization accuracy, which is similar to earlier state-of-the-art systems with manually built pipelines. Instead of depending solely on these manually created modules, they creatively implement the utilization of multiple deep neural network topologies to provide a learning-based strategy [18]. Today, it is thought of as a highly strategic goal to create effective fuel cell hybrid vehicles (FCHVs), to have them deployed as widely as possible across the entire transportation sector, and to fully satisfy well-known ecological and regulatory constraints on a global scale [19]. The growing volume of traffic is destroying cities all around the world. Smart cities are a recent development that is viewed as a successful approach to dealing with several serious urban issues like traffic, pollution, energy usage, and waste treatment [20].

## 10.2    Methods

A depth analysis was done to maximize the advantages of autonomous vehicle distribution. Unfortunately, the current industry does not employ autonomous vehicles, making it impossible to gather empirical data through the use of established methods like surveys or interviews. Real-world data obtained from the most successful distribution strategies in conjunction with cutting-edge technologies must be thoroughly analyzed. A computer simulation was run using the data collected to determine the potential levels of efficiency for the suggested competitiveness approach. The research was adopted to produce quantitative proof to support the suggested framework. Because simulations offer precise constraints and assumptions, using a contribution to the scientific literature was still legitimate—thanks to a computation method created by a computer. Additionally, the chosen method allowed for the evaluation of multiple scenarios, which was not possible with qualitative methods. The information was used to model a dynamic logistic network. The Monte Carlo (MC) simulated annealing process was used to simulate partial goods logistics, choosing the optimal routes and suppliers at random. The possible advantages of autonomous vehicles were learned from corporate sources and other publications. The final paragraph of the method reveals a more thorough step-by-step breakdown.

## 10.2.1    Competition and Sustainable Supply Chains at Odds

The introduction of manufacturing lines to the sector is linked to the industrial age, which began in Britain. The need for a labor force has altered as a result of the invention of machines and motors. Job workshops and batch manufacturing were the two main methods of production employed in the past. The laborer must be skilled and specialized in a variety of activities during that time. The working population was forced to become an expert in particular objectives and devote more attention to single jobs as a result of the industrial revolution's increased usage of mass manufacturing on the market. The fourth industrial revolution, often known as Industry 4.0, is taking place right now. It is known as the digital revolution. However, it is crucial to comprehend what brought about the industry's drastic change before analyzing the unique characteristics of the modern industrial revolution. Because manufacturing costs were reduced by the development of new inventive technologies, consumers began to demand more individualized production. It made it feasible for people to buy a variety of goods for a low price, which was before impossible. Due to the abundance of supply for various products, customers adopted a demanding rather than suppliant stance. Customers began to request more customized products for their use, thus the manufacturing process had to change once more. In earlier times, when customers did not have the option of choosing from a wide range of manufacturers, mass production was advantageous. As a result, the current industrial revolution offers means of producing more customized goods. On the one hand, Industry 4.0 empowers producers to provide consumers with what they want. Cycle times are getting shorter and customer order amounts are dropping. Short-notice orders are being sent to production in increasing numbers. On the opposite hand, investments are necessary to match the technology with what businesses are already doing. The price of the product may rise as a result of the incorporation of cutting-edge technologies into business operations, which could result in the loss of the competitive advantage. The cost of production makes up a very small portion of the product's total cost. Marketing, sales, distribution, and customer service are further factors. The distribution issue is the primary emphasis of this essay. Another important component of current consumer demand is distribution. Internet access and e-commerce have made acquiring goods even simpler, and it is typical to see customers buying goods from different continents. As a result, the local market must now contend with the global market. There is just one market in the globe, according to some, and a regional or global market no longer exists. Naturally, not every industry is covered by this. The worldwide distribution of the quickly paced consumer goods sector serves as the best illustration. Low distribution costs are necessary to sustain a competitive edge, but product demand additionally relies on the price of the product. In addition, the manufacturing and delivery lead times are highly important. Present-day customers want their items immediately; therefore, careful demand planning is necessary. Furthermore, due to trends, shifting consumer demand, or expiration dates, many items cannot be kept on hand for an extended period. Small production orders are a significant problem in the quickly evolving consumer goods sector.

### 10.2.2 Industry's Effect Application of the 4.0 Idea to Business Operations

The emergence of the fourth industrial revolution has significantly altered business operations. To maintain sustainable and low management, an effective competitiveness strategy must be developed while simultaneously implementing the Industry 4.0 idea. Businesses that fail to adapt to the changing environment will go out of business. The notion of Industry 4.0 has multiple components. Fundamentally, it implies that everything is interconnected and that total connection and openness of data and information are crucial. More sophisticated business decisions have been made as a result of this type of technical progress, including flexible business operation adaptation and flexible human resource planning. Only via a creative integration of all these technologies can Industry 4.0's advantages become apparent. The Internet of Things (IoT) technology is one of the cornerstones of Industry 4.0 principles. The IoT is a communication innovation that connects everything using several technologies and makes it easier for communication devices to connect. The concept of the Internet of Things opens significant opportunities for visualizing supply chain operation procedures. With the use of this method, real-time business activity scheduling, monitoring, and control are all possible for food enterprises. It can help them reduce food waste, manage risk from unforeseen deviations, and keep up with food safety laws. The Internet of Things idea can be used when planning a transit system. Big data analytics is the flip side of the Industry 4.0 notion. To find new patterns or eliminate weaknesses, data analysis is important; simply collecting data from the environment is not sufficient. Utilizing the data that are currently available effectively provides a thorough overview of business operations. Future items can be completely suited to the needs of the customer—thanks to the study of the client's wants. Descriptive, predictive, diagnostic, and prescriptive statistics are some of the disciplines that make up big data analytics. Making smarter decisions can only be assisted by real-time information. Given that agricultural products have a limited shelf life, this is especially useful. Diagnose statistics is used to model different business processes and provide a statistical justification for how the market could influence the choices made. Finally, everything needs to be condensed and translated into business terms. The notion of Industry 4.0 needs to be modified for operational and commercial strategy. Big data models for process control, for instance, can be used to build the most effective strategies for enhancing the environmental effectiveness of sustainable supply chain management and for managing natural resources sustainably. Even larger advancements have resulted from the concepts of big data analysis and IoT. It is now possible to use autonomous vehicles in the industry. Figure 10.1 depicts the overall competitiveness approach. There are four steps in the method. Operations of those involved in the supply chain must be defined and visualized during the initial phase. The activities include several distinct components, including purchasing, warehousing, and several modes of transportation. A more thorough organization study should be carried out during the second stage to identify the willing businesses that would be most suited to create a logistical cluster. The entire supply chain should have its activities computerized during the third phase. The management strategy's main considerations should be the potential for gathering, processing, and utilizing information. Key components of the cluster should be continuously assessed and watched during the final phase. The cluster can achieve higher levels of cost-effective efficiency and long-term viability by incorporating self-driving cars and big data analysis into organizational procedures. Big data analytics and autonomous vehicles both can improve flexibility and redundancy in the management process. Continuous analysis of the strategy would develop adaptive capabilities, which would aid in making better decisions in the present. Since autonomous vehicles can sense their navigation without input from humans, they are more environmentally friendly than traditional cars. As a result, costs, emission levels, and working hours can all be significantly decreased. Aside from long distances, autonomous vehicles can also be used at the operational level of the supply chain. Some nations have acknowledged the invention of autonomous vehicles as a significant economic growth factor. Recently, regulators in the USA said that the artificial intelligence system used by Google Cars would qualify as a driver under federal law. The introduction of driverless vehicles has many potential advantages. Transport makes up a sizable portion of the supply chain. There is a chance that the cargo will be harmed during shipment. Therefore, the use of self-driving cars can lower the amount of damaged goods. According to statistics, drivers are to blame for up to 90% of traffic accidents. On the other hand, because less fuel is used, there is less of an influence on the environment. Furthermore, by consistently driving short distances, which is not always achievable with regular ground vehicles, the amount of fuel used can be further decreased. It is difficult to quantify the possible environmental advantages, though. There is currently no method of fuel economy testing that can accurately assess fuel economy ratings, the energy consumption and environmental damage caused by light automobiles. When traveling in convoys, preliminary fuel economy studies have shown that fuel efficiency can increase by up to 10%. The current economy testing process lacks the means to assess how autonomous vehicle technologies would affect fuel efficiency ratings. As a result, it is necessary to perform more precise calculations for the exact autonomous vehicles. The evaluation of the literature, however, can show that autonomous vehicles have positive effects on the economy and the environment. The utilization of transport is a key factor in autonomous vehicle development. The trucks are typically not utilized well. After all, the rest period is also deleted when the driver is removed. Additionally, there is a chance for the logistic cluster members to share the autonomous vehicles. Shared autonomous vehicles may offer affordable transportation options. A logistic cluster could use the sharing technique mentioned in the paper as well. Additionally, combining autonomous drive technologies with big data analysis, cloud computing, and the Internet of Things can increase safety on the roads while making transport more easily accessible to customers and suppliers. The cloud-based option enables the storage of far more past information than an independent system and provides sufficient accuracy to comprehend trends in fuel usage and to help users make deft judgments. Analysis tools for cloud computing allow for the conversion of fuel use to expenses or $CO_2$ emissions, the analysis of energy use per tonne used in production, and the monitoring of energy consumption by each vehicle.

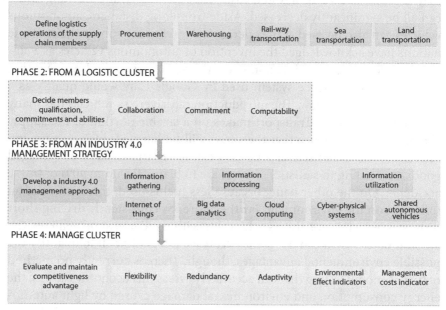

**Figure 10.1** Framework for logistic clusters that limits supply chain management trade-offs.

## 10.3   Results

The data used to create the logistic network model for the food industry were obtained through professional interviews. Fifty Lithuanian businesses involved in the continent's food industry took part in the interview. Invoices and other significant data have been acquired, and several supply chain-related questions have been raised. A significant portion of the interview's results were previously published. Table 10.1 shows a sample of the collected data. The primary finding from the conversation was that tiny markets frequently use partial goods. Typically, businesses have between 5 and 20 pallets of cargo that need to be imported or exported. The cost per pallet when shipping a full truck is roughly 50 euros; however, when transporting lower quantities, the cost per pallet might increase three to four times. These findings compel the establishment of logistic clusters of small- and medium-sized businesses, which will share resources like transportation and information. For some sectors, partial goods transit might be a challenge. In this instance, we emphasized the results in light of the food business. The food sector was selected as a reference sector because

Table 10.1 Example of demand and supply data from expert interviews with the food industry.

| Loading country-city | Quantity of cargo, Euro pallets | Delivery country-city | Required temperature | Product name |
|---|---|---|---|---|
| Belgium-Geel | 32 | Lithuania-Šiauliai | Chilled | Vegetables |
| Belgium-Aalst | 15 | Lithuania-Vilnius | None | Tea, coffee |
| Belgium-Alken | 8 | Lithuania-Vilnius | None | Cereal, flakes |
| Belgium-Alken | 11 | Lithuania-Vilnius | None | Spices and herbs |
| Belgium-Kortrijk | 9 | Lithuania-Kaunas | Chilled | Vegetables |
| Belgium-Antwerp | 13 | Lithuania-Šiauliai | Chilled | Dairy products |
| Germany-Kiel | 23 | Lithuania-Šiauliai | None | Spices and herbs |
| Germany-Löhne | 11 | Lithuania-Šiauliai | None | Cereal, flakes |
| Germany-Bielefeld | 18 | Lithuania-Šiauliai | Chilled | Bread |
| Germany-External | 17 | Lithuania-Šiauliai | None | Dairy products |
| Germany-Melle | 16 | Lithuania-Šiauliai | Chilled | Spices and herbs |
| Germany-Lügde | 12 | Lithuania-Šiauliai | None | Nuts and seeds |
| Netherlands-De Kwakel | 16 | Lithuania-Šiauliai | Frozen | Fruits |

*(Continued)*

**Table 10.1** Example of demand and supply data from expert interviews with the food industry. (*Continued*)

| Loading country-city | Quantity of cargo, Euro pallets | Delivery country-city | Required temperature | Product name |
|---|---|---|---|---|
| Netherlands-Veenendaal | 12 | Lithuania-Šiauliai | None | Fish |
| Netherlands-IJsselmuiden | 32 | Lithuania-Šiauliai | Frozen | Spices and herbs |
| Netherlands-Purmerend | 5 | Lithuania-Šiauliai | Frozen | Fats |
| Netherlands-Veldhoven | 6 | Lithuania-Šiauliai | None | Fats |
| Netherlands-Helmond | 12 | Lithuania-Šiauliai | Chilled | Spices and herbs |
| United Kingdom-London | 15 | Lithuania-Vilnius | Chilled | Meat |
| United Kingdom-London | 16 | Lithuania-Vilnius | Frozen | Bread |
| United Kingdom-Aylesford | 12 | Lithuania-Kaunas | Chilled | Meat |
| United Kingdom-London | 16 | Lithuania-Kaunas | None | Meat |
| United Kingdom-Bristol | 16 | Lithuania-Kaunas | None | Bread |
| United Kingdom-Cambridge | 16 | Lithuania-Kaunas | None | Cereal, falkes |

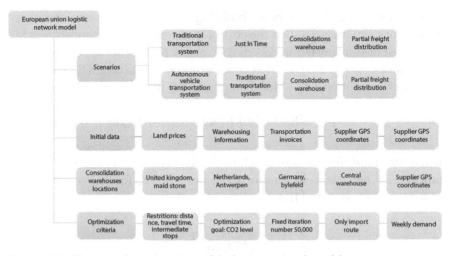

**Figure 10.2** Illustrates the assumptions of the logistic network model.

it frequently uses temperature-controlled transportation methods, which have a greater negative impact on the environment than would other industries Figure 10.2.

Only the immediate consolidated storage facility and partial freight collecting distribution procedures are considered in this model, which starts with the first warehouse sites. The initial one is timely, which mimics direct distribution from suppliers to the end destination by removing warehouses from the model. The second tactic is known as consolidation warehouses, in which merchandise is collected from the area and taken to the closest warehouse before being transported from the warehouse to a central warehouse in Lithuania. Last but not least, the simulated annealing principle is used to program the partial freight optimization strategy. The $CO_2$ emission level computation was the optimization objective; transportation costs, warehouse management costs, and warehouse building costs were also taken into account. Based on the journey distances, in this study, the amount of emissions brought on by supply chain transportation has been independently determined.

The model is best expressed as follows:

$$SMD = \sum_T \sum_L UDD(C,OR,S) + \sum_j UGD(C,ORS,) + \sum_j SD(C,ORS,EDQ))$$

$$(10.1)$$

where UDD stands for warehouse building costs, and SMD stands for overall network expenses. UGD is the cost of managing the warehouse, and SD is the cost of transportation. Given the variety of situations, L is the warehouse index (L = 1, 2, 3) and OR is the number of pallets. EDQ stands for energy consumption rate, C for distance, and S for a type of temperature.

$$FK = BF * (C * FEDQ + SS * SEDQ) \qquad (10.2)$$

where FK stands for emission level, BF for average $CO_2$ emission, C for distance, FEDQ for fuel consumption of engines, SEDQ for fuel consumption of heat, and SS for travel time.

$$SS = \frac{C}{BT} + 11 * CJX\left(\left(\frac{\frac{C}{BT}}{9}\right), 0\right) \qquad (10.3)$$

where BT denotes the mean speed, and CJX denotes an operator that only leaves whole numbers.

The obtained emission level data were then updated on the assumption that the cargo was consolidated onto one truck. The path with the lowest $CO_2$ emissions has been chosen. The optimal route that was chosen has been eliminated from the list of suppliers. The procedure was carried out repeatedly until the best routes were allocated to all of the suppliers in the supplier set. The suppliers have been individually added to the end objective functions without being combined, with the understanding that they have been withdrawn without being assigned to specific routes. Due to optimization limits, some suppliers cannot be consolidated. For instance, there are restrictions on distance, a truck's maximum load capacity is 32 containers, the transit time cannot be longer than 30% of the time required for direct delivery, etc. In both situations, the traditional system of distribution and the independent distribution system, the optimum paths for every supplier have been chosen, after this method has been used 50,000 times (Figure 10.3).

The usual consumption rates and working hours have been used to examine these three situations and two options. During the first approach, a traditional system of distribution has been simulated. The second method involved modeling an autonomous distribution system. The distribution model for autonomous vehicles has been simulated by varying

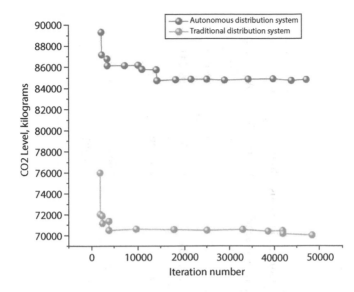

**Figure 10.3** Distribution model simulations with simulated annealing.

fuel consumption and travel times. The simulation's findings demonstrated that shorter lead times and more effective utilization of fuel rates were made possible by convoy driving. Convoy driving also makes better use of available road space and minimizes the demand for parking. Instead of 50 meters between each connected vehicle in a platoon, only 15 meters are needed. The aerodynamic drag is significantly reduced by this much shorter distance. Although it is difficult to predict the extent to which fuel consumption and $CO_2$ emissions might be reduced by up to 10% by deploying autonomous vehicles in actual use.

The outcomes of simulations based on selected scenarios are displayed in Table 10.2. In essence, the findings indicate that distribution in a timely approach has the highest transportation expenses, but there are no costs associated with building or managing warehouses. Thus, this kind of strategy, which is more focused on individual businesses than on clusters, is suitable if there is a shortage of available land or starting money. In comparison to the just-in-time case, the transportation costs for the consolidation warehouse are reduced by 19%, and the costs associated with the partial goods gathering strategy are reduced by 41%. The partial goods scenario has the greatest $CO_2$ emission level, whereas the consolidation warehouse case has the lowest. This is a result of the driver's rest period, which must be at least 10 hours long after each 90 minutes of driving.

**Table 10.2** Provides an analysis of the logistic network situation.

| Type | Independent distribution system | | | Conventional distribution method | | |
|---|---|---|---|---|---|---|
| | Just-in-sequence (JIS) | Distribution center | A portion of the cargo | Just-in-sequence (JIS) | Distribution center | A portion of the cargo |
| Transport expenses, € | 142 006 | 110 151 | 102 555 | 152 042 | 121 755 | 108 048 |
| CO$_2$ level, kg | 141 856 | 91 182 | 3 911 | 181 931 | 10 255 | 109 241 |
| Warehouse construction costs, € | 0 | 341 550 | 207 942 | 0 | 116 756 | 3 904 |
| Travel time, hours | 1958 | 1 074 | 3081 | 3 281 | 1 664 | 271 931 |
| Warehouse management costs, € | 0 | 10 263 | 3 904 | 0 | 339 581 | 5 024 |

$CO_2$ is constantly generated during the period of rest because the caravan's temperature control must be maintained so that the amount of time left to the destination remains constant. This scenario can be explained by the longer trip duration.

## 10.4    Conclusions

According to research, using consolidation warehouses in supply chains can lead to a more environmentally friendly system with just-in-time distribution, which has $CO_2$ emissions that are 55% higher and transportation costs that are 19% lower. While larger markets with larger order quantities should concentrate on the just-in-time distribution strategy to optimize their distribution systems, this approach is more appropriate for smaller cargo quantities. Although the cost of transport may be reduced by 18.4% as a result of this strategy, $CO_2$ emissions may rise by 43%. By establishing logistics clusters to share transportation and use autonomous vehicles, this problem can be solved while cutting transportation costs and $CO_2$ emissions by 5% and 23%, respectively, in comparison to conventional distribution models. Industry 4.0, big data analytics, and the Internet of Things implementation can aid in demand forecasting, cargo optimization, and food waste reduction while boosting the cluster's adaptability and competitiveness. Autonomous cars can be utilized to distribute goods in huge volumes across vast distances using consolidation warehouses and regionally gathered partial goods. The study notes several theoretical contributions, such as the significance of a methodical approach to technology use, the requirement for information utilization skills in management, and the contribution of organizational factors to technical advantages. The study's quantitative evidence, however, is restricted to the system's complexity and does not take into account outside variables like policies or economic trends. Therefore, to validate the suggested strategy, further study should adopt a complexity theory perspective.

## References

1. Zhang, S. *et al.*, Self-sustaining caching stations: Toward cost-effective 5G-enabled vehicular networks. *IEEE Commun. Mag.*, 55, 11, 202–208, 2017, doi: 10.1109/MCOM.2017.1700129.

2. Zhong, Z. *et al.*, Multiobjective optimization framework for cooperative adaptive cruise control vehicles in the automated vehicle platooning environment. *Transp. Res. Rec.*, 2625, 1, 32–42, 2017, doi: 10.3141/2625-04.

3. Shahian Jahromi, B. *et al.*, Real-time hybrid multi-sensor fusion framework for perception in autonomous vehicles. *Sensors (Basel)*, 19, 20, 4357, 2019, doi: 10.3390/s19204357.

4. Jones, E.C. and Leibowicz, B.D., Contributions of shared autonomous vehicles to climate change mitigation. *Transp. Res. D*, 72, 279–298, 2019, doi: 10.1016/j.trd.2019.05.005.

5. Feng, S. *et al.*, Safety assessment of highly automated driving systems in test tracks: A new framework. *Accid. Anal. Prev.*, 144, 105664, 2020, doi: 10.1016/j.aap.2020.105664.

6. Hao, M. and Yamamoto, T., Shared autonomous vehicles: A review considering car sharing and autonomous vehicles. *Asian Transp. Stud.*, 5, 1, 47–63, 2018.

7. Phan, D. *et al.*, Intelligent energy management system for conventional autonomous vehicles. *Energy*, 191, 116476, 2020, doi: 10.1016/j.energy.2019.116476.

8. Ding, J. *et al.*, A rule-based cooperative merging strategy for connected and automated vehicles. *IEEE Trans. Intell. Transp. Syst.*, 21, 8, 3436–3446, 2019, doi: 10.1109/TITS.2019.2928969.

9. Mohamed, A.A.S. *et al.*, Planning optimization for inductively charged on-demand automated electric shuttles project at Greenville, South Carolina. *IEEE Trans. Ind. Appl.*, 56, 2, 1010–1020, 2019, doi: 10.1109/TIA.2019.2958566.

10. Chen, S. *et al.*, Solving the first-mile ridesharing problem using autonomous vehicles. *Comput. Aided Civ. Infrastruct. Eng.*, 35, 1, 45–60, 2020, doi: 10.1111/mice.12461.

11. Lin, N., Zhao, Q., Zhao, L., Hawbani, A., Liu, L., Min, G., A novel cost-effective controller placement scheme for software-defined vehicular networks. *IEEE Internet Things J.*, 8, 18, 14080–14093, 2021.

12. Yu, H. *et al.*, Towards energy-efficient and cost-effective DC nanaogrid: A novel pseudo hierarchical architecture incorporating V2G technology for both autonomous coordination and regulated power dispatching. *Appl. Energy*, 313, 118838, 2022, doi: 10.1016/j.apenergy.2022.118838.

13. Cai, W. *et al.*, A review on methods of energy performance improvement towards sustainable manufacturing from perspectives of energy monitoring, evaluation, optimization and benchmarking. *Renew. Sustain. Energy Rev.*, 159, 112227, 2022, doi: 10.1016/j.rser.2022.112227.

14. Lu, Y. *et al.*, Real-time performance-focused localization techniques for autonomous vehicle: A review. *IEEE Trans. Intell. Transp. Syst.*, 23, 7, 6082–6100, 2021, doi: 10.1109/TITS.2021.3077800.

15. Feng, S. *et al.*, Testing scenario library generation for connected and automated vehicles, part I: Methodology. *IEEE Trans. Intell. Transp. Syst.*, 22, 3, 1573–1582, 2020, doi: 10.1109/TITS.2020.2972211.

16. Li, G. *et al.*, Detection of road traffic participants using cost-effective arrayed ultrasonic sensors in low-speed traffic situations. *Mech. Syst. Signal Process.*, 132, 535–545, 2019, doi: 10.1016/j.ymssp.2019.07.009.

17. Abduljabbar, R. *et al.*, Applications of artificial intelligence in transport: An overview. *Sustainability*, 11, 1, 189, 2019, doi: 10.3390/su11010189.

18. Lu, W. *et al.*, L3-net: Towards learning based lidar localization for autonomous driving, in: *Proc. IEEE/CVF Conference on Computer Vision and Pattern Recognition*, pp. 6382–6391, 2019, doi: 10.1109/CVPR.2019.00655.

19. Sorrentino, M. *et al.*, Development of flexible procedures for co-optimizing design and control of fuel cell hybrid vehicles. *Energy Convers. Manage.*, 185, 537–551, 2019, doi: 10.1016/j.enconman.2019.02.009.

20. Seuwou, P. *et al.*, The future of mobility with connected and autonomous vehicles in smart cities, in: *Digital Twin Technologies and Smart Cities*, pp. 37–52, 2020, doi:10.1007/978-3-030-18732-3_3.

# 11

# Adapting Underground Parking for the Future: Sustainability and Shared Autonomous Vehicles

**Vamsidhar Talasila[1]\*, Madala Pavan Pranav Sai[1],**
**Gade Sri Raja Gopala Reddy[1], Vempati Pavan Kashyap[1], Gunda Karthik[1]**
**and K. V. Panduranga Rao[2]**

*[1]Department of Computer Science and Engineering, Koneru Lakshmaiah Education Foundation, Vaddeswaram, Guntur, India*
*[2]Department of Computer Science and Engineering, Sree Vahini Institute of Science and Technology, Tiruvuru, India*

## Abstract

A significant field of worldwide science and technical innovation is the creation of shared autonomous vehicles (SAVs). SAVs' ability to drastically minimize the requirement for parking is one of its most coveted qualities in urban areas. Particularly in densely populated metropolitan areas, the town's underground parking space (UPS) is presently the biggest fixed-traffic area. The requirement for UPS renewals will become more urgent in the SAV situation. However, due to its unique form attributes, which are significantly constrained by outside factors, the UPS is challenging to renew, requiring aimed techniques and tactics. To gather information for this study, fieldwork was initially done to examine the geographical morphology and operating circumstances of typical UPSs in various parts of Ningbo. The time series assessment technique and functional substitution choice models for the sustainable renewal of subterranean parking were developed dependent on the driver status reaction and the multiple-purpose feature models. The study also analyzes the best design approaches for combining common examples' spatial features with their operational substitution objectives. The findings will offer scientific direction for builders' and city designers' upcoming designs in SAVs.

*\*Corresponding author*: talasila.vamsi@kluniversity.in

Kanak Kalita, Narayanan Ganesh and S. Balamurugan (eds.) Metaheuristics for Machine Learning: Algorithms and Applications, (235–252) © 2024 Scrivener Publishing LLC

**Keywords:** Area of underground parking, autonomous vehicle shared, revitalize methods, design techniques

## 11.1   Introduction

The number of automobiles on our roadways is growing in tandem with city expansion and urbanization, which causes traffic jams, air pollution, and other environmental and social issues. Parking issues in crowded metropolitan areas have been successfully solved by underground parking buildings. However, underground parking facilities are now facing novel possibilities as well as obstacles as the transportation sector changes in response to the introduction of discussed autonomous vehicles (AVs) [1]. We must modify subterranean parking infrastructure to meet the demands of shareable and driverless vehicles if we are to create a sustainable future. By integrating technology and designing parking structures with flexibility in mind, we can create parking facilities that are more efficient, cost-effective, and sustainable [2].

Implementing dynamic parking systems, which enable many people to utilize a single parking space at various times, is a way to adjust to the demands of shared vehicles. Automatic parking structures that arrange and shift cars as required or shared parking applications that let users book and share parking spaces can also be used to do this. Designing parking lots with the adaptability to accept the various sizes and forms of these cars is another option to satisfy the demands of autonomous vehicles [3]. This can be done by establishing modular, readily reconfigurable parking spaces or by constructing parking spaces with flexible proportions. In addition to these modifications, modifying subterranean parking facilities for shared and driverless cars has positive financial and ecological consequences. We can lessen the negative effects of urban mobility on the natural world and save money on infrastructural expenditures by minimizing the demand for parking spaces and maximizing the use of existing facilities [4, 5].

In this article, we will look at how subterranean parking garages may be revitalized to better meet the demands of shared and autonomous vehicles and, eventually, build an environmentally friendly transport network for cities. We will look at how technologies may be incorporated into these facilities, the benefit of multiuser parking, and the possible financial and ecological advantages of making these changes. Underground parking garages have a chance to play a significant role in the development of a more sustainable and effective urban transportation system by adjusting to the requirements of shared and self-driving vehicles. The way we view urban transportation has the potential to change as a result of shared and autonomous cars. These cars can assist in lowering the need for private automobile possession, cutting down on emissions of carbon dioxide, and improving the atmosphere. However, we also need to reconsider how we approach parking if we want to fully realize these advantages.

The structure of the paper is as follows. The associated work is shown in Section 11.2. Algorithms for the methodology are described in Section 11.3. The analysis produced is shown in Section 11.4, and the conclusion is presented in Section 11.5.

## 11.2 Related Works

The paper [6] examines the current literature on the benefits of the renewal of urban public parking spaces and suggests the four primary problems entailed: the amount to get renewed (i.e., forecasting demand assessment), when to renew (i.e., update time series evaluation), what to renew (i.e., function replacement decision), as well as how to keep up (i.e., design empirical research). Additionally, it presents a rough idea for and develops a research framework for beneficial renewal techniques for parking spaces within the shared autonomous vehicle (SAV) situation. To make cities smarter and to shape the future of urban travel, this presentation will present a cutting-edge examination of several connectivity projects. These are both newly developed processes with promoting acceptance thus far and a far greater ability to assist in a shift to an improved transportation framework or they remain in an early phase of growth and have not yet been accepted as potent processes that could change travel behavior norms [7]. The paper [8] provides an overview of the historically cars-oriented design and the world's century-long capitulation to vehicle culture. It then goes into further detail about various self-driving technology and how they could affect how cities look. The approach is used in a case study on Regensburg, a historically significant German city. Findings indicate that the dedicated lane for buses causes a pollution decrease of 3.25% to 6.65% and a mode shift of approximately 1.6% from auto modes to public transportation (PT). It has been determined that a shuttle service enhances the current PT system by boosting the volume of PT trips in the service region [9]. The study [10] shows how policies have a significant impact on the transportation sector's supply, but human expectations also have a role in determining the framework in which the sector's demand will operate. The efforts that have been examined emphasize the need for multifaceted sustainable transportation measures to reduce dependence on automobiles and accomplish broader sustainability objectives.

The study [11] examines the interaction in Korea between the general pollutants in the air and the behavior of Bike-Sharing System (BSS) riders. They investigated the relationships between exposure to airborne particles and BSS enrollment across time. The study [12] aims to explain the current state of the European cooperation programs that concentrate on the growth of the AV industry and to illustrate in detail the difficulties faced by urban planners and auto manufacturers. A competitive plan is taken into account in the article, as it supports sustained and effective cost control. The chain of supply has to change and transition from conventional to more environmentally friendly approaches. Long-term competitive edge may be maintained with the use of the Internet of Things, big data analytics, online computing, cyber-physical networks, autonomous cars, and logistic clusters [13]. The paper [14] aims to give a mechanism for future studies to employ realistic flow models to achieve more precise forecasts on SAV benefits. In this study, a based-on-events approach for including SAV actions in current traffic simulation frameworks is presented. The study [15] uses current taxonomy types from literature to describe the generally defined AV fleet administration problem, adds new, or more nuanced, dimensions to existing taxonomic categories, and introduces new taxonomy types to categorize particular AV fleet management obstacles.

## 11.3   Methodology

### 11.3.1   Framework for Research

First, a field study is used to gather information for the study on the physical characteristics and operational circumstances of underground parking spaces (UPSs). According to these characteristics, the collected items were categorized. Following that, a technique to evaluate the time frame of UPSs within the SAV situation is developed for analyzing the creating time series of various kinds of UPSs, and a library for operating substitutes is developed by professional opinions and literature research. The attribute-based multiple goals-making choices model determines the future role of each type of UPS. The topic of sustainability is finally brought up about renewal methods.

### 11.3.2   Area of Research

To speed up SAV in real-world applications, China is working to create modern AI technologies. China's east coast is home to the sizable town of

Ningbo, which has an advanced economy and a dense population. Digital equipment is widely embraced in Ningbo. Meanwhile, the use of SAVs will be more appealing given the elevated level of automobile ownership and lack of parking spaces.

### 11.3.3  Collection of Data

The geographical makeup, architectural kinds, and uses of structures above the ground all have an immediate impact on UPS's renewal. Additionally, UPS service circumstances in various parts of a city may vary. Consequently, we carried out direct UPS inquiries across multiple Ningbo urban areas to gather more complete and varied data. The final sample information gathered includes several indicative regions in each of Ningbo's seven administrative regions, including Haishu, Jiangbei, Beilun, Zhenhai, Yinzhou, Fenghua, and Xiangshan. Industrial shop structures, workplaces, lodgings, and other structures with above-ground uses are examples. In Ningbo, 200 samples of UPSs were eventually collected. Graphics were also used to assess the structure of their area.

### 11.3.4  Analysis of Clusters

Various UPS groups were autonomously created by two-step clustering based on the characteristics of the UPS. Additionally, the primary distinctions between the categories were made clear. Each category's renewal period and functionality substitution are covered individually. The benefit of spreading in two steps is that it allows for concurrent spreading using continuous and categorized factors and can calculate an ending amount of categories. The two phases of the clustering method are the creation of a cluster features tree and the merging of the leaf nodes using a clustering algorithm.

### 11.3.5  DSR Model

The DSR model includes solid principles for management and is strongly tied to ecologically sustainable urban development objectives. The study enhances the component arrangement in the current DSR layout through the uniqueness of the UPS. The updated model highlights the crucial part capital area renewal plays in sustainable growth while maintaining the rational connection among indices. One of them, "Drivers" (D) refers to the requirement for the renovation of the parking space as a result of external factors, such as city evolution; "Status" (S) refers to the present state of the parking space construction, surroundings, underground space, and natural surroundings, expressing the area's potential for revitalization; and "Response" (R) refers to the UPS owners' views on reconstruction. The study improves and establishes the requirements, elements, and signal levels associated with the UPS renewal by the level of execution. The surroundings ("location, use of the ground building, mix of uses, and spatial connectivity"), the geometry arrangement ("number of floors, the scale of UPS, structural span, space height, and coverage of ground building"), and effective features (i.e., "whether it is a civil air defense basement") are all considered driver indicators. The kind of UPS property owner is what defines the response index. Table 11.1 contains a list of each indicator's nature and particular meanings.

**Table 11.1** Index of the driver, status, and response model system.

| Standards | Nature | Index | Factors | Implication of index |
|---|---|---|---|---|
| Responses (RE) | Unfavorable | UPS's rights of ownership and their nature (RE1) | Renewal desire | Kind of UPS operator |
| Status (ST) | Unfavorable | Number of floors (ST1) | Spatial structure | Quantity of subterranean floors |
| | Favorable | Size of UPS (ST2) | | Quantity of parking spaces overall |
| | Favorable | Structure's length (ST3) | | The mean distance between the sections |
| | Favorable | Area height (ST4) | | Every floor's median height |
| | Favorable | Proportion of ground-to-building exposure (ST5) | | The proportion of elevated to subsurface floor space |

*(Continued)*

**Table 11.1** Index of the driver, status, and response model system. (*Continued*)

| Standards | Nature | Index | Factors | Implication of index |
|---|---|---|---|---|
| | Favorable | Underground defense from the air (ST6) | Functional attributes | If it is an underground facility for the urban defense of the air |
| Drivers (DR) | Unfavorable | Parking charge price (DR1) | Operation status | A per-hour parking charge |
| | Unfavorable | Parking lot rate of change (DR2) | | The proportion of each day's parking lot entries to all parking lot entries |
| | Favorable | Location (DR3) | The atmosphere outside | It matters if the UPS is near a hub for city transit |
| | Favorable | Use of ground-level floor (DR4) | | Functional category of a ground-level structure |
| | Favorable | Several functions (DR5) | | If additional covert operations are combined with the UPS |
| | Favorable | Connection (DR6) | | If UPS has access to the nearby subterranean area |

Every index is a measure's assessment level and is split into two groups and given 1 or 2 points by the pertinent regional criteria and the peculiarities of the UPS. The math is made simpler, and two-step clustering is made easier by separating the groups into only two. Study professionals present the criteria for evaluating an index and, following several revisions, establish the quantitative assessment criteria for every indicator. For more information, see Table 11.2. Utilizing the conclusions of professional

Table 11.2 The DSR indexes' weights and value attributions.

| Index | Index evaluation standard and score | | Weight |
| | 2 | 1 | |
| --- | --- | --- | --- |
| ST1 | 1 Floor | Greater than 1 floor | 0.182 |
| ST2 | More than 100 parking spaces together | Every parking space under 100 | 0.200 |
| ST3 | A mean column spacing of at least 6 meters | Less than 6 meters between columns on average | 0.211 |
| ST4 | Net height of at least 3 meters | Less than 3 meters in net height | 0.153 |
| ST5 | Less than 50% of a building's area is on the ground. | Greater than 50% of a building's area is on the ground | 0.141 |
| ST6 | Basement for non-civil air defense | Basement civil air defense | 0.113 |
| RE | Mixed ownership | Single ownership | 1.000 |
| DR1 | Charge an hourly rate of more than 10 yuan. | Charge a rate that is less than 10 yuan per hour. | 0.303 |
| DR2 | More than two times every day are changed. | A daily turnover rate of no more than two occurs. | 0.215 |
| DR3 | Urban traffic node area | Region of non-urban traffic nodes | 0.139 |
| DR4 | Public | Civil | 0.096 |
| DR5 | Not combined with other activities | Combined with additional operations | 0.130 |
| DR6 | Connected | Unconnected | 0.117 |

evaluation, the "AHP" technique is also utilized to evaluate the metric of the size of drivers and statuses. The outcomes are then checked for accuracy. The driving forces and the condition of the specimens were assessed in the study using a weighted total approach. In this research, the driving force stage and state stage assessment outcomes are coupled using the four-quadrant technique, and renewal interest is divided into three groups, ranging from elevated to inadequate: higher driving forces with a high status indicates recent growth; higher driving forces with a low status indicates the short-term growth; and a weak driving force with a weak state indicates long-term growth.

## 11.3.6    Model with Multiple Objectives

A classic multiple-goals issue is choosing an appropriate substitute for UPSs. Its traits include the incompatibility of the objectives and the inconsistency of the numerous quality markers. To thoroughly assess and rate the plans of a small number of UPSs that need to be substituted, choice-makers study the choice facts and example data that are already available. The two components of multiple goals attribution choice-making are options and choice characteristics. The following formula describes the choice-making process:

$$\underset{w\in W}{CQ}[b1(W), b2(W), \dots bm(W)] \tag{11.1}$$

$$w\varepsilon W = [w / w_{ji} = e(b_j, v_i), j = 1, 2, \dots n, i = 1, 2, \dots] \tag{11.2}$$

$b_j$ is the case of No. $j$, $v_i$ is the attribute of No.$i$, and $w_{ji} = e\ (b_j, v_i)$ is the utility function value of case $j$ for attribute $i$. $CQ$ is the decision criterion in this scenario. Equation 11.2 may be used to evaluate and order different UPS service choices based on the selection criteria. Various utility function matrices and criteria for making decisions lead to matching mega-attribute processes for making decisions. The function substitute evaluation for UPS entails six steps, all of which are by the general procedure of multiple goals and mega-attribute-making choices: (i) setting up the selection matrices, (ii) creating a recursive hierarchy, (iii) normalizing the values of the attributes, (iv) determining the index's weight, (v) calculating the complete characteristic usefulness value, and (vi) ranking the various possible schemes.

We first create substitute libraries for the UPS functionality. The renewal purpose possibilities for city UPS are arranged and described, presenting regional rules, industrial standards for design, and possible uses in future urbanization.

By various function objectives and the DSR model, the study then creates matching qualities and weights. The expert's AHP approach is used in the weighing technique to determine how to determine whether the 10 functional objectives are appropriate. The optimal substitution goal for every UPS case is chosen after replacing the values of the attributes of the various UPS cases (Figure 11.1) by contrasting the total amount size replacements function. For instance, the following formula is used to determine the importance of the operational goal Commercial (F1):

$$E1 = 0.11Dr1 + 0.07Dr2 + 0.11Dr3 + 0.01Dr5 + 0.22Dr6 + 0.07St1$$
$$+0.05St2 + 0.10St2 + 0.04St4 + 0.02St5 + 0.02St6 + 0.04Re1$$

$$(11.3)$$

| | S1 | S2 | S3 | S4 | S5 | S6 | R1 | D1 | D2 | D3 | D4 | D5 | D6 |
|-----|----|----|-----|----|----|----|----|----|----|-----|----|----|----|
| G1 | 7 | 5 | 10 | 4 | 2 | 1 | 4 | 11 | 7 | 11 | 15 | 1 | 22 |
| G2 | 13 | 9 | 17 | 20 | 12 | 7 | 3 | 3 | 4 | 2 | 4 | 2 | 6 |
| G3 | 12 | 3 | 17 | 3 | 6 | 6 | 3 | 3 | 7 | 23 | 7 | 7 | 3 |
| G4 | 10 | 4 | 6 | 13 | 3 | 14 | 7 | 9 | 7 | 8 | 5 | 6 | 8 |
| G5 | 12 | 5 | 14 | 7 | 6 | 2 | 6 | 8 | 2 | 15 | 14 | 6 | 3 |
| G6 | 9 | 2 | 11 | 5 | 7 | 21 | 2 | 1 | 4 | 3 | 13 | 19 | 3 |
| G7 | 9 | 13 | 13 | 10 | 2 | 3 | 13 | 12 | 2 | 12 | 2 | 5 | 4 |
| G8 | 4 | 14 | 4 | 6 | 2 | 4 | 5 | 15 | 20 | 3 | 9 | 2 | 12 |
| G9 | 12 | 7 | 1 | 1 | 6 | 12 | 6 | 4 | 1 | 21 | 12 | 6 | 11 |
| G10 | 4 | 5 | 10 | 10 | 9 | 6 | 4 | 6 | 12 | 4 | 14 | 12 | 4 |
| Sum | 92 | 67 | 101 | 79 | 55 | 76 | 53 | 72 | 66 | 102 | 95 | 66 | 76 |

**Figure 11.1** Weight matrix of attributes.

## 11.3.7    Statistical Data

Radar graphs are utilized for contrasting the characteristics of various UPS kinds, multiple regression analyses are utilized to examine the connection between Driver indices and Status indices for different types of UPSs, communication evaluation is used to determine the connection between renewal time and associated UPS characteristics, and intersect-tabs are utilized to contrast the renewal times in instances of various substituted purposes.

# 11.4    Analysis

## 11.4.1    Feature Types

The mean of the 13 indications was 1.52 for all 200 instances. The mean value of 200 instances for each of the six Driver indices was 1.64 (Dr1), 1.43 (Dr2), 1.8 (Dr3), 1.53 (Dr4), 1.32 (Dr5), and 1.13 (Dr6), accordingly. The mean values for all instances for each of the six Status indices were correspondingly 1.36 (St1), 1.52 (St2), 1.53 (St3), 1.67 (St4), 1.75 (St5), and 1.43 (St6). The reaction index had an average value of 1.87. The Drivers index had a weighted mean of 1.48. The current state indices' weighted mean was 1.52.

The two-step clustering algorithm separates 200 examples into four groups based on 13 category factors. Figure 11.2 displays the parameter ordering of categorization relevance. Parking lot cost is the most crucial factor, then the spot, the level of parking changeover, and floor level. According to the information, the identifying factor of categorization accuracy was 0.26, which is satisfactory. These kinds have unique characteristics. For example, the initial group includes 40 cases where 100% of the parking prices are under or exactly match 10 yuan/hour, where 45% of the destinations are close to traffic nodes, and where 65% have an elevated parking rate of turnover. The next group consists of 50 cases, with 96% of the parking costs above 10 yuan/hour, 92% of the locations being close to traffic nodes, and all of the parking rates of turnover falling into one of two categories: either very high or very weak. There are 74 examples in the third group, of which 62.2% have a weak rate of parking changeover, 89.2% are geographically located in traffic node regions, and 91.9% have parking rates of more than 10 yuan/hour. There are 36 examples in the fourth category, of which 72.2% have parking fees that are under or equal to

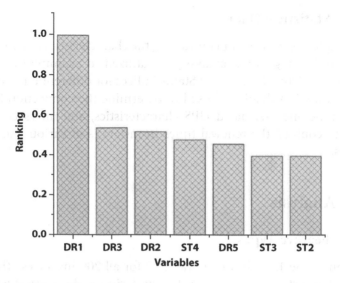

**Figure 11.2** Ranking of the factors.

10 yuan/hour, 83.3% have sites that are outside of traffic nodes, and 72.2% have significant parking turnover rates.

The mean values of the signals for the various UPS kinds are displayed on the radar chart in Figure 11.3. The indicator readings of D, S, and R for the four categories are quite distinct, as shown in Figure 11.3. While the outcomes of the S indices of type 3 are more comparable to those of other kinds, the readings of the D indices of type 2 are more dissimilar than those of the other kinds. The D, S, and R readings for the first type are 1.31,

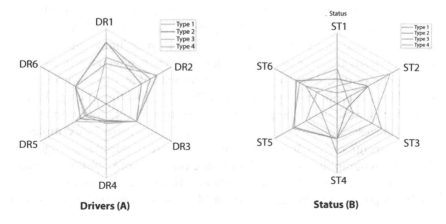

**Figure 11.3** UPS-type characteristics.

1.49, and 1.90, accordingly. The D, S, and R readings for the second type are 1.48, 1.40, and 1.93; for the third type, they are 1.60, 1.66, and 1.77; and for type 4, they are 1.47, 1.51, and 2.01, accordingly. It is clear that the third category's D and S are often greater than those of the other categories.

## 11.4.2    Timing of Renewal

A UPS will be considered recent expansion if D has a higher value than 1.494 and S is bigger than 1.539; middle-term expansion if Dr is bigger than 1.494 and St is bigger than 1.539; and long-term expansion if D is lower than 1.494 and S is lower than 1.539, as per Chapter 3.4. This usual procedure creates four parts on the outside of Figure 11.4's two-axis values.

The green region in the top right side represents the current phase of growth, the yellow regions at the higher left and bottom right sides indicate the medium-term phase of expansion, and the red region in the lowered left corner represents the long-term phase of expansion. Figure 11.4 reveals that a total of 92 instances have been categorized as medium-term expansion, of which 30 are type 3 instances and 26 are type 2, 48 instances have been categorized as short-term expansion, of which 18 are type 2 instances and 10 are each of types 1, 3, and 4. Of the 60 instances categorized as recent expansion, 34 are type 3 instances and 14 are type 4, while 30 are type 3 instances and 26 are type 2, and there are 92 instances categorized as medium-term expansion. Nearly half of type 3 (44%) is growing rapidly compared to more than one-third of type 2 (37%) and half of types 1, 2, and 3. Figure 11.4 also demonstrates the varied relationships between the Dr and St. Type 3 Dr and St have a lesser positive association, whereas Dr and St of other kinds have lesser opposing interactions.

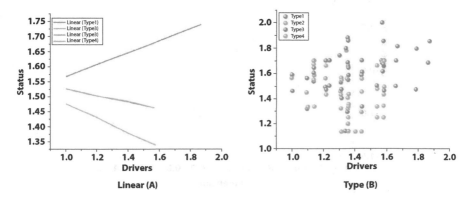

**Figure 11.4** Renewal time outcomes.

For the 13 DSR model indices and renewal time, numerous connection types of research are used in this work. The relationship research chart (Figure 11.5), which highlights the association among the parameters, reflects the findings. The level of each strewn point in Figure 11.5 corresponds to a particular parameter. If the dispersed spots have a nearer level, they are near together. The variable renewal timing features are discovered and assigned to various regions in Figure 11.5 based on the description of the associated analysis graph. Long-term growth and recent growth exhibit distinct features because they diverge greatly from their points of origin. Instances without a subterranean connection, a modest lower-level location, and no additional integrated obligations are the main characteristics that are ideal for medium-term expansion. The top building's usage for civil purposes, together with its narrow essential spans and minimal height, is the main characteristic of long-term expansion scenarios.

### 11.4.3 Replacement of Function

The mass matrix structures as shown in Figure 11.1 are the basis for the weighing calculations and assessment of every alternative function for every instance kind. The calculations are done to correspond with the mean value of 13 sustainable criteria for every instance kind. Table 11.3 is a list of the outcomes. Various types have varying capacities for

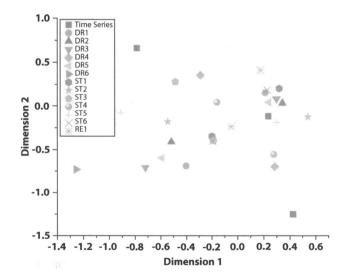

**Figure 11.5** Analyzing renewal timing and UPS properties.

practical adaptation. For the first type, business operations, educational institutions, and libraries are a better option; for the second type, clt & ent, logistics, and libraries are the best substitute functions; and for type 4, data centers, cultural entertainment, and libraries are the best substitute functions. Table 11.3 aggregates the many types of acceptable performances as well as the suitability of each function for distinct sorts. The commercial function is the least ideal of the 10 jobs, as can be shown, while the screen is the most versatile.

One by one, we statistically analyzed the substitution of 200 functions to determine the renewal distribution of time ratio for various function kinds. The exhibition is the most frequent role for renewal in 46 cases, while commercial and office are the least frequent (only four of each). This is seen in Figure 11.6. Most of the business operations, together with everything related to the school, library, and half of the office, are in the short-term expansion phase. The office operation is nearing its conclusion. Most of the scenarios that are ideal for libraries and logistics centers are in the long-term expansion phase, whereas libraries and data centers make up the largest and lowest percentage of mid-term renewals.

Table 11.3 Rankings of function replacement for each UPS type.

| Functions | Type 2 | Type 4 | Ranking | Type 1 | Type 3 |
|---|---|---|---|---|---|
| Culture & Entertainment | 4 | 9 | 19 | 2 | 4 |
| Office | 5 | 8 | 23 | 5 | 5 |
| DataCenter | 1 | 10 | 25 | 7 | 7 |
| Laboratory | 7 | 3 | 19 | 3 | 6 |
| Exhibition | 2 | 2 | 13 | 8 | 1 |
| Logistics | 9 | 1 | 27 | 9 | 8 |
| Commercial | 6 | 5 | 30 | 10 | 9 |
| Stadium | 8 | 4 | 16 | 1 | 3 |
| School | 3 | 6 | 17 | 6 | 2 |
| Library | 10 | 7 | 31 | 4 | 10 |

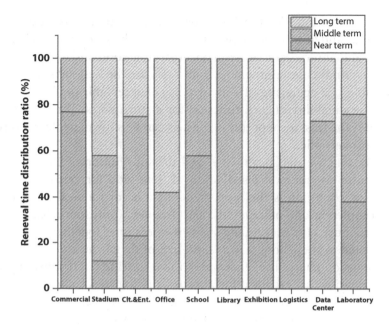

**Figure 11.6** Distribution of renewal times.

## 11.5   Conclusion

This study performed a preliminary investigation on sustainable renewal procedures and plans for urban subterranean parking spaces based on the SAV situation. The next findings were reached: The subterranean parking space with the extension of a broad building and for public use of the top-most growing is acceptable for early regrowth, but the examples with a short architectural span and minimal amenities and the above structure for civil purposes are largely suitable for long-term expansion. Most of the situations have a successful location for exhibition replacement, and certain situations also have effective roles as educational institutions and athletic facilities. Instances, where laboratories work well, tend to be those that are short- and medium-term solutions. The lighting and ventilation of underground rooms represent the primary sustainable design inconsistency for the majority of parking garages. Contradictory architectural elements can be efficiently resolved with the use of inset lighting, ventilation shafts, and squares.

A rising in groundwater owing to leaks or mishaps is one risky technical and geological occurrence that might result from replacing the UPS as a building. This study does not take into account the technical and geographical features of UPSs, in addition to the dependability of buildings in terms of accountability and obligations, which are closely tied to how the underground space operates. As a result, from a design perspective, the practical adaptation of this research is simply a reference.

Regardless of its shortcomings, this research has a significant amount of value. It provided an evaluation of feasibility and potential answers while exposing the new issues regarding physical rejuvenation brought on by the shift toward electronic towns by building an empirical foundation. To use the results of science to free the process of design, further studies will be connected to low-carbon, environmentally friendly, and other aims, improve the structure of buildings with a variety of reasons, and combine it into innovative ideas in a more acceptable way. Future studies will also focus on the backdrop of the digital city and the features of urban system spaces, develop more efficient design techniques, and execute real-world project presentations.

# References

1. Tscharaktschiew, S. and Reimann, F., Less workplace parking with fully autonomous vehicles? *J. Intell. Connected Veh.*, 5, 3, 283–301, 2022, doi: 10.1108/JICV-07-2022-0029.
2. Papa, E. and Lauwers, D., Smart mobility: Opportunity or threat to innovate places and cities. In *20th International Conference on Urban Planning and Regional Development in the Information Society (REAL CORP 2015)*, pp. 543–550, 2015.
3. Clark *et al.*, The impacts of autonomous vehicles and e-commerce on local government budgeting and finance. *Urbanism Next, Sustainable Cities Initiative University of Oregon*, 2017, https://cpb-us-e1.wpmucdn.com/blogs. uoregon.edu/dist/f/13615/files/2017/07/Impacts-of-AV-Ecommerce-on-Local-Govt-Budget-and-Finance-SCI-08-2017-2n8wgfg.pdf
4. Victor, T. *et al.*, When autonomous vehicles are introduced on a larger scale in the road transport system: The Drive Me project, in: *Autom. Driving Safer More Effic. Future Driving*, pp. 541–546, 2017, doi:10.1007/978-3-319-31895-0_24.
5. Baumgardner, W., Cassidy, C., Ruhl, M., The promise of seamless mobility: Autonomous vehicles and the mobility-as-a-service revolution. In *Disruptive Transport Driverless Cars, Transport Innovation and the Sustainable City of Tomorrow*, W. Riggs (Ed.), pp. 11–20, Routledge Taylor & Francis Group, London, UK, New York, NY, USA, 2019.
6. Xia, B. *et al.*, Sustainable renewal methods of urban public parking spaces under the scenario of shared autonomous vehicles (SAV): A review and a proposal. *Sustainability*, 13, 7, 3629, 2021, doi: 10.3390/su13073629.

7. Nikitas, A. *et al.*, How can autonomous and connected vehicles, electromobility, BRT, hyperloop, share-use mobility, and mobility-as-a-service shape transport futures in the context of smart cities? *Urban Sci.*, 1, 4, 36, 2017, doi: 10.3390/urbansci1040036.

8. Noyman, A. *et al.*, Road map for autonomous cities: Sustainable transformation of urban spaces, 2017.

9. Ceder, A., Urban mobility and public transport: Future perspectives and review. *Int. J. Urban Sci.*, 25, 4, 455–479, 2021.

10. Ortegon-Sanchez, A. *et al.*, Car-free initiatives from around the world: Concepts for moving to future sustainable mobility, in: *TRB 96th Annual Meeting Compendium of Papers*, Washington, DC, 2017, Jan.

11. Park, J. *et al.*, Air pollution and public bike-sharing system ridership in the context of sustainable development goals. *Sustainability*, 14, 7, 3861, 2022, doi: 10.3390/su14073861.

12. Ágnes, S.P.F., Autonomous vehicles from the EU perspective, 2020.

13. Gružauskas, V. *et al.*, Minimizing the trade-off between sustainability and cost-effective performance by using autonomous vehicles. *J. Cleaner Prod.*, 184, 709–717, 2018, doi: 10.1016/j.jclepro.2018.02.302.

14. Levin, M.W. *et al.*, A general framework for modeling shared autonomous vehicles with dynamic network-loading and dynamic ride-sharing applications. *Comput. Environ. Urban Syst.*, 64, 373–383, 2017, doi: 10.1016/j.compenvurbsys.2017.04.006.

15. Hyland, M.F. and Mahmassani, H.S., Taxonomy of shared autonomous vehicle fleet management problems to inform future transportation mobility. *Transp. Res. Rec.*, 2653, 1, 26–34, 2017, doi: 10.3141/2653-04.

# 12

# Big Data Analytics for a Sustainable Competitive Edge: An Impact Assessment

**Rajyalakshmi K.[1]\*, Padma A.[2], Varalakshmi M.[3], Suhasini A.[4] and Chiranjeevi P.[5]**

[1]*Department of Computer Science and Engineering, Koneru Lakshmaiah Education Foundation, Vaddeswaram, Guntur, India*
[2]*Chaitanya Bharathi Institute of Technology, Hyderabad, India*
[3]*Department of Humanities and Sciences, Vardhaman College of Engineering, Shamshabad, Hyderabad, India*
[4]*Sri Durga Malleswara Siddhartha Mahila Kalasala, Vijayawada, India*
[5]*Department of Mathematics and Humanities, R V R and J C College of Engineering, Chowdavaram, Guntur, India*

## Abstract

One of Industry 4.0's key components is big data analytics (BDA), a cornerstone. It has developed into an effective instrument for boosting businesses' competitive advantages by improving data-driven performance. While this is happening, the global resource problem is forcing corporations to take a commission based on sustainability seriously. According to the literature, BDA and innovation can increase a company's productivity and provide a competitive advantage. According to this study, a sustainable competitive advantage (SCA) might be produced by combining big data analytics capabilities (BDACs) with elevated levels of data availability (DA). Research from the past and the dynamic capacity hypothesis support this claim. PLS-SEM, a statistical method that uses partial least squares to model structural equations, was utilized to analyze the results of this study's survey of 117 manufacturing companies. According to the findings, BDAC significantly boosts internal consistency (IC) and is highly dependent on DA. Additionally, statistics show that compared to BDAC, IC directly impacts a firm's SCA. This study provides important theoretical and practical insights into the challenges of BDA application to achieve suitable procedures, promoting industrial organizations to improve their sustainable business performance (SBP).

\*Corresponding author: rajyalakshmi.kottapalli@gmail.com

Kanak Kalita, Narayanan Ganesh and S. Balamurugan (eds.) Metaheuristics for Machine Learning: Algorithms and Applications, (253–266) © 2024 Scrivener Publishing LLC

*Keywords*: Sustainable competitive advantage (SCA), data availability (DA), big data analytics (BDA), firm performance (FPER)

## 12.1   Introduction

Big data (BD) research is growing in popularity in both academic and business research. With the assistance of the appropriate tools and systems, BD and predictive analytics (BDPA) are analytical techniques that include accessing, identifying, retrieving, storing, processing, visualizing, and managing vast amounts of complex data [1]. When compared to the current state of conventional data processing systems, this form of data demonstrates a large quantity and speed of data processing, which might provide frequent compensation and settlement. The second is utilizing business analytics (BA) to monitor and decide on organizations. BAs are prepared with the knowledge and abilities to assess organizational strategy efforts and create successful business planning [2]. E-commerce companies can use BD to handle the massive volumes of data accessible to identify market trends, anticipate customer needs, and assess consumer buying habits. Undoubtedly, BD's contribution to the innovation process is becoming more visible in practice and acknowledged in research [3]. The definition of big data customer (BDC) activity may be concealed in BD, and consumer analytics is the practical use of this information, even though in the contemporary economy, BD is viewed as a new type of capital. Businesses must allocate enough organizational, human, and physical capital resources to BD to benefit from this new type of capital [4]. By enhancing time, management, and market transaction costs such as those associated with online buyer–seller interactions, big data analytics (BDA) may assist e-vendors. Especially in the case of e-commerce, business intelligence (BD) enables businesses to monitor consumer behavior and identify the best strategies for turning one-time clients into devoted ones. Comparing a company's value chain to its rivals, one that employs BD analytics sees a 5%–6% increase in productivity [5]. This study covers the impact of BDA in supplying a long-lasting competitive edge.

The remaining portions of the paper are given below: Section 12.2 summarized the literature, Section 12.3 described the suggested strategy, and Section 12.4 presented and discussed the experimental data sets and simulation findings. The analysis is concluded in Section 12.5, which also recommends further study.

## 12.2    Related Works

The research [6] investigated the relationship between the elements of internal consistency (IC) and the competitive advantage (CA) of the hotel industry by mediating the influence of service innovation and moderating the impact of BDA capabilities. The study [7] developed a paradigm to examine how exploitative, explorative, and ambidextrous innovation techniques result in big data customer (BDC). Additionally, it will look at how it can provide a company with a sustainable competitive edge. By utilizing the dynamic capacity theory to examine how data analytics capabilities (DACs) work as a mediating element, the study [8] investigated how the deployment of BDA influences the quality of judgments. The article [9] introduced BDA to understand the interactions between competitive advantage (CA) and supply chain management practices (SCMPs) in Jordanian manufacturing firms. The article [10] introduced the concept of sustainable smart manufacturing by fusing the fundamental technologies of intelligent manufacturing with pervasive servitization over the whole life span. The research [11] intends to investigate how wearable technology usage has affected Indian health insurance companies. To gain a competitive edge, it emphasizes the essential dynamic skills that health insurance companies need to develop to handle massive data produced by wearable technologies. The article [12] shows how BDA may give IT businesses a competitive advantage and boost business performance. China and India are the subjects of the research. The study [13] enhanced by evaluating the direct effects of big data analytics capabilities (BDACs) on firm performance (FPER) and the mediating effects of process-oriented dynamic capabilities (PODCs) on the relationship between BDAC and FPER. Madhani [14] created a variety of frameworks to demonstrate how BD and BDA are being used to alter the supply chain further digitally. One of these frameworks examines how BD-enabled supply chains' competitive objectives support the expansion of customer value and, as a result, aid in creating competitive advantages. The article [15] employed BDA to analyze thoroughly and research business sustainability plans.

## 12.3    Hypothesis and Research Model

### 12.3.1    Theoretical Model

The proposed model designed for this study is exposed in Figure 12.1, and it comprises the four reflecting components data availability (DA), BDAC,

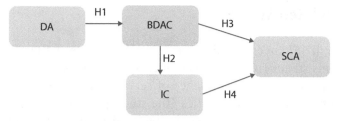

**Figure 12.1** Suggested research design.

IC, and sustainable competitive advantage (SCA). The foundation for the idea is the dynamic capabilities concept, which maintains that businesses must create new strategic talents to keep up with the market's growth rate of technology advancements and shifting customer preferences. This model, founded on the theory that DA, when supported by BDAC and creative processes, may improve organizations' sustainable performance, illustrates the dynamic potential of BDAC and IC. Finally, the characteristics above will increase organizations' SCA.

### 12.3.1.1   Hypothesis 1 (H1)

BDAC is a dynamic capability because it exhibits emotional capability traits like repeatability, making an experience hard to replicate and, consequently, providing valuable assets that increase competitive advantage. However, data must be accessible to use BDA; otherwise, overall performance and competitive advantage may suffer. Furthermore, deleted data cannot be recovered even after they are discovered. Therefore, businesses strive to make their data as accessible as possible to improve their BDAC by addressing relevant concerns, including data source, size, and gathering technique. Massive volumes of data may be delivered over the Internet of Things (IoT) through cyber-physical systems, proximity sensors, radio-frequency identification (RFID), and other advanced Industry 4.0 production technologies, which can then be connected to the cloud to ensure DA. BDA might be linked to enterprise resource planning (ERP) and other management information systems. We thus suggest that DA is a BDAC facilitator, as higher DA encourages improved data analysis. The following is the situation that we offer:

H1: DA may improve BDAC.

### 12.3.1.2    BDAC as a Facilitator for IC (H2)

Businesses may boost their IC in items, processes, and markets by integrating BDA with additional data sources like customer research, strategy, and equipment monitoring. BDAC might improve IC by simplifying routine processes and the work of an innovation team. Additionally, they demonstrated how BDAC positively affected IC. Consequently, we suggest the following:

H2: BDAC benefits IC in an optimistic way.

### 12.3.1.3    The Contribution of BDAC and IC to Raising SCA (H3) and (H4)

BDAC is an important center for the creation of knowledge, to start. This is accomplished using various data sources, such as those about consumers, processes, and production, to help organizations make better decisions, enhance performance, and preserve a competitive edge. For instance, BDA has a substantial influence on the social and environmental sustainability of a corporation. In hypotheses 3 and 4, the primary impacts of BDA on businesses' financial performance were examined in more detail. Second, the dynamic ability of innovation substantially contributes to raising sales, profitability, and performance excellence by creating new products and processes.

Furthermore, an innovation that facilitates quicker market change adaptation promotes competitive advantage development. As a result, IC dramatically impacts a company's ability to operate profitably and competitively. Adaptable talents by strengthening and maintaining their competitive edge and overall performance, BDA and innovation both help businesses overcome external obstacles and competencies. We thus put forth the following hypotheses:

H3: Businesses' SCA is positively impacted by BDAC's dynamic capacity.

H4: The SCA of an organization is positively affected by IC, since it is an emotional competence.

### 12.3.1.4    Sustainable Competitive Advantage

A company gains a competitive edge when it outperforms its present or future rivals in terms of success. Modern technologies like BDA also provide sustained performance by supporting data-driven performance. Finding an advantage in competition usually requires contrasting the success of a business to that of its rivals. In light of this, we operationalize SCA as a standard for outperforming competitors regarding environmental and social outcomes. This design is the first to consider the three sustainability components at the business level, according to prior research that forms the foundation of the competitive advantage framework.

## 12.3.2   Proposed Method

Business decision analysis is the process of sifting through enormous complicated information in search of patterns, correlations, and insights that may be utilized to impact choices and acquire valuable data. Large amounts of structured and unstructured data must be subjected to the most up-to-date analytics techniques and algorithms in order to extract useful information and provide insights that may be put into practice.

### 12.3.2.1   Layout Assessment

The fundamental presumptions and methods of the study were evaluated using a web-based questionnaire. Each of the 15 survey questions received a score from respondents on a 5-point Likert scale, with 1 being a great deal of unhappiness and 5 a great deal of agreement. The previous material was used as a guidance for creating the questionnaire. The four components of the four multi-item reflecting measures for the research model were created using the questions. The G*Power 3.1 program set the minimum sample size at 117 samples. As a result, 5%, 90%, and 0.3 were chosen as the power, effect size, and significant threshold parameters, respectively.

### 12.3.2.2   Analysis Method and Data Collection

This study concentrated on manufacturing firms from various industrial sectors that were aware of and had some experience with Industry 4.0 technology in order to test the hypothesis. The service sectors were not included in the study, since several survey questions were only intended to be addressed by respondents from the industrial sectors. The secondary objective of the questionnaire was to collect data to evaluate the theories behind the structures. To strengthen the validity of the data gathered, the members of management at the highest levels were strongly encouraged to reply to the questionnaire. This study employed PLS-SEM, since it is a statistical software tool for DA that is effective at analyzing data from tiny sample sizes, mediating factors, and indirect correlations. SmartPLS may also directly assess reliability, discriminant, and convergent validity.

It delivers graphical outputs and a user interface that is attractive to the eye. Compared to other software packages, it has a more flexible manufacturing process.

## 12.4 Results

The conceptual model is subjected to two analyses using PLS-SEM software: first, the measurement model is assessed, and then the structural model is taken into account. The two following subsections go into considerable detail about the results and rationale for both acts.

### 12.4.1 Evaluation of Validity and Reliability

Evaluation of the reflected measurement models requires the conduct of validity and reliability tests for the constructs. Passing both tests is necessary for the structural model exam. By evaluating the values of all variables to those of their related signals with the legitimacy of the questionnaire problem, these evaluations attempt to determine the internal coherence of the data provided by those who responded. While Cronbach's alpha, especially composite reliability (CR) testing, was used to assess the IC or dependability, discriminate and convergent validity tests were utilized to determine the reliability.

To ascertain an item's internal coherence inside a construct, use CA. Both the item and factor reliability scores must be at least 0.60. Additionally, for the combination of reliability, which is used to verify the IC, values better than 0.8 are required. Due to matching CA values above 0.8 with compound reliability scores over 0.8, the results displayed in Table 12.1 indicate the dependability of all structures. The outcomes confirm the acceptability and reliability of the IC for each conception.

**Table 12.1** Results of validity and reliability tests.

| Construct | $R^2$ | CA | CR | AVE |
|-----------|-------|-------|-------|-------|
| DA | | 0.639 | 0.804 | 0.580 |
| BDAC | 0.168 | 0.743 | 0.837 | 0.564 |
| IC | 0.241 | 0.711 | 0.818 | 0.531 |
| SCA | 0.440 | 0.743 | 0.839 | 0.567 |

Figure 12.2 shows Cronbach's alpha. A scale or questionnaire's internal consistency or reliability is measured by the statistic known as CA. Lee Cronbach, an American psychologist, is credited with coming up with the concept. The range of the Cronbach's alpha coefficient (CAC) is 0 to 1. The alpha value is nearer to 1, the more internally consistent the scale's components are. When the alpha is more significant, the items on the scale are more closely related to one another, indicating that they are evaluating the same underlying notion. The CA (0.743) value will be bigger than CR and average variance extracted (AVE).

In Figure 12.3, CR measures the proportion of actual score variance to the construct's overall variation. By dividing the total squared loadings (factor loadings) of the items on the construct by the total squared loadings plus the total residual variances (measurement error) of the items, the coefficient of determination (CR) is determined. Equation 12.1 may be written as follows.

*CR = (Sum of square loadings) / (Sum of Squared loadings + sum of residual variances)*

$$(12.1)$$

In structural equation modeling (SEM), the AVE statistic is employed to evaluate the convergent validity of a construct or latent variable. It gauges how much variation is captured by a construct's items compared to how much variance results from measurement error in Figure 12.4. The average of the squared correlations between each item and the other items in the

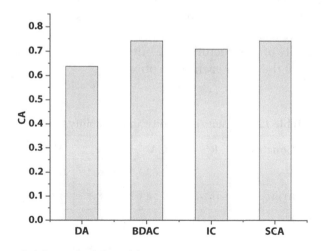

**Figure 12.2** Reliability and validity of the CA.

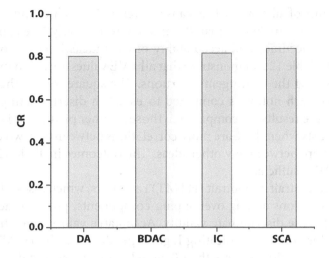

**Figure 12.3** Reliability and validity of the CR.

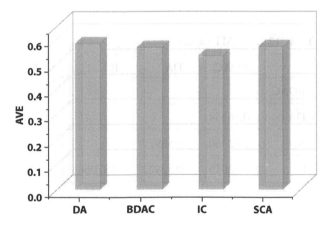

**Figure 12.4** Reliability and validity of the AVE.

same construct determines the AVE, which is then divided by the total variance of the things. Equation 12.2 may be written as follows:

$$AVE = (Sum\ of\ squared\ item - factor\ correlations)\ /\ (sum\ of\ item\ variances)$$

$$(12.2)$$

The composite reliability requires values greater than 0.7 to verify the internal consistency. The findings in Table 12.2 demonstrate the dependability of all constructs because matching CA values and combined reliability values are higher than 0.7 and 0.8, respectively. The conclusions attest to the accuracy and acceptability of each idea's internal coherence. The data in Table 12.3 demonstrate that all AVE values are much more than 0.6, supporting the convergent assertions. The square root of the average variance of each notion is computed to establish discriminating validity (DV), and the results are compared to those of other pictures. It is asserted that DV exists when there are more correlations between any two concepts than there are between any other ideas. The outcomes in Table 12.2 show that the DV is sufficient.

These heterotrait-monotrait (HTMT) ratio tests, which assess the intensity of distinctions among overlapping components, provided additional evidence for the discriminate validity. Acceptable values range from 0 to 1, with values under 1 indicating high dependability. The HTMT values for this investigation are less than 0.90, which supports the discriminate validity, as shown in Table 12.2.

**Table 12.2** HTMT values.

|       | BDAC    | DA      | IC      | SCA |
|-------|---------|---------|---------|-----|
| BDAC  |         |         |         |     |
| DA    | 0.56554 |         |         |     |
| IC    | 0.62260 | 0.48970 |         |     |
| SCA   | 0.53015 | 0.32422 | 0.87068 |     |

**Table 12.3** Examine the legitimacy of differences.

|   |      | 1    | 2    | 3    | 4    |
|---|------|------|------|------|------|
| 1 | BDAC | 0.75 |      |      |      |
| 2 | DA   | 0.41 | 0.76 |      |      |
| 3 | IC   | 0.49 | 0.33 | 0.73 |      |
| 4 | SCA  | 0.4  | 0.23 | 0.66 | 0.75 |

When the indication was most recently produced, the acceptable values for external loadings had to be less than 0.7 but greater than 0.4. Otherwise, they must be more than or equal to 0.7. To validate the significance of the outer loads in the model, the t-statistics must be checked with values more than 2.00. The signals are therefore significant, according to the findings of the exterior loading of the t-test.

## 12.4.2    Structural Model of Coefficient of Determination ($R^2$)

$R^2$ is a mathematical indicator with permissible values between 0 and 1 that shows how much variance in the exogenous constructions can be explained by the exogenous constructs. According to Table 12.2, where the $R^2$ value for SCA is 0.439, the BDAC and IC constructs account for 45.0% of the conflict in the SCA constructs. Table 12.4 demonstrates that the bootstrapping method also used PLS-SEM to calculate the t-value and assess the structural model.

Verifying the path coefficient values or the statistical significance of the relationships between the latent variables in the structural framework is crucial for assessing the offered hypothesis. The t-value, significance level, and the path's related standardized coefficients (B-value), which must be at or higher than 0.1 to be deemed significant, are calculated using the 0.05 threshold of importance.

DA considerably and positively impacts IC, while BDAC significantly influences IC but not SCA, according to the model fit findings in Table 12.4. SCA is significantly and favorably affected by IC. However, the findings imply that IC has the greatest influence on SCA. The findings in Table 12.4 are consistent with H1, H2, and H4. The theory that BDAC and SCA are connected, however, is unsupported by any data.

**Table 12.4** The model's fit outcomes.

|     | $t$-value | $B$-value | STDEV | $p$-value | $T$ statistics |
| --- | --- | --- | --- | --- | --- |
| H2  | 6.062 | 0.491 | 0.081 | 0 | 6.06 |
| H1  | 5.256 | 0.41 | 0.078 | 0 | 5.238 |
| H4  | 8.897 | 0.605 | 0.068 | 0 | 8.922 |
| H3  | 1.178 | 0.106 | 0.09 | 0.237 | 1.183 |

### 12.4.3   Discussion

This study looked into the relationship between a firm's SCA and dynamic skills like BDA and innovation. The results of the study suggest that BDAC has a major impact on IC and that IC improves SCA capabilities but not BDA. The study's findings add to the body of knowledge in this area by presenting a number of new viewpoints. This work is the first to assess the relationship between the DA level and BDAC as well as the contribution of BDAC and IC to the formation of SCA. Our findings show that an increase in DA level favors BDAC, and the results of the conceptual model are compatible with H1. Data availability will considerably rise when a company's system is connected to BDA, since all components are connected to the IoT and the backup mechanism is effective, boosting BDAC. However, IoT technology enablers must be used to assist the DA in industrial firms if the BDAC is to be enhanced. This paradigm can be used, and it works incredibly well when cutting-edge products with high levels of customization generate a lot of data. BD will not aid manufacturers in proportion to the amount of money invested in this industry, and conventional mass manufacturing processes do not require highly customized products. Thus, this approach could be more effective in these situations. The technique is also useless when organizations lack the IT infrastructure or agility to meet a broad range of market demands or all client expectations. The IC may not be impacted by the BD and BDAC in such circumstances; therefore, the SCA may not be improved. The same is true for businesses that operate in competitive markets. The study also examines network needs as a precondition for BDA when looking at DA concerns. Furthermore, by emphasizing emotional skills as crucial facilitators for SCA at the organizational level in the industrial sector, this research assists managers' decisions regarding allocating resources and making investments.

## 12.5   Conclusion

The findings support the hypothesis in the study's research questions that DA significantly affects BDAC, substantially improving the interaction with IC. However, BDAC plays a tiny part in raising a company's SCA. The findings also suggest that IC significantly influences the association between BDAC and SCA. Based on the outcomes of each hypothesis, a corporation could make a decision. Businesses must digitalize their manufacturing, operational, and corporate processes in order to expand the data that are accessible to BDA. In H1, DA significantly and favorably affects

BDAC. By incorporating goods, machinery, and other intelligent objects into the IoT network and feeding a stream of data to BDA, businesses may digitalize their production processes. In H3, it was demonstrated that BDAC, a dynamic capability, influenced enterprises' SCA in a favorable way. According to our analysis, BDAC has little impact on an organization's SCA. The dynamic capacity known as IC in H4 substantially and positively impacts an enterprise's SCA. This encourages individuals making decisions to invest money in technology that supports innovations. This study offers a helpful framework for addressing various difficulties, including how DA, BDAC, and IC support manufacturing businesses' SCA. Since the methodology of this study only permits generalizing findings to the service industry, there is still room for improvement. Given this, future research may employ a sector-based study design, concentrating on the industrial or service sectors. This strategy may target distinct qualities in each industry by incorporating more particular criteria in the research questions, producing more detailed findings and a more accurate sector differentiation analysis. To achieve sustainability in processes, this research provides significant theoretical and practical insights into these problems. The long-term competitive advantage of industrial enterprises may be strengthened using these insights. But future research could benefit from this study's constraints and flaws.

# References

1. Nilashi, M. et al., How can big data and predictive analytics impact the performance and competitive advantage of the food waste and recycling industry? Ann. Oper. Res., 1–42, 2023, doi:10.1007/s10479-023-05272-y.
2. Bag, S. et al., Big data analytics as an operational excellence approach to enhance sustainable supply chain performance. Resour. Conserv. Recycl., 153, 104559, 2020, doi:10.1016/j.resconrec.2019.104559.
3. Sazu, M.H., Does big data drive innovation in e-commerce: A global perspective? SEISENSE Bus. Rev., 2, 1, 55–66, 2022, doi:10.33215/sbr.v2i1.797.
4. Erevelles, S. et al., Big data consumer analytics and the transformation of marketing. J. Bus. Res., 69, 2, 897–904, 2016, doi:10.1016/j.jbusres.2015.07.001.
5. Le, T.M. and Liaw, S.Y., Effects of pros and cons of applying big data analytics to consumers' responses in an E-commerce context. Sustainability, 9, 5, 798, 2017, doi:10.3390/su9050798.
6. Alkhatib, A.W. and Valeri, M., Can intellectual capital promote a competitive advantage? Service innovation and big data analytics capabilities in a moderated mediation model. Eur. J. Innov. Manag., 2022, doi:10.1108/EJIM-04-2022-0186.

7. Zhang, Z. *et al.*, Big data capability and sustainable competitive advantage: The mediating role of ambidextrous innovation strategy. *Sustainability*, 14, 14, 8249, 2022, doi:10.3390/su14148249.

8. Li, L. *et al.*, Evaluating the impact of big data analytics usage on the decision-making quality of organizations. *Technol. Forecast. Soc. Change*, 175, 121355, 2022, doi: 10.1016/j.techfore.2021.121355.

9. Baqleh, L.A. and Alateeq, M.M., The impact of supply chain management practices on competitive advantage: The moderating role of big data analytics. *Int. J. Prof. Bus. Rev.*, 8, 3, e0679–e0679, 2023, doi:10.26668/businessreview/2023.v8i3.679.

10. Ren, S. *et al.*, A comprehensive review of big data analytics throughout product lifecycle to support sustainable smart manufacturing: A framework, challenges, and future research directions. *J. Cleaner Prod.*, 210, 1343–1365, 2019, doi:10.1016/j.jclepro.2018.11.025.

11. Nayak, B. *et al.*, Integrating wearable technology products and big data analytics in business strategy: A study of health insurance firms. *J. Syst. Inf. Technol.*, 21, 2, 255–275, 2019, doi:10.1108/JSIT-08-2018-0109.

12. Behl, A., Antecedents to firm performance and competitiveness using the lens of big data analytics: A cross-cultural study. *Manage. Decis.*, 60, 2, 368–398, 2022, doi:10.1108/MD-01-2020-0121.

13. Wamba, S.F. *et al.*, Big data analytics and firm performance: Effects of dynamic capabilities. *J. Bus. Res.*, 70, 356–365, 2017, doi:10.1016/j.jbusres.2016.08.009.

14. Madhani, P.M., Big data usage and big data analytics in supply chain: Leveraging competitive priorities for enhancing competitive advantages. *IUP J. Supply Chain Manag.*, 19, 2, 1–35, 2022.

15. Zhang, W. *et al.*, Research on the mechanism of the sustainable development model of enterprises based on big data analysis model. *Mob. Inf. Syst.*, 2021, 1–12, 2021, doi:10.1155/2021/4469255.

# 13

# Sustainability and Technological Innovation in Organizations: The Mediating Role of Green Practices

Rajyalakshmi K.[1*], Rajkumar G. V. S.[2], Sulochana B.[3], Rama Devi V. N.[4] and Padma A.[5]

[1]*Department of Computer Science and Engineering, Koneru Lakshmaiah Education Foundation, Vaddeswaram, Guntur, India*
[2]*Department of Computer Science and Engineering, GITAM Deemed to be University, Visakhapatnam, India*
[3]*Department of Humanities and Sciences, Chebrolu Hanumaiah Institute of Pharmaceutical Sciences, Chowadaram, Guntur, India*
[4]*Department of Mathematics, GRIET, Hyderabad, India*
[5]*Chaitanya Bharathi Institute of Technology, Hyderabad, India*

## Abstract

A few of an organization's goals are innovation, large profits, and continued survival. Even so, sustainability has evolved into a rigorous activity for both commercial and charity organizations, since it pushes businesses to greater effectiveness. Sustainability requires enough funds and expertise. The factors that impact sustainability were examined in previous studies, but innovation is rarely considered from this angle. The present study investigates the connection among organizational performance, technical innovation, and management creativity, with sustainability acting as a mediating element. We tested the model using structural equation modeling in the analysis of moment structures (AMOS) using actual information collected from 304 CEOs and top managers in various countries. The findings suggest that incorporating new management practices and technologies into an organization may greatly enhance its effectiveness and longevity. Sustainability acts as a mediator between management innovation and organizational performance and between organizational performance and technical

*Corresponding author*: rajyalakshmi.kottapalli@gmail.com

Kanak Kalita, Narayanan Ganesh and S. Balamurugan (eds.) Metaheuristics for Machine Learning: Algorithms and Applications, (267–284) © 2024 Scrivener Publishing LLC

innovation. To improve long-term viability and success, we urge CEOs and other senior managers to invest in management and technical innovation.

*Keywords:* Organizational performance, technology innovation, management innovation

## 13.1   Introduction

The connection among management and technical innovation may be significantly impacted by sustainability. The goal of sustainability is to provide for current needs without compromising future generations' ability to do the same. This implies that technology advancements and sustainable management techniques are created with consideration for the environment, social justice, and economic viability [1]. A mediating factor is a variable that accounts for the process by which one variable affects the other to explain the connection between the two other factors. A variable that aids in explaining how management and technological innovation impact organizational performance would be a mediating factor in the context of the interaction between management and technological innovation on organizational performance. The working population's expertise and ability capacity are one potential intermediary influence. To be embraced and utilized successfully, advances in technology often need novel abilities and knowledge [2]. The adoption and application of emerging technologies may thus be facilitated by management approaches that encourage learning and growth, which can boost organizational performance. The degree of interaction and collaboration inside the company is yet another possible mediating element. The discovery and implementation of novel innovations that may improve the efficiency of an organization can be facilitated through effective communication and cooperation across individuals, groups, and divisions [3].

The magnitude and uncertain environments limit technology innovation, companies now depend more on IT. Due to changes in the corporate environment, to attain and retain productivity, boost performance, and survive in today's challenging markets. The innovation-related activities that are technology-based and aimed at enhancing performance are driven by these developments. Numerous research surveys have shown that with the increasing adoption of ICT by enterprises across a number of industries, many firms fail to advance beyond the company phase of the life cycle [4]. In general, businesses may design strategies to improve the way they handle management and technology innovations for optimal organizational performance by recognizing intermediary elements in the interaction among management and technical innovation on organizational performance [5]. This research is one of the first to take into account such a complicated framework for investigating links among many diverse dimensions by assessing the suggested model and testing the relevant predictions. This connects acceptance, creation, and routinization of big data with developments in sustainability benefits in rivalry, economic and ecological results, management and other belonging points of view, business ethical conduct, consumer appetite for environmentally friendly products, and human capital businesses [6]. Despite the growing interest in information management and innovation, only a small number of studies, particularly those that looked at developing countries, have shown tangible proof connecting the use of knowledge management with firm-level innovation. For theoretical and strategic reasons, it is crucial to concentrate about the connection between innovation and knowledge management. First, it is significant because, as intangible assets like intellectuals capital, as well as expertise, have become increasingly accepted as being necessary to recognize, oversee, and improve to promote and improve company value, investigators have noted that there is a lack of scientific evidence that guides how these intangible resources can be managed [7]. In this research, we analyze and investigate the impact of sustainability as a mediating factor in the relationship between "management innovation (MI) and technological innovation (TI)" on organizational performance.

## 13.2   Related Work

The study [8] examined how knowledge management (KM) factors affect organizational sustainability. It compares the results of companies that have earned the ISO 9001 standard with those that have not. Data from 156 private sector employees in Iraq's Kurdistan Region was used in the study. Utilizing a partial least squares method, we evaluate the proposed model and investigate the variances among ISO 9001-certified and noncertified organizations. The findings demonstrate the importance of knowledge storage in the creation, exchange, and use of knowledge. Additionally, it has been shown that knowledge management significantly affects an organization's capacity to remain viable. The research [9] analyzed that entrepreneur innovativeness affects the relationship between technological innovation and company success in Kenya. The investigation made use of structural equation modeling (SEM) and a sample of 240 businesses. The results show that technological innovation has a favorable impact on business success. According to the survey, entrepreneurs should create cutting-edge plans to improve business performance. The impact of organizational innovation (OI) and technical innovation capabilities (TICs) on business performance is evaluated in this research.

The paper [10] determined that TICs mediated the effects of OI on firm performance using a sample of 265 manufacturing enterprises from the Pearl River Delta in China. Additionally, they looked at how OI affected the link between TICs and firm performance. The association between OI and company performance was shown to be partly mediated by TICs according to the findings of structural equation modeling investigations. Similar to the way TICs and business performance were correlated, OI somewhat mitigated this association. The study [11] examined the root causes and effects of open technology in small and medium-sized enterprises (SMEs). To evaluate the assumptions, we gathered multisource data from 404 SMEs and employed structural equation modeling. The study [12] suggested an approach to clarify the function that information creation plays as a connecting link between knowledge management enablers and organizational success. Cooperation, T-shaped skills, education, and technology support are all factors that might affect an organization. The research argues that the way decisions are made might attenuate the correlation between knowledge creation and business success. A collection of statements that represent an empirically driven research aim and also identify the relationships among the variables of interest is offered to aid the audience in comprehending within an organization context. To examine [13] the connection between an organization's culture, total quality management (TQM), and performance within the context of (SMEs) is mentioned. More specifically, it suggests a framework outlining potential connections between organizational culture, TQM measures, and achievement within the organization. Data from functionality representatives of Indian automotive module SMEs that are members of the Auto Component Manufacturer's Association of India were collected using a survey approach. Utilizing the path evaluation methods of modeling structural equations with AMOS, estimation of parameter data analysis, and the fit of goodness data have been utilized for evaluating the suggested conceptual framework. The study [14] used an approach built on data envelopment analysis (DEA), and it is applied to a group of SMEs in the nation's Eastern region. Financial, functional, environmental, and social factors are regarded as output criteria of the suggested framework, whereas agile and sustainable development-oriented inventions are viewed as input criteria. The DEA separates ineffective SMEs and proposes benchmarking at least one of them. The research then uses a qualitative approach to identify methods of enhancement for the underperforming SMEs. The survey [15] shows that eco-conscious proprietors who improve the efficiency of the firm are impacted by technological innovation. Effective businesses that go above and beyond their financial responsibilities to support sustainability projects and social well-being may generate much more money. Management innovation and employee participation in environmental protection efforts have the potential to boost both the financial health and the business's position among its constituents. The study [16] analyzed how corporate sustainability (CS) and total quality management (TQM) are structurally related, as well as whether TQM methods might help businesses accomplish CS goals. The research investigates how knowledge management provides an essential part in the link between TQM and CS and how KM mediates that relationship.

### 13.2.1 Hypothesis Development

Hypothesis (H1) Creativity among executives enhances organizational success.
Hypothesis (H2) The efficiency of organizations is enhanced by advances in technology.
Hypothesis (H3) Creativity in leadership enhances sustainability.
Hypothesis (H4) Advancement in technology enhances organizational sustainability.
Hypothesis (H5) Sustainability enhances the effectiveness of organizations.
Hypothesis (H6) The interaction of MI and organizational performance is mediated by sustainability.
Hypothesis (H7) The interaction of TI and organizational performance is mediated by sustainability.

## 13.3 Methodology

The study will use a quantitative approach by surveying a cross section of businesses. Random sampling will be used to choose the sample, and structural equation modeling will be used to evaluate the collected data. The survey will include questions designed to gauge administration, technological innovation, sustainability, and the efficiency of businesses. Items pertaining to their leadership, strategic planning, and decision-making abilities will be evaluated. Items that capture the extent to which a company invests in R&D, adopts new technology, and implements innovative procedures will be used to gauge technological innovation.

### 13.3.1   Sample and Population

Using the application of a standard survey, Companies with activity in various countries submitted empirical information for this research via the use of a conventional questionnaire. It is challenging to find information about management, innovation, and technical projects in different countries. Because most of the businesses fail to report every one of their expenditures in their annual mentions, there is a measurement problem. Additionally, stated (subjective) measures are advocated as offering more trustworthy statistics in developing countries like China, India, and Pakistan. Key cities in various countries were picked as targets since they are home to the majority of enterprises. We collected data from companies that engage in production, commerce, and services. The 700 randomly selected organizations that made up the distribution of the 700 surveys each received one survey. Directors were requested to answer the survey, since they have a better understanding of the plans and policies of their companies. The survey explicitly said the information was not going to be published publicly and was only going to be utilized for research. In this study, 304 valid responses or a response rate of 43.43% were received. A sample size of at least 300 is necessary in the cited cities to produce valid results. Table 13.1 lists the different types of firms that participated in the study.

### 13.3.2   Techniques

One variable that is dependent, organization performance and sustainability, was employed as a mediating variable in this study along with two separate independent variables, MI and TI. Today's most common products are unquestionably available in a range of sizes and the six elements are used it is divided into three groups: management processes (items 1 and 2), management procedures (items 3 and 4), and structure (items 5 and 6).

Technology innovation also lacks a general description or set of measures. We utilized the nine elements, one of the nine being "We use the most recent innovations for fresh product advancement" to handle the numerous aspects. "Our competitors believe us to be a pioneer in the area of sustainability" is one of the five statements from their prior survey that we used as a case item for assessing sustainability.

The success of a company is frequently measured using metrics like "return on assets (ROA)," "return on equity (ROE)," "return on investment (ROI)," and sales growth. This survey frequently uses accounting records in

**Table 13.1** Description of the companies.

| Variables | % | Period |
|---|---|---|
| **Organizations' mean years** | | |
| 21 and above years | 36.5 | 111 |
| 10 years and less | 28.3 | 86 |
| 11–20 years | 35.2 | 107 |
| **Education of CEOs/ managers** | | |
| Master | 41.8 | 127 |
| Intermediate and below | 22.7 | 69 |
| Bachelor | 28.0 | 85 |
| PhD etc. | 7.6 | 23 |
| **Nature of industry** | | |
| Trading | 32.89 | 100 |
| Total | 100.0 | 304 |
| Manufacturing | 34.21 | 104 |
| Services | 32.89 | 100 |

the evaluation of the efficiency of businesses. In this study, organizational performance was evaluated using the exact method (self-reported) as was used to evaluate the other components of organizational performance. On the basis of indicators like ROA, ROE, and ROI, CEOs and other top executives were asked to assess the performance of the company.

### 13.3.3  Control

We adjusted for the educational backgrounds of executives and managers as well as the age of the businesses to reduce erroneous findings. These variables have a big impact on performance. According to the structural model, there is a considerable relationship between CEOs' and managers' educational backgrounds and the success of organizations.

### 13.3.4 Data Analysis

To determine averages, standard deviation (SD), and information normality, we used descriptive statistical methods. The findings indicate that MI has the lowest mean value, and organization performance has the greatest average level. Given that all of the variables' skewness and kurtosis values are within the suggested ranges, our results appear fair ±2 ranges per George and Mallery. The results are represented in Table 13.2.

### 13.3.5 Verifying Factor Evaluation

To verify the accuracy and dependability of the variables utilized, confirmatory factor analysis (CFA) was carried out. First, we evaluated an estimation method (Figure 13.1) that took into account every factor. The average value of chi sq./df is 2.135, which is less than 3 as required. We discovered an appropriate model fit. In accordance with other examinations of alternative models that fit: Software tools: GFI, AGFI, CFI, TLI, and NFI provided satisfactory results. These values indicate that the model is valid: chi sq./df = 2.235; GFI = 0.87; AGFI = 0.84; CFI = 0.94; TLI = 0.89; NFI = 0.89; root mean squared error (RMR) = 0.015; root mean squared error of approximation (RMSEA) = 0.061. Similarly, RMR and RMSEA also provided appropriate values demonstrating a satisfactory model fit. On each of their respective constructs, all of the variables were substantially weighted (p = 0.01) (Table 13.3).

We examined the average variance extracted (AVE), also known as convergent validity. To achieve adequate validity for convergence, AVE value should be greater than 0.50. The reality that all of the variables have respectable values (e.g., larger than 0.5) confirms that the variables account for a substantial amount of variation in the pertinent components. We also assessed discriminant validity to see whether the items

**Table 13.2** Presentation of illustrative information.

| Parameters | Threshold | Peak performance | Average | SD | Skewness | Kurtosis |
|---|---|---|---|---|---|---|
| Organization performance | 1.24 | 4.95 | 3.7062 | 0.45160 | −1.105 | 1.100 |
| Management innovation | 1.44 | 4.4 | 3.2684 | 0.39568 | −0.376 | 1.737 |
| Technology innovation | 1.38 | 5.05 | 3.6157 | 0.44017 | -0.427 | 1.507 |
| Sustainability | 1.41 | 4.56 | 3.3183 | 0.40734 | -0.174 | 1.684 |

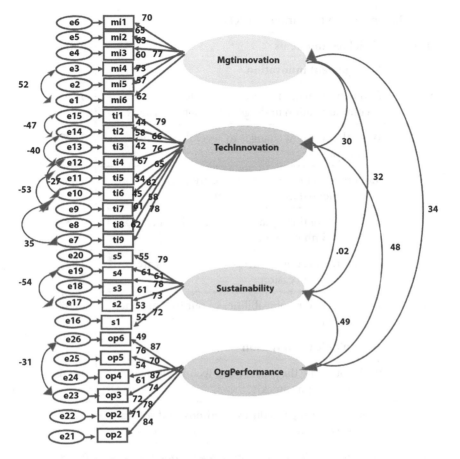

**Figure 13.1** Method of measuring model.

were not overlapping and explained distinct variances in the specific constructs. The value obtained from (Table 13.4) provide the satisfactory and valid results.

To determine if the things are trustworthy and in line with one another, we also examined compound reliability. All of the elements' averages exceeded the cutoff value of 0.70, which was supported by the findings.

### 13.3.6    Standard Technique Bias

The standard technique bias (STB) was examined using SPSS and the Harman one-factor test. Four of the components we discovered had eigenvalues higher than 1. Additionally, the first component only described 33.97% of the variance, which was under 50%. As a result, it was shown

**Table 13.3** Impact on the various aspects.

| Sl. no. | Variables and items | Estimate |
|---------|---------------------|----------|
| | **Management innovation** | |
| mi5 | Company system of internal and external communication undergoes frequent revisions. | 0.863 |
| mi6 | We make constant changes to several systemic components. | 0.847 |
| mi3 | Modern systems for governance are often implemented in our company. | 0.805 |
| mi4 | In the span of three years, there have been changes to the reimbursement policy. | 0.757 |
| mi1 | In our organization, policies and processes are updated on occasion. | 0.847 |
| mi2 | The duties and responsibilities of our staff are often modified. | 0.807 |
| | **Technological innovation** | |
| ti8 | We incorporate the most recent technology breakthroughs quickly. | 0.648 |
| ti9 | In our business, procedures, methods, and software evolve quickly. | 0.874 |
| ti3 | The rate at which novel items are developed is sufficiently rapid and viable. | 0.768 |
| ti4 | There are plenty fresh items on sales right now. | 0.645 |
| ti5 | We are currently marketing items that are initial business adopters. | 0.854 |
| ti1 | We have the capacity to generate goods having unique characteristics. | 0.772 |
| ti2 | When creating new products, we use the most recent technologies. | 0.674 |
| | **Sustainability** | |
| s2 | Our competition observes us as a top business in the environment sector. | 0.737 |

(Continued)

**Table 13.3** Impact on the various aspects. (*Continued*)

| Sl. no. | Variables and items | Estimate |
|---|---|---|
| s5 | We provide social and moral requirements a more detailed response than our rivals. | 0.784 |
| s3 | We create novel products and facilities or enhance already existing ones that are thought to be beneficial for the environment and for community. | 0.772 |
| s4 | Our track record for durability is superior than that of other companies in this area. | 0.824 |
| s1 | We are the initial business in the sector to provide goods and services that are ecologically conscious. | 0.731 |
| | **Organization performance** | |
| op1 | Profit from properties | 0.835 |
| op5 | Trade percentage | 0.746 |
| op6 | Ultimately profitable | 0.854 |
| op2 | Income from stocks | 0.789 |
| op3 | Profit from capital | 0.726 |
| op4 | Revenues rise | 0.858 |

that typical bias in methods is not a concern. Additionally, we examined the impact of a usual implicit section of the measurement structure and found that the STB in no way put our investigation's conclusions at risk.

## 13.3.7   Correlation

The findings of the Pearson correlation in SPSS are shown in Table 13.4. Both the association among MI and organizational performance and the relationship between MI and sustainability were determined to be significant. TI is substantially connected to sustainability and organization performance. It is a significant connection between sustainability and organizational effectiveness. None of the correlation coefficients above 0.80 indicated the lack of multicollinearity.

**Table 13.4** Credibility, dependability, and relevance.

| Factors | AVE | CR | I | II | III | IV | V | VI |
|---|---|---|---|---|---|---|---|---|
| Qualification | - | - | 1 | | | | | |
| Years | - | - | 0.074 | 1 | | | | |
| Org. performance | 0.64 | 0.91 | 0.202 ** | 0.440 ** | 0.366 ** | 0.514 ** | 0.525 ** | 0.86 |
| Sustainability | 0.58 | 0.88 | 0.047 | 0.192 ** | 0.346 ** | 0.460 ** | 0.76 | |
| Management innovation | 0.64 | 0.92 | 0.071 | 0.110 | 0.80 | | | |
| Technology innovation | 0.50 | 0.89 | 0.112 | 0.219 ** | 0.325 ** | 0.70 | | |

## 13.3.8   Robustness Checks

We carried out the processes in SPSS to test the robustness. First, we looked at how MI and TI affected sustainability, and we discovered that both had a positive impact. The results confirmed those of AMOS. We looked at how MI and TI affected company efficiency and found that there was a critical direct influence.

Additionally, the connections between TI and company efficiency as well as between MI and organizational efficiency were shown to be strengthened when viability served as an intermediary. As a result, we contend that there was no apparent distinction between the results of SPSS and AMOS.

## 13.3.9   Interaction Analysis

To verify that the relationship between sustainability in MI and TI is represented, we added an extra model. The regression techniques are showing the immediate indications and significant interaction affects for both MI and TI, indicating that the signs linked to these values propose the exact direction that MI and TI are likely to affect organizational performance.

In the same way, TI also altered throughout the sustainability interaction period, going from 0.255 to -0.831. Sustainability was important as a mediator. Sustainability's relationship term with MI produced a poor outcome, while it produced a good result with TI. The substantial values of both interaction terms demonstrated that sustainability had an impact on and had the power to alter efficiency. The scale and methods used to quantify the components meant that the change was not ensured.

**Table 13.5** Inferential statistics.

| | Unreliable parameters | | Standard parameters | | |
|---|---|---|---|---|---|
| Model | Standard Error | B | Beta | T | Sig. |
| (Constant) | 0.206 | 1.281 | | 6.221 | 0 |
| Tech. innovation | 0.049 | 0.359 | 0.388 | 7.377 | 0 |
| Mgt. innovation | 0.054 | 0.226 | 0.220 | 4.171 | 0 |

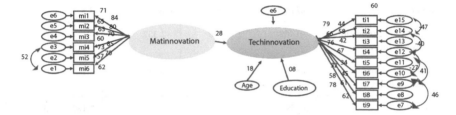

**Figure 13.2** Model of structure.

Although a formal hypothesis was not put out to test whether MI causes TI, MI may cause TI. A structural model is used to determine if the case for better TI as a result of MI efforts should be made. The findings in Table 13.5 showed that MI strongly contributed to TI. Therefore, we contend that there is a good likelihood that MI will integrate TI into enterprises. Figure 13.2 shows the model of structure. The evaluation of interactions is shown in Table 13.6.

## 13.4  Discussion

In this study, the impact of TI and MI on organizational effectiveness was investigated. The goal of this study is to put the model to the test using data in a developing country. We provide evidence that sustainability considerably enhances financial performance in the developing economies. Opposing views put out by Yu and Zhao [17] may be adequately addressed by our study, which concludes that sustainability and financial success are significantly positively correlated. Our results are also very supportive of the resource-based view of the firm (RBV) theory, demonstrates how a company with special and beneficial assets and abilities may create

**Table 13.6** Evaluation of interactions.

| Coefficients | | | | | |
|---|---|---|---|---|---|
| | Unreliable parameters | | Standard parameters | | |
| Model | B | Std. Error | Beta | t | Sign |
| Years | 0.165 | 0.027 | 0.298 | 7.217 | 0 |
| Qualification | 0.047 | 0.095 | 0.137 | 2.988 | 0.004 |
| Management innovation | 1.778 | 0.375 | 1.525 | 5.248 | 0.000 |
| Technological innovation | −0.828 | 0.224 | -0.856 | -3.157 | 0.002 |
| Sustainability | 0.718 | 0.208 | 0.647 | 3.538 | 0 |
| Management innovation × Sustainability | −0.489 | 0.100 | −2.357 | −4.864 | 0 |
| Technological innovation × Sustainability | 0.377 | 0.028 | 1.859 | 4.125 | 0 |
| Years | 0.159 | 0.089 | 0.328 | 7.185 | 0 |
| Qualification | 0.047 | 0.059 | 0.157 | 3.056 | 0.058 |
| Management innovation | 0.157 | 0.089 | 0.157 | 3.089 | 0.002 |
| Technological innovation | 0.257 | 0.056 | 0.277 | 5.256 | 0 |
| Sustainability | 0.324 | 0.052 | 0.297 | 6.210 | 0 |
| (Persistent) | −0.689 | 0.625 | | −0.959 | 0.387 |
| Years | 0.158 | 0.056 | 0.357 | 7.368 | 0 |
| Qualification | 0.057 | 0.026 | 0.147 | 2.756 | 0.007 |
| Management innovation | 0.247 | 0.089 | 0.203 | 4.347 | 0 |
| Technological innovation | 0.347 | 0.04 | 0.362 | 7.671 | 0 |
| (Persistent) | 0.715 | 0.199 | | 3.589 | 0 |
| (Persistent) | 3.024 | 0.083 | | 36.628 | 0 |
| Years | 0.236 | 0.028 | 0.427 | 8.386 | 0 |
| Qualification | 0.083 | 0.025 | 0.171 | 3.350 | 0.001 |
| (Persistent) | 1.127 | 0.199 | | 5.658 | 0 |

an edge in order for competing better in a market. There is much to be done to more completely conceive and then experimentally analyze this field in order to discover the distinctive effect of each invention. For the same reason, we only employed six dimensions to assess organizational success. Future research should take into account other factors to further explain the findings. In order to thrive over the long term, business organizations, particularly those operating in volatile markets, require creative strategies. Countries like India, Pakistan has many characteristics with other nations; therefore, the consequences apply equally to developing and mature economies.

## 13.5   Conclusions

This study offers a clear image of opposing hypotheses about the connection between sustainability and financial success, as well as the RBV hypothesis. Because of the inconsistent findings of other research, this study aims to assess the impact of management innovation and technology innovation on the efficiency of companies with an intermediary function for sustainability. To assess our strategy, we used a model made up of structural equations in AMOS and SPSS to analyze information gathered from 304 executives and other senior executives. Our investigation revealed that TI is more crucial than MI for the viability and success of businesses in developing countries' emerging economies. Firm leadership should pay close attention to how MI is configured across divisions, since doing so significantly improves performance and longevity. Companies would do well to focus on MI and TI rather than relying on just one, as they are the primary markers of long-term viability and financial success. In conclusion, we advocate for CEOs and executives to give MI and TI implementation the time and care it needs in order to succeed in the long run.

## References

1. Cheng, Y. *et al.*, How do technological innovation and fiscal decentralization affect the environment? A story of the fourth industrial revolution and sustainable growth. *Technol. Forecast. Soc. Change*, 162, 120398, 2021, doi: 10.1016/j.techfore.2020.120398.
2. Pan, X. *et al.*, Dynamic relationship among environmental regulation, technological innovation and energy efficiency based on large scale provincial

panel data in China. *Technol. Forecast. Soc. Change*, 144, 428–435, 2019, doi: 10.1016/j.techfore.2017.12.012.

3. Garousi Mokhtarzadeh, N. *et al.*, Investigating the impact of networking capability on firm innovation performance: Using the resource-action performance framework. *J. Intellect. Cap.*, 21, 6, 1009–1034, 2020, doi: 10.1108/JIC-01-2020-0005.

4. Teece, D.J., A capability theory of the firm: An economics and (strategic) management perspective. *N. Z. Econ. Pap.*, 53, 1, 1–43, 2019, doi: 10.1080/00779954.2017.1371208.

5. Parida, V. *et al.*, Reviewing literature on digitalization, business model innovation, and sustainable industry: Past achievements and future promises. *Sustainability*, 11, 2, 391, 2019, doi: 10.3390/su11020391.

6. El-Kassar, A.N. and Singh, S.K., Green innovation and organizational performance: The influence of big data and the moderating role of management commitment and HR practices. *Technol. Forecast. Soc. Change*, 144, 483–498, 2019, doi: 10.1016/j.techfore.2017.12.016.

7. Ode, E. and Ayavoo, R., The mediating role of knowledge application in the relationship between knowledge management practices and firm innovation. *J. Innov. Knowl.*, 5, 3, 210–218, 2020, doi: 10.1016/j.jik.2019.08.002.

8. Demir, A. *et al.*, Links between knowledge management and organizational sustainability: Does the ISO 9001 certification have an effect? ISO 9001. *Knowl. Manage. Res. Pract.*, 21, 1, 183–196, 2023, doi: 10.1080/14778238.2020.1860663.

9. Chege, S.M. *et al.*, Impact of information technology innovation on firm performance in Kenya. *Inf. Technol. Dev.*, 26, 2, 316–345, 2020, doi: 10.1080/02681102.2019.1573717.

10. Chen, Q. *et al.*, Effects of organizational innovation and technological innovation capabilities on firm performance: Evidence from firms in China's Pearl River Delta. *Asia Pac. Bus. Rev.*, 26, 1, 72–96, 2020, doi: 10.1080/13602381.2019.1592339.

11. Singh, S.K. *et al.*, Top management knowledge value, knowledge sharing practices, open innovation and organizational performance. *J. Bus. Res.*, 128, 788–798, 2021, doi: 10.1016/j.jbusres.2019.04.040.

12. Abubakar, A.M. *et al.*, Knowledge management, decision-making style and organizational performance. *J. Innov. Knowl.*, 4, 2, 104–114, 2019, doi: 10.1016/j.jik.2017.07.003.

13. Sinha, N. and Dhall, N., Mediating effect of TQM on relationship between organisational culture and performance: Evidence from Indian SMEs. *Total Qual. Manage. Bus. Excell.*, 31, 15-16, 1841–1865, 2020, doi: 10.1080/14783363.2018.1511372.

14. De, D. *et al.*, Impact of lean and sustainability oriented innovation on sustainability performance of small and medium sized enterprises: A data envelopment analysis-based framework. *Int. J. Prod. Econ.*, 219, 416–430, 2020, doi: 10.1016/j.ijpe.2018.07.003.

15. Chege, S.M. and Wang, D., The influence of technology innovation on SME performance through environmental sustainability practices in Kenya. *Technol. Soc.*, 60, 101210, 2020, doi: 10.1016/j.techsoc.2019.101210.
16. Abbas, J., Impact of total quality management on corporate sustainability through the mediating effect of knowledge management. *J. Cleaner Prod.*, 244, 118806, 2020, doi: 10.1016/j.jclepro.2019.118806.
17. Yu, M. and Zhao, R., Sustainability and firm valuation: An international investigation. *Int. J. Account. Inf. Manage.*, 23, 289–307, 2015, https://doi.org/10.1108/IJAIM-07-2014-0050.

# 14

# Optimal Cell Planning in Two Tier Heterogeneous Network through Meta-Heuristic Algorithms

Sanjoy Debnath[1]*, Amit Baran Dey[2] and Wasim Arif[2]

*Department of ECE, VelTech Rangarajan Dr. Sagunthala R&D Institute of Science and Technology, Tamil Nadu, India*
*Department of ECE, National Institute of Technology Silchar, Assam, India*

## Abstract

This work comprises optimal cell planning of a two-tier heterogeneous network that consists of macro and small cells with mobile and machine type user in emergency. The optimum cell planning is a promising work to be solved for efficient resource allocation of a wireless network. Cell planning deals with the optimum placement of cells while maximizing the overall network utility. Here, the development of utility function comprises intercell interference and user throughput satisfaction. This work deals with the maximization of network utility of a two-tier heterogeneous network under the constraints of minimum power consumption, user coverage, and satisfaction fulfillment. The user satisfaction could be thought of as user association with the optimal cell while fulfilling the demanded data rate. The effectiveness of the developed model is analyzed through optimal allocation of resources among emergency and normal users, while maximizing network utility.

*Keywords*: Heterogeneous network, network slicing, cell planning, resource allocation, user association

## 14.1 Introduction

Heterogeneous network (HetNet) is a phrase that relates to the use of numerous devices and techniques in a wireless connection. In order to give

*Corresponding author*: drsanjoydebnath@veltech.edu.in

Kanak Kalita, Narayanan Ganesh and S. Balamurugan (eds.) Metaheuristics for Machine Learning: Algorithms and Applications, (285–300) © 2024 Scrivener Publishing LLC

network coverage in an area with a broad variety of cellular service zones, such as an open outdoors environment, office buildings, dwellings, and subterranean places, a Wide Area Network can employ a combination of macrocells, picocells, and femtocells. A HetNet is a service that connects complicated interoperation between macrocell, small cell, and, in some circumstances, Wi-Fi network parts to produce a mosaic of coverage, with handoff capabilities across network elements. The ARCchart. analysis predicts that HetNets would help propel the worldwide mobile infrastructure market to roughly US\$57 billion in spending by 2017 [3]. Wireless connection is being used extensively in networks. Whether it is mobile communications, fixed telephony via WLL, or wireless personal communication, the possibilities are endless. The accessible spectrum is limited, making it a valuable resource. It must be utilized with caution in order to achieve the network operator's goals. The key principles for cell planning in mobile networks, particularly the LTE network, are discussed here.

In HetNet, a femtocell is considered as a low-power small cell that is often used in a home or small company. Small cell is a broader term used in the corporate world, with femtocell being a subset. Current designs often allow 4–8 constantly operational mobile phones in a home environment, depending solely on version number and femtocell hardware, and 8–16 concurrently active mobile phones in corporate settings, again depending solely on version number and femtocell hardware. A femtocell aids the service provider in increasing access within or even at the cell edge, particularly in areas where connection would otherwise be usually absent. Although WCDMA has gotten a lot of press, the concept is applicable to each and every protocol, notably GSM, CDMA2000, TD-SCDMA, and WiMAX.

Cell planning in a wireless communication network is considered as one of the challenging problems, which has to consider for each and every type of network design. In [1], the Gazzai et al., discussed the LTE cell planning problem and solved the same with the metaheuristic particle swarm optimization techniques. It was observed that the optimal deployment of cells mostly depends on the user distribution in a particular geographical area and their demanded data rate. Optimal cell planning in a multi-RAT network is discussed in [2], where Debnath et al., proposed an energy-efficient scheme to find the optimal resource allocation in a multi-RAT network under the constraint of user allocation and fulfillment of demanded data rate. To meet the increasing user demand in the cellular network, multi-RAT HetNet is one of the solutions. To improve the energy efficiency of the network, a multi-objective framework for the resource allocation in HetNet is analyzed through Pareto optimal solution [3].

On the other hand, spectrum sharing is an important feature for utilizing the wireless resource effectively [4]. In [4], Ye *et al.*, analyzed the schemes of optimal allocation of resource slices in the base station (BS) for quality-of-service (QoS) improvement. As optimum cell planning also offers effective resource allocation in wireless communication, thus the concept of resource slicing is merged with optimization for effective allocation of resources [5]. It was observed that network slicing scheme maximizes the overall bandwidth resource utilization.

Providing the best algorithm for solving strategy policy, upper subchannel allocation, uplink maximum transmission allocation, and computational resource scheduling, Melendex *et al.*, in 2017 used a technique called joint computation offloading and resource allocation optimization. The advantages in this scheme is lower complexity, time saving, and reduction of energy consumption [6]. However, the computational time and accuracy both are equally important in optimization, one of the ways are to offload the computation and maximize the overall efficiency of the network management [6]. In [7], Wang *et al.*, discuss on the computation offloading and intercell interference minimization while managing effective resource allocation. Whereas minimization of energy consumption in offloading is also a part of concern in wireless communication [8]. Thus, considering task offloading, the resource allocation and spectrum efficiency improvement work is discussed in [9].

It is also observed that the NOMA-based HetNet could also be considered for the maximization of spectrum efficiency and resource allocation [10]. As both spectrum efficiency and resource allocation are important for optimal network utility, we utilize a metaheuristic algorithm for energy-efficient spectrum allocation to serve emergency users. For a guaranteed QoS, the strategy of NOMA is highly important to minimize the energy consumption of all users. Thus, the application of a heuristic algorithm in NOMA-based HetNet for the maximization of overall network utility will provide balanced energy and spectrum efficiency. The advantage of NOMA includes optimal power distribution, QoS-oriented user fairness, suitable user pairing, and good link adaptations. To achieve the desired throughput in 5G communication techniques, NOMA is one of the desirable techniques that meet both energy and spectrum efficiency [11]. NOMA is basically of two types, namely, power domain and code domain. Scheduling and performing the power description adaptation in the downlink, power domain NOMA is a suitable technique. In [12], Liu *et al.*, discussed and analyzed the power domain NOMA in respect of user throughput and power allocation strategy. It was observed that the proposed joint transmission-based NOMA model offers improved user coverage and throughput [12].

For the maximization of the network utility that consists of both spectrum efficiency and energy efficiency, metaheuristic algorithms are getting high importance. For finding the near-optimal solutions because of the non-convexities, a technique called mixed-integer nonlinear programs can also be utilized, but these techniques have some complexities [13]. The particle swarm optimization (PSO) with less complexity and high exploration capability of the search space is well suited to find the optimal solution in the complex communication problems [14]. Due to simplicity and ease of implementation, the PSO and its supplementary algorithms like the gravitational search algorithm (GSA), grey wolf algorithm (GWO), and whale optimization algorithm (WOA) are very popular among the researcher [14]. Afterward, to improve the balancing between the exploration and exploitation rate, a hybrid version of the algorithms is suggested [15]. To get the solution of the complex problem accurately and effectively, a hybrid version of the algorithms is preferred [16].

The application of hybrid meta-heuristic algorithm to maximize the energy efficiency is found effective and promising in wireless communication. Towards that a hybridize algorithm based on PSO and GSA is proposed for the maximization of energy efficiency in a cognitive radio network is proposed in [17]. A computational efficient hybrid differential evolution with learning (HDEL) is used for utility maximization in un-manned aerial vehicle network [16]. Still the problem of network planning for emergency user coverage and network utility maximization is not addressed in the literature. Thus, we are motivated to perform this work to solve the said problem with the highly computational efficient DADE algorithm.

The rest of the paper is arranged as follows. Section 14.2 of this paper includes proposed methodology, section 14.3 presents results and discussion, followed by section 14.4 that draws the conclusion of the paper.

## 14.2  System Model and Formulation of the Problem

As shown in the Figure 14.1, consider a NOMA-assisted two-tier HetNet comprises one macro base station (MBS) and $K$ number of SBS. Assume that all SBSs are NOMA assisted and connected to one another through a fusion center (FC). The task of the FC is to accumulate the channel state information and allocate the resource accordingly. Consider that there are $M$ numbers of NUs and $F$ numbers of EUs randomly distributed over the coverage region of the MBS. It is also assumed that for $w$ allocated bandwidth, $S$ numbers of channels are allocated.

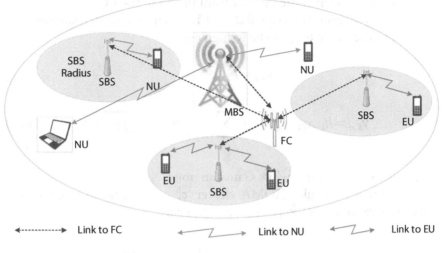

**Figure 14.1** System model.

The index sets of all of the assumed parameters are denoted as follows for the SBS: $k = \{k \,\|\, 1 \leq k \leq K\}$, for NU: $M = \{m \,|\, 1 \leq m \leq M\}$, for EU: $F = \{f \,|\, 1 \leq f \leq F\}$, and for S: $S = \{s \,|\, 1 \leq s \leq S\}$. At any particular instant of time, the possibility of one channel is free or idle is as follows:

$$p(s) = \frac{e\left(T_s^I\right)}{e\left(T_s^I\right) + e\left(T_s^B\right)} \qquad (14.1)$$

where $e\left(T_s^I\right)$ is the average idle time and $e\left(T_s^B\right)$ is the busy time of s$^{th}$ channel.

The number of channels assigned to SC may not be sufficient for allocating to all the EU of the SC zone. Assume that F number of EU multiplexed over an idle block of spectrum, and the EUs multiplexed over the same channel form a NOMA cluster. Considered that the set of NOMA cluster under $k^{th}$ SC is $C_k$. Thus for total N number of NOMA clusters $1 < n < N$, one cluster could be represented as $C_k^n$.

One EU tries to communicate to the SBS, and the interchange modulated symbol $x_{k,i}$ between the $k^{th}$ SBS and $i^{th}$ EU can be represented as follows:

$$x_{k,n} = \sum_{i \in C_k^n} x_{k,i} \sqrt{P_{k,i}} \qquad (14.2)$$

where $P_{k,i}$ is the transmitted power from the BS to the EU.

The received modulated signal at the EU, when the channel gain between the BS and the EU is $h_{k,i}$, can be written as:

$$y_{k,i} = h_{k,i} x_{k,n} + z_0 \tag{14.3}$$

$$y_{k,n} = h_{k,i} x_{(k,n)} \sqrt{P_{k,i}} + \sum_{i \neq j \in C_k^n} h_{k,i} x_{k,j} \sqrt{P_{k,j}} + N_0 \tag{14.4}$$

where $N_0$ is the additive white Gaussian noise.

Thus, for a particular NOMA cluster $c_k^n$, the signal-to-interference-plus-noise ratio (SINR) $\gamma_{k,i}$ can be computed as:

$$\gamma_{k,i} = \frac{P_{k,i} \left| H_{k,i} \right|^2}{\omega_k^n + I_k} \tag{14.5}$$

where $\left| H_{k,i} \right|^2$ is the normalized channel response of the $i^{th}$ EU. $I_k$ is the interference received from the other EUs from the same NOMA cluster and can be represented as:

$$I_{k,i} = \sum_{j \neq i \; j \in C_k^n} \left| H_{k,i} \right|^2 P_{k,j} \tag{14.6}$$

Selection parameter $\alpha_{n,k}$ for one EU to choose a particular SBS and NOMA cluster is represented as:

$$\alpha_{k,i}^n = \begin{cases} 1, & i \in C_k^n \\ 0, & ortherwise \end{cases} \tag{14.7}$$

Based on that, the throughput of $i^{th}$ EU of cluster $c_k^n$ can be computed as:

$$R_{k,i} = \alpha_{k,i}^n \omega_k^n \log_2 \left( 1 + \bar{\gamma}_{k,i} \right) \tag{14.8}$$

where $\bar{\gamma}_{k,i}$ can be represented as:

$$\bar{\gamma}_{k,i} = \frac{\left(p_{k,i} * |H_{k,i}|^2\right)}{\omega_k^n + \sum_{\substack{j=1 \\ j<i}}^{i-1} \alpha_k^n * p_{k,j} * |H_{k,i}|^2} \tag{14.9}$$

Now, based on the Shannon capacity formula, the network utility for the SB network can be written as:

$$R_t = \sum_{k=1}^{K} \sum_{n=1}^{N} \sum_{i=1}^{F_k} \alpha_{k,i}^n \omega_k^n \log_2\left(1 + \bar{\gamma}_{k,i}\right) \tag{14.10}$$

$$R_t = \sum_{k=1}^{K} \sum_{n=1}^{N} \sum_{i=1}^{F_k} R_{k,i} \tag{14.11}$$

Accordingly, the optimization problem for resource allocation can be formulated as:

$$\max_{\alpha_k^n, \omega_k^n, p_{k,i}} \sum_{k \in K} \sum_{C_k^n \in C_k} \sum_{i \in C} R_{k,i} \tag{14.12}$$

S.t.

$$C1 : \alpha_{k,i}^n \in \{0,1\}, \quad \forall k,i,n, \tag{14.13}$$

$$C2 : \sum_{k=1}^{K} \sum_{n=1}^{N} \omega_k^n \leq S, \tag{14.14}$$

$$C3 : 1 \leq \omega_k^n \leq S, \quad \forall k,n \tag{14.15}$$

$$C4 : \sum_{n=1}^{N} \alpha_{k,i}^n \leq 1, \quad \forall k,i \tag{14.16}$$

$$C5{:}\bigcup_{n=1}^{N} C_k^n \subseteq \mathcal{F}, \quad \bigcap_{n=1}^{N} C_k^n = \phi, \quad \forall k, \qquad (14.17)$$

$$C6 : \left| C_k^n \right| \leq F_c, \quad \forall k,n, \qquad (14.18)$$

$$C7 : 0 \leq \sum_{n=1}^{N} \sum_{i=1}^{F_c} \alpha_{k,i}^n p_{k,i} \leq p_k, \quad \forall k, \qquad (14.19)$$

$$C8 : \sum_{n=1}^{N} \alpha_{k,i}^n R_{k,i} \geq R_{k,i}^{min}, \quad \forall k,i \qquad (14.20)$$

*Description of the constraint:*

Equation 14.13 represents the limitation of the selection parameter $\alpha_{n,k}$.

Equations 14.14 and 14.15 discuss the bandwidth constraint, where it says that the total number of channels should be greater than the idle channel.

Equations 14.16 and 14.17 deal with the clustering constraint, where one EU can associate with only one NOMA cluster in one SBS. Equation 14.17 describes that the entire set of $C_k$ NOMA clusters is a subset of $F$.

Constraint 6 (Equation 14.18) deals with the successive interference cancellation (SIC) implementation complexity.

Equation 14.19 states that the power allocated to all of the EUs is less than the total budget of the power $p_k$.

Lastly Equation 14.20 provides a guarantee that one EU acquires minimum data rate.

Consider a large geographical area where we can deploy n number of base stations in order to distribute data among the users. So here, we have to ensure to check all of the parameters before we deploy them into the geographical area. We can say that parameters are nothing but the macro base stations, small base stations, primary users, and emergency users. So, we need to check where we have to deploy all of these parameters in the large geographical area. We can randomly insert the user position as our wish. Now, we should take a random value as an iteration count. It denotes the number of iterations taken to complete the process. Figure 14.2 shows the flowchart of the proposed model.

After the initialization of user position and parameters, we have to randomly deploy macro base stations and small base stations into the large geographical area. Here, we have some rules to follow that the macro base

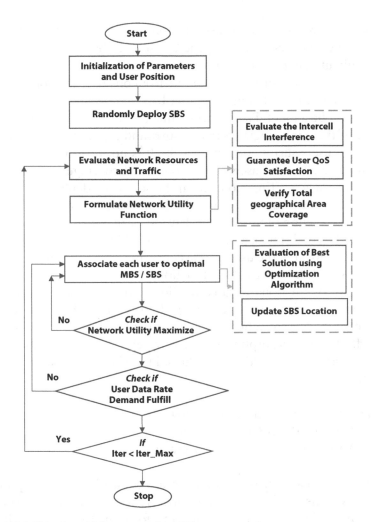

**Figure 14.2** Flowchart of the proposed model.

station should be placed at the center of the large geographical area. After placing a macro base station at the center of the large geographical area, we have to cordially place the SBSs with respect to the MBS. It looks like neighboring BSs regardless of both macro and small base stations. After arranging both the base stations in their respective positions, we have to evaluate network resources and air traffic.

Where the network resources are nothing but the power and the bandwidth used in any communication. We should evaluate about how much power is transmitted through the entire process or how much power is there for the process of transmission. Coming to bandwidth, we have to evaluate how much bandwidth is generally utilized by one communication node while utilizing channels in this entire process. Now, coming to air traffic, it is the data transferred in the air from one user to another user or may be from one base station to another base station.

There will be a lot of disturbances while the information is passed. For example, if there is a single BS in our surroundings and there are total $N$ numbers of users surrounded by that BS. It is not possible for one BS to accommodate all of the users in the concerned coverage area because of its resource capacity. This problem can be solved by deploying more BSs in that area. So, we have to evaluate both network resources and air traffic. After completion of this step, we have to formulate the network utility function. The condition of a network in availability of resources and capability to cater to all of the users in the concerned area in terms of end user perceived QoS is known as utility function.

These utility functions are used to allocate resources and manage data rates. The original notion is expanded by the network utility function (NUF) concept presented here. As a measure of network connections, the NUF reflects signal absorption as well as the efficiency and utility of a service. Network utility function is evaluated based on three steps. They are as follows:

1. Evaluate the inter-cell interference
2. Guarantee user QoS satisfaction
3. Verify total geographical coverage

The rapid expansion of communication networks over the previous decade has set new aspirational expectations about future wireless connections to meet the ever-increasing demand for user. However, the fundamental limitations of communication channels in cellular operators make achieving the goals impossible. Better spectral reuse performance between cells is essential to deal with the huge cost and shortage of acceptable wireless spectrum, which contributes to increasing levels of interference. Thus, the concept of QoS comes in the communication network for resource monitoring and framework designed to prevent interference such as information leakage, jitter, and latency. QoS also establishes limits and targets for sources of data that travel as high bandwidth traffic through networks.

After the above two steps, we have to check the total geographical area for the association of deploying BSs and users. After the completion of the above three steps, we can formulate the network utility function. In order to assign each user to the nearest BS optimally, we have to follow two steps. They are as follows:

1. Search for optimal solution based on a metaheuristic
2. Update MBSs and SBSs locations

Utilize a metaheuristic algorithm for finding optimal location of BSs (SBS and MBS) while maximizing network utility. The proposed algorithm will check if the utility function is maximum or not. If it is maximum, then it is processed to the next step of process until all of the iteration has completed. If the utility function is low, it will again come and check the locations of the BS and the location is updated accordingly under the constraint of user data rate satisfaction. Here, user data demand is nothing but the amount of data rate a normal user required when the user start communication. If it is full, then it is processed to the next step. If it is not full, then it will go back and the locations of the base stations are updated again until it reaches the user demand. The next step is the iteration count should be less than the maximum iteration count.

## 14.3    Result and Discussion

In simulations, assume the coordinates for the MBS as (2500, 2500), and SBSs are chosen randomly in the geographical area. A total of 1,300 users including 900 mobile and 400 machine-type devices (MTDs) were randomly deployed. Here, MTDs are the devices generating constant data traffic for communication like IoT devices. Analyze the resource allocation and user association model in two data suits having different data rates for NU/EU and MTD. The parameter assumptions for the simulation are listed in Table 14.1.

In general, users within the coverage area of one SBS also come under the coverage of the MBS. Thus, received power-based association gives the first priority to SBS, whereas demand fulfillment has to be taken care of with the SINR. Thus, user's association has to perform with SBS or MBS based on received power and data rate. In case a device is free to choose its association with a BS. The association with the SBSs is established on a first-come, first-served basis. When the threshold is reached, the users are connected to the MBS regardless of their geographical location.

The analysis of the optimal user association to BS is presented in Figures 14.3 and 14.4. Observe that the users are optimally associated with the nearby BSs on the basis of their data rate demand.

**Table 14.1** Parameter values.

| Parameters | Value |
|---|---|
| QoS exponent | 3 |
| Frequency of operating carrier signal, $f$ | 1800 MHz |
| Total bandwidth resources, $w$ | 20 MHz |
| Noise power, | -104 dBm |
| Packet data size, | 9000 bits |
| Machine data packet size, | 2000 bits |
| Transmit power of MBS, $P_k$ | 46 dBm |
| Transmit power of SBS, $P_k$ | 23 dBm |
| Data Suit-1 | |
| Data rate demand for NU/EU | 128 Kbps |
| Data rate demand for MTD | 56 Kbps |
| Data Suit-2 | |
| Data rate demand for NU/EU | 256 Kbps |
| Data rate demand for MTD | 128 Kbps |

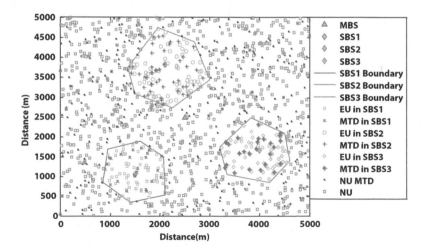

**Figure 14.3** Optimal user association to BSs with data suit-1.

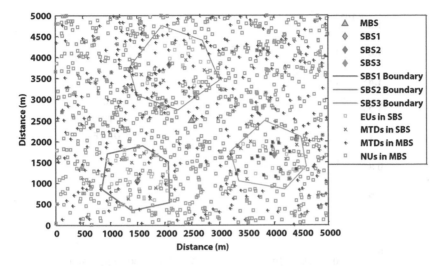

**Figure 14.4** Optimal user association to BSs with data suit-2.

From Figure 14.3, it is observed that the users are associated with the BSs according to their geolocation and data rate demand. The practical capacity of one SBS is limited and not have sufficient ability to cater much user. Thus, for the maximization of network utility, users have to be optimally associated with the BS having higher capacity and ability to fulfill the demanded data rate. Thereafter, we analyze the same with higher demanded data rate of users. Figure 14.4 shows the association of optimal users following demanded data rate suit-2.

From Figure 14.4, it is observed that the smaller number of users is associated with the SBS as compared to the previous case of data suit-1. Results observed are intuitively justified, as the capacity of one SBS is limited and this limitation provides the variation in network accessibility on the basis of demanded user data rate. Thus, in this case, SBSs are optimally deployed to the same place with less number of associated users.

In this work, we analyze the optimal user association to optimal BS by three well-known metaheuristic optimization algorithms, namely, the PSO, GWO, and DADE. Results of Figure 14.5 depicts that the maximum network utility achieved with the GWO and DADE is 1.65E+04 and the maximum network utility achieved with the PSO is 1.66E+04. It is also observed that the convergence characteristics of the DADE is superior to those of the GWO and PSO.

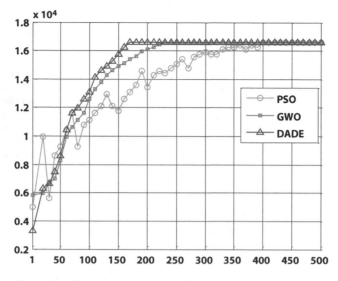

**Figure 14.5** Network utility maximization graph.

## 14.4   Conclusion

In this paper, we analyzed optimal cell planning in a two-tier heterogeneous network keeping the emergency user on high priority than the normal user. It was observed that optimal user association to optimal cell is highly required for user data rate satisfaction. It is also observed that optimal resource allocation while balancing emergency user and normal user association provides maximum network utility. It was observed that prioritizing emergency users and finding the optimal location of SBS for catering EU/NU provide satisfactory resource utilization. In the future, considering network function virtualization, the performance of the network utility is analyzed under the constraint of user satisfaction.

## References

1. Ghazzai, H., Yaacoub, E., Alouini, M. -S., Dawy, Z., Abu-Dayya, A., Optimized LTE cell planning with varying spatial and temporal user densities, in *IEEE Transactions on Vehicular Technology*, vol. 65, no. 3, pp. 1575–1589, March 2016, doi:10.1109/TVT.2015.2411579, https://ieeexplore.ieee.org/abstract/document/7056465.
2. Debnath, S. *et al.*, Energy efficient optimal resource allocation in multi-RAT heterogeneous network. *Appl. Artif. Intell.* Taylor & Francis, 35, 15, 2246–2275, 2021, doi: 10.1080/08839514.2021.1998300.

3. Yu, G. *et al.*, Multi-objective energy-efficient resource allocation for multi-RAT heterogeneous networks. *IEEE J. Sel. Areas Commun.*, 33, 10, 2118–2127, 2018, doi: 10.1109/JSAC.2015.2435374.

4. Ye, Q. *et al.*, Dynamic radio resource slicing for a two-tier heterogeneous wireless network. *IEEE Trans. Veh. Technol.*, 67, 10, 9896–9910, 2018, doi: 10.1109/TVT.2018.2859740.

5. Bahlke, F. *et al.*, Optimized cell planning for network slicing in heterogeneous wireless communication networks. *IEEE Commun. Lett.*, 22, 8, 1676–1679, 2018, doi: 10.1109/LCOMM.2018.2841866.

6. Melendez, S. and McGarry, M.P., Computation offloading decisions for reducing completion time, in: *Proc. 14th IEEE Annu. Consum. Comm. Netw. Conf. (CCNC)*, Jan. 2017, pp. 160–164, doi: 10.1109/CCNC.2017.7983099.

7. Wang, C. *et al.*, Joint computation offloading and interference management in wireless cellular networks with mobile edge computing. *IEEE Trans. Veh. Technol.*, 66, 8, 7432–7445, Aug. 2017, doi: 10.1109/TVT.2017.2672701.

8. Zhang, K. *et al.*, Energy-efficient offloading for mobile edge computing in 5G heterogeneous networks. *IEEE Access*, 4, 5896–5907, 2016, doi: 10.1109/ACCESS.2016.2597169.

9. Xu, C. *et al.*, Energy-minimization task offloading and resource allocation for mobile edge computing in NOMA heterogeneous networks. *IEEE Trans. Veh. Technol.*, 69, 12, 16001–16016, 2020, doi: 10.1109/TVT.2020.3040645.

10. Shin, W. *et al.*, Non-orthogonal multiple access in multi-cell networks: Theory, performance, and practical challenges. *IEEE Commun. Mag.*, 55, 10, 176–183, Oct. 2017, doi: 10.1109/MCOM.2017.1601065.

11. Islam, S.M.R. *et al.*, Power-domainnon-orthogonal multiple access (NOMA) in 5G systems: Potentials and challenges. *IEEE Commun. Surv. Tutorials*, 19, 2, 721–742, Apr.-Jun. 2017, doi: 10.1109/COMST.2016.2621116.

12. Liu, C. and Liang, D., Heterogeneous networks with power-domain NOMA: Coverage, throughput, and power allocation analysis. *IEEE Trans. Wirel. Commun.*, 17, 5, 3524–3539, May 2018, doi: 10.1109/TWC.2018.2816923.

13. Burer, S. and Letchford, A.N., Non-convex mixed-integer nonlinear programming: A survey. *Surv. Oper. Res. Manage. Sci.*, 17, 2, 97–106, Apr.-Jun. 2012, doi: 10.1016/j.sorms.2012.08.001.

14. Clerc, M. and Kennedy, J., The particle swarm-explosion, stability, and convergence in a multidimensional complex space. *IEEE Trans. Evol. Comput.*, 6, 3, 58–73, Feb. 2008, doi: 10.1109/4235.985692.

15. Debnath, S. *et al.*, A hybrid memory based dragonfly algorithm with differential evolution for engineering application. *Eng. Comput.*, Springer, 37, 4, 2775–2802, 2021, doi: 10.1007/s00366-020-00958-4.

16. Debnath, S. *et al.*, Computationally efficient Hybrid differential evolution with learning for engineering application. *Int. J. Bio*, 19, 1, 29–39, 2022, doi: 10.1504/IJBIC.2022.120744.

17. Eappen, G. and Shankar, T., Hybrid PSO-GSA for energy efficient spectrum sensing in cognitive radio network. *Phys. Commun.*, 40, 101091, 2020, doi: 10.1016/j.phycom.2020.101091.

# 15

# Soil Aggregate Stability Prediction Using a Hybrid Machine Learning Algorithm

**M. Balamurugan**

*Department of Computer Applications, Acharya Institute of Graduate Studies*
*Bengaluru, India*

## Abstract

The concept of soil aggregate stability (SAS) is utilized as a criterion for soil composition because several soil ecosystem functions depend on the presence of stable aggregates. Predictive models have gained increased attention as a replacement for direct measurements because aggregate stability is rarely recorded in soil surveys. In order to anticipate soil aggregate stability, this work aims to develop a novel machine learning (ML) technique called the hybrid tree-based twin-bounded support vector machine (HT-TBSVM). Unexpected discoveries were made by examining soil records that provided information on soil properties such as structure, soil nutrient concentration, alkalinity, and moisture aggregates. This collection includes 109 soil samples from Chile's hyperarid, arid, and semiarid regions, as well as humid areas, including cultivated fields, grasslands, and tree plantations. The most prevalent soil types in this dataset were clay loam, sandal loam, and loam, and the values for each soil attribute ranged widely. The mean absolute error (MAE), $R^2$, normalized root mean square error (nRMSE), and root mean square error (RMSE) are used as different indicators to determine the effectiveness of the given prediction. We evaluated these measurements in comparison to conventional approaches to predicting SA stability. The experimental results show that the proposed approach outperforms conventional approaches in terms of outcomes.

*Keywords*: Soil, soil aggregate stability (SAS), deep neural network (DNN), support vector machine (SVM)

*Email*: balamurugan2833@acharya.ac.in

Kanak Kalita, Narayanan Ganesh and S. Balamurugan (eds.) Metaheuristics for Machine Learning:
Algorithms and Applications, (301–314) © 2024 Scrivener Publishing LLC

## 15.1   Introduction

The management of soil must be sustainable to protect it for future generations, given the increasing environmental pressures it is facing. This management cannot be carried out without an in-depth knowledge of the diverse features and properties of the soil. Aggregate stability, which influences water storage and the stabilization of organic carbon (OC), is a crucial component of soil conservation, along with the preservation of its environmental functions. Increased soil structural stability may also result in increased resistance to corrosive agents and compaction. Stable soil aggregates (SAs) create a solid soil structure that allows for the best potential gas, water, and nutrient transport and storage. Therefore, soil aggregate stability (SAS) may serve as a valuable indication for assessing soil quality [1]. The challenging process of soil aggregation involves the complex interplay of the soil's organic and mineral components, resulting in a microaggregate (0.25 mm) within a macroaggregate [2]. SAS is essential for soil resilience to mechanical stresses such as those brought on by surface runoff and rainfall, which, in turn, contributes to soil resistance to water erosion. As SA degrades, finer particles are created. Since these particles are effectively transported by water and wind flow, they tend to clog soil pores and create crusts when re-sedimented [3]. Soil aggregate stability distribution (SASD) data are typically statistically quantified using the mean weight diameter (MWD) and the geometric mean diameter (GMD). Because these mass fractions ($m_i$) of SA depend on different ($d_i$) resemble probability distribution functions (PDFs), higher-order moments, such as standard deviation ($\sigma$) and skewness coefficient, are used to characterize soil aggregate size distribution (SASD) data in addition to their mean values [4]. However, the dynamic and complicated relationship between SAS and soil factors cannot be captured by the linear regression model, which typically produces inferior prediction accuracy [5].

The following is the paper's primary contribution:

1. The hybrid tree-based twin-bounded support vector machine was proposed.

The following is the paper's organization: Section 15.2 reviews the relevant works, Section 15.3 explains the suggested approach, Section 15.4 presents the results and discussions, and Section 15.5 presents the conclusions.

## 15.2   Related Works

Cooke *et al.* [6] studied the value of digestates as organic soil additions and how it varies based on process variables and posttreatments. Pavlů *et al.* [7] investigated whether the same approach can be applied to different types of soils, including Haplic Luvisol, two Haplic Cambisols, and a Calcaric Leptosol. Xu *et al.* [8] explored the interplay between fluoranthene's actions and soil aggregate structure, while *Shi et al.* [9] showed the potential of hyperspectral imagers for assessing SAS and aggregating size fractions on a massive scale. Liu *et al.* [10] analyzed the impact of monovalent cations on aggregate stability and splash erosion, and Zhou *et al.* [11] studied the effect of soil binders on aggregate stability in urban forest soils with organic mulch. Ma *et al.* [12] used Gaussian geostatistical simulation and multivariate empirical mode decomposition techniques to investigate the geographical distribution and scale-specific implications of water-stable aggregates (WSA) content. Xue *et al.* [13] conducted a multiyear investigation to understand the variables that affect SAS in a rice-rape agricultural system, and Tang *et al.* [14] examined how different land use practices influence SA stability and aggregate-associated OC and total nitrogen (TN) concentrations.

## 15.3   Proposed Methodology

Soil aggregation refers to the joining and holding together of aggregates of various sizes by various organic and inorganic components. It encompasses

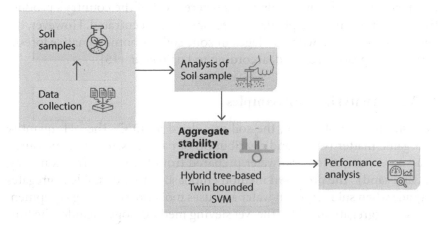

**Figure 15.1** Block diagram of soil aggregation.

both the formation and stability processes, which run continuously and even act simultaneously in the field. As a result, it can be challenging to distinguish their interrelated impacts. Some writers attribute the development of soil aggregation primarily to physical forces, while others argue that a variety of elements, including the quantity and quality of inorganic and organic stabilizing agents, are responsible for its stabilization. Figure 15.1 shows a block representation of the proposed method.

### 15.3.1   Soil Samples and Characteristics

To collect a diverse set of data for the soil characteristics used in this research, the sampling area was designed to include a variety of soil types, land uses, and climate variables. The study collected 109 soil measurements from the ground in Chile between the latitudes of 27°43'S and 51°20'S at a depth of 0–17 cm. The research area is located in four of Chile's eight soil zones, including the Magellan, arid Mediterranean (37 sites), and desert (19 sites), with 23 sites in total. The study area covers a range of climates, from humid to hyperarid. The desert zone, for example, has an annual precipitation of only 43 mm, making it hyperarid, while the Mediterranean region has an arid climate with an annual precipitation of no more than 440 mm. The Mediterranean and Magellan zones, on the other hand, receive annual rainfall totals of 1,220 mm and 238 mm, respectively, and are classified as such. The soil orders examined in the study include Alfisols, Andisols, Histosols, Inceptisols, Mollisols, and Ultisols. The study found an increase in Andisol presence from the Mediterranean to the Magellan zones. The majority of the samples taken from the desert, wet, and moist Mediterranean zones were found in the middle valley, which has the majority of cultivated soils and is where most of the country's productive land, grassland, and plantation regions are concentrated. However, the Serrano River Basin, with its Magellan zone soils, is home to native forests, shrubs, and peaty scrubland, according to Luzio *et al.* [15].

### 15.3.2   Analyzing Soil Samples

At a sieving size of 2 mm, the soil was dried at 40°C. The pH, quantity of organic matter (OM), and distribution of particle sizes were measured in a suspension of soil and water prepared from the sieved fraction (clay, silt, and sand). The proposed method emphasizes that unstable aggregates degrade when submerged in water and uses moisture screening equipment to assess aggregate stability. The wet sieving methodology includes the fundamental mechanisms of aggregate dispersion, slaking, and mechanical dispersion, simulating the pressures associated with water infiltration into SA in the field. A 0.25-mm filter holding distilled water and 4.0 g of solid crystals between 1 and 2 mm is repeatedly raised and lowered for 3 minutes during the experiment. Stable aggregates that pass through the sieve during the 3-minute wet sifting procedure are collected in the distilled water container below the sieve. After the sieves have been cleaned until only sand and small root fragments remain, the canisters are reinstalled and filled with a dispersing solution. Both sets of cans are then dried at 110°C after dewatering. Distilled water and dispersing solution are added to the canisters, and the weights of the water-filled can and its contents are calculated and subtracted. The weight of the stable materials is calculated by subtracting the weight of the dispersing solution and 0.2 g of that solution from the weight of the container containing the aggregates. The weight of the stable aggregates obtained in the cans of dispersing solution is then divided by the sum of the weights of the stable and unstable aggregates in Equation 15.1, where 100% indicates that no aggregates were broken and 0% indicates that all aggregates were broken. The WSA index is then calculated using the percentage of stable aggregates.

$$WSA = \left( \frac{W_{ds}}{W_{ds}} + w_{dw} \right).100 \qquad (15.1)$$

where WSA is the number of particles evenly distributed in distilled water (g), the total weight (%) dispersed in the dispersing solvent $w_{ds}$ along with the $w_{dw}$ is the aggregates' weight(%) (g).

### 15.3.3    Hybrid Tree-Based Twin-Bounded Support Vector Machine-Based Model

The process of learning hybrid trees (HTs) from training sets of class labels is referred to as hybrid tree induction. HT is used in this approach because the greedy strategy employed by C5.0 and the top-down recursive approach are only suitable for decision tree construction.

#### 15.3.3.1    Hybrid Tree Algorithm-C5.0

HT is often used to address data classification problems. The HT algorithm typically involves two phases: the training phase, which constructs the decision tree using the chosen training data sample, and the prediction phase, which uses the HT created during the training phase to forecast the target data. Developing an HT is a key step in creating data classification rules.

The following data formula uses the most popular decision tree algorithm, C5.0:

$$GainRation\,(s,a) = \frac{Gain\,(s,a)}{SplitInformation(a)} \qquad (15.2)$$

$$SplitInformation(s,a) = -\sum_{t}^{c} \frac{|s_t|}{|s|} log_z \frac{|s_t|}{|s|} \qquad (15.3)$$

The C5.0 algorithm is composed of the following steps (Figure 15.2):

1. Assuming the conditional qualities are as stated, determine the original data's information gain ratio.
2. Select the property $A_i$ with the highest ratio value as the base node of the decision tree.
3. Sort these actual data into groups based on the root node.
4. Calculate the information gain ratio for the starting data in each category under the given circumstances, and then choose a greater value as the decision node.
5. Recursively calling these aforementioned methods until all of the original data are categorized.

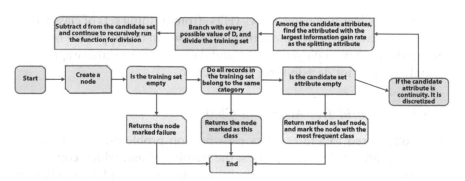

**Figure 15.2** C5.0's algorithm flow.

### 15.3.3.2 Twin-Bounded Support Vector Machine-Based Model

Assume that $A \in R^{m_1 \times n}$ represents the data points in class +1 and $B \in R^{m_i \times n}$ represents the data points in class 1, respectively. Each row in both matrices corresponds to a data sample.

The nonparallel hyperplanes are located via the twin-bounded support vector machine (TBSVM) in linear form by Equation 15.1.

$$f_1(x) = w_1^T x + b_1 = 0 \text{ and } f_2(x) = w_2^T x + b_2 = 0 \qquad (15.4)$$

Such that each hyperplane is closer to and further distant from the data points of one class than the data points of the other. It is given the class name +1 or 1 depending on how close together the two hyperplanes' data samples are. TBSVM resolves the two quadratic programming problems (QPPs) by using the objective function of one class and constraints related to the other class.

$$min_{w_1,b_1,\xi,\xi^*} \frac{1}{2} c_3 \left( \| w_1 \|^2 + b_1^2 \right) + \frac{1}{2} \xi^{*T} \xi^* + c_1 e_1^T \xi$$
$$s.t., A w_1 + e_1 b_1 = \xi^* - (B w_1 + e_2 b_1) + \xi \ge e_2, \xi \ge 0 \qquad (15.5)$$

and

$$min_{w_2,b_2,\eta,\eta^*} \frac{1}{2} c_4 \left( \| w_2 \|^2 + b_2^2 \right) + \frac{1}{2} \eta^{*T} \eta^* + c_2 e_1^T \eta$$
$$s.t. \ B w_2 + e_2 b_2 = \eta^* - (A w_2 + e_1 b_2) + \eta \ge e_1, \eta \ge 0 \qquad (15.6)$$

where the positive factors $c_1, c_2, c_3,$ and $c_4$ are present in Equations 15.5 and 15.6.

We must obtain the dual formulations as follows to solve Equations 15.4 and 15.5.

The QPP (15.4) Lagrangian is provided by:

$$L(w_1, b_1, \xi, \alpha, \beta) = \frac{1}{2} c_3 (\| w_1 \|^2 + b_1^2) + \frac{1}{2} \| A w_1 + e_1 b_1 \|^2 + c_1 e_2^T \xi + \alpha^T (B w_1 + e_2 b_1 - \xi + e_2) - \beta^T \xi,$$

$$(15.7)$$

where the vectors with $\alpha = \alpha_1,......\alpha_{m_2}$ and $\beta = \left(\beta_1,.....,\beta_{m_2}\right)$ are the Lagrange multipliers and for $\alpha, \beta, \xi, w_1, and\ b_1$, the Karush-Kuhn-Tucker (KKT) conditions are given as Equations 15.7–15.13.

$$\nabla_{w_1} L = c_3 w_1 + A^T \left(Aw_1 + e_1 b_1\right) + B^T \alpha = 0, \qquad (15.8)$$

$$\nabla_{b_1} L = c_3 b_1 + e_1^T (Aw_1 + e_1 b_1) + e_2^T \alpha = 0 \qquad (15.9)$$

$$\nabla_\xi L = c_1 e_1^T - \beta^T - \alpha^T = 0 \qquad (15.10)$$

$$-(Bw_1 + e_2 b_1) + \xi \geq e_2, \xi \geq 0 \qquad (15.11)$$

$$\alpha^T (Bw_1 + e_2 b_1 - \xi + e_2) = 0, \beta^T \xi = 0 \qquad (15.12)$$

$$\alpha \geq 0, \beta \geq 0. \qquad (15.13)$$

Since $\beta \geq 0$, Equation 15.9 gives us:

$$0 \leq \alpha \leq c_1$$

Equations 15.8 and 15.9 give us:

$$\left([A^T e_1^T][Ae_1] + c_3 I\right)[w_1 b_1]^T + [B^T e_2^T]\alpha = 0 \qquad (15.14)$$

Here is the identity matrix, etc. Equation 15.14 becomes true if $V_1 = [w_1, b_1]^T$, $H = [Ae_1]$ and $G = [Be_2]$

$$(H^T H + c_3 I)v_1 + G^T \alpha = 0 \text{ or } v_1 = -(H^T H + c_3 I)^{-1} G^T \alpha. \quad (15.15)$$

The dual of the QPP can be found by combining Equation 15.15 with Equations 15.8 through 15.13 in the Lagrangian.

$$max\, \alpha\, e_2^T \alpha - \frac{1}{2}\alpha^T G(H^T H + c_3 I)^{-1} G^T \alpha \qquad (15.16)$$

$$s.t. \quad 0 \leq \alpha \leq c_1.$$

In a similar vein, QPPs dual is given as Equation 15.17:

$$max\, \alpha\, e_1^T \gamma - \frac{1}{2}\gamma^T H(G^T G + c_4 I)^{-1} H^T \gamma \qquad (15.17)$$

$$s.t. \quad 0 \leq \gamma \leq c_2.$$

where $\gamma$ the Lagrange multiplier is used. If $V_2 = [w_2, b_2]^T$, then the augmented vector can be written as Equation 15.18.

$$v_2 = (G^T G + c_4 I)^{-1} H^T \gamma. \qquad (15.18)$$

The test sample is given one of the class labels $i(i = +1, -1)$ depending upon its distance from the two hyperplanes $(w_1, b_1)$ *and* $(w_2, b_2)$ as the solutions to the QPPs and are found by solving the QPPs (15.16) and (15.17).

$$Class\, i = arg\, min\, k = 1,2 \frac{\left| w_k^T x + b_k \right|}{\| w_k \|}, \qquad (15.19)$$

The class i sample is derived in Equation 15.19.
where the absolute value is $|.|$.

## 15.4   Result and Discussion

The details of the soil prediction for SA stability findings are covered in this section. The variables used to evaluate the effectiveness of the suggested method are the mean absolute error (MAE), normalized root mean square error (nRMSE), and the coefficient of determination ($R^2$). To assess the effectiveness of the suggested method, the current random forest (RF), k-nearest neighbors (kNN), support vector machine, and artificial neural network (ANN) [16, 17] techniques are compared.

The RMSE represents the standard deviation of the residuals (prediction errors). Residuals measure the distance between data points and the regression line, and the RMSE measures the spread of these residuals. Equation 15.20 illustrates the formula for calculating the RMSE.

$$
RMSE = \left[ \frac{\sum_{j=1}^{N} [Z(X_i) - Z^*(X_i)]^2}{N} \right]^{\frac{1}{2}}
\tag{15.20}
$$

Figure 15.3 demonstrates that for the RMSE, the suggested method (0.11%) outperformed the results of the current methods of RF (0.17%), KNN (0.33%), SVM (0.21%), and ANN (0.32%). It shows the suggested system's good performance.

The coefficient of determination ($R^2$), which has a range of 0 to 1, is employed to measure how accurately a statistical model predicts an outcome. The $R^2$ number is the proportion of variation in the dependent variable that the statistical mode forecasts. Equation 15.21 illustrates the $R^2$ formula.

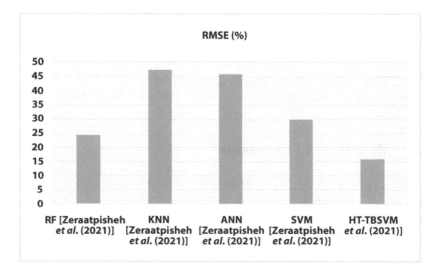

**Figure 15.3** Comparative analysis of the RMSE.

$$R^2 = 1 - \frac{\sum_{i=1}^{N} [Z(X_i) - Z^*(X_i)]^2}{\sum_{i=1}^{N} [Z(X_i) - \underline{Z}(X_i)]^2} \quad (15.21)$$

Figure 15.4 demonstrates that for the $R^2$, the suggested method (0.82%) outperformed the results of the current methods of RF (0.74%), KNN (0.21%), SVM (0.28%), and ANN (0.15%). It shows the suggested system's better performance.

Comparing the models of different scales using the root mean square normalized error (nRMSE) is simplified by using the RMSE. The normalized RMSE connects the observed range of the variables with the RMSE. The nRMSE expresses the RMSE as a percentage of the overall range that the model typically resolves. Equation 15.22 illustrates the formula for calculating the nRMSE.

$$nRMSE = \frac{RMSE}{\underline{Z}(X)} \times 100 \quad (15.22)$$

Figure 15.5 demonstrates that for the nRMSE, the suggested method (15.84%) is significantly lower than the results of the current methods of RF (24.28%), KNN (47.14%), SVM (45.71%), and ANN (30.00%). It shows the suggested system's better performance.

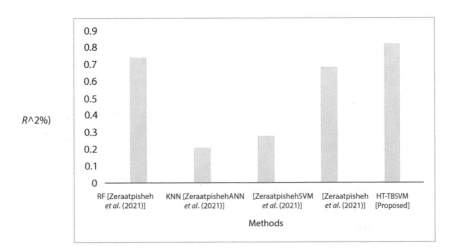

**Figure 15.4** Comparative analysis of the $R^2$.

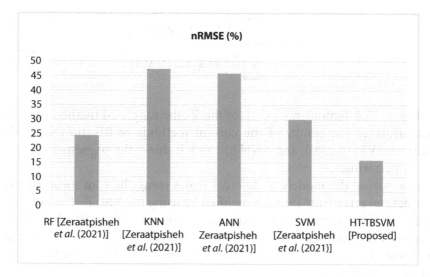

**Figure 15.5** Comparative analysis of the nRMSE.

The MAE score is obtained by averaging the absolute error data. Absolute is a mathematical operation that converts a negative integer into a positive one. When calculating the MAE in Equation 15.22, the difference between an expected value and a forecasted value could be either positive or negative.

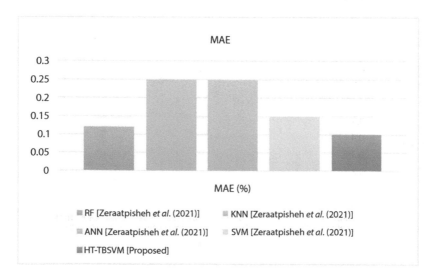

**Figure 15.6** Comparative analysis of the MAE.

$$MAE = \frac{1}{N} \sum_{i=1}^{N} \left[ | Z(X_i - Z^*(X_i)| \right] \qquad (15.23)$$

Figure 15.6 demonstrates that for the MAE, the suggested method (0.10%) is lower than the results of the current methods of RF (0.12%), KNN (0.25%), SVM (0.25%), and ANN (0.15%). It shows the suggested system's good performance.

## 15.5  Conclusion

The stability of the soil aggregate directly affects the sustainability of the soil and crop output. This paper provides a general overview of the mechanisms and forces involved in the growth and stability of SA. Therefore, the goal of this research was to create a novel model based on HT-TBSVM to predict SAS. Measuring the amounts of soil organic carbon (SOC) and SAS indices in various aggregate sizes takes a lot of time, money, and labor. In this study, four machine learning models (RF, SVM, kNN, and ANN) were evaluated for their ability to predict SAS and SOC in variations in aggregate fractions. When dealing with large datasets, hybrid tree-based twin-bounded SVM may not perform well due to a longer required training time. In future studies assessing the contributions of soil biota to soil aggregation, species combinations should also be considered.

## References

1. Bouslihim, Y. et al., Machine learning approaches for the prediction of soil aggregate stability. Heliyon, 7, 3, e06480, 2021, doi: 10.1016/j.heliyon.2021. e06480.
2. Rivera, J.I., and Bonilla, C.A., Predicting soil aggregate stability using readily available soil properties and machine learning techniques. CATENA, 187, 104408, 2020, doi: 10.1016/j.catena.2019.104408.
3. Besalatpour, A.A. et al., Estimating wet soil aggregate stability from easily available properties in a highly mountainous watershed. CATENA, 111, 72–79, 2013, doi: 10.1016/j.catena.2013.07.001.
4. Purushothaman, N.K. et al., National-scale maps for soil aggregate size distribution parameters using pedotransfer functions and digital soil mapping data products. Geoderma, 424, 116006, 2022, doi: 10.1016/j. geoderma.2022.116006.

5. Blomquist, J. *et al.*, Soil characteristics and tillage can predict the effect of structure lime on soil aggregate stability. *Soil Res.*, 60, 4, 373–384, 2022, doi: 10.1071/SR21022.

6. Cooke, J., Girault, R., Busnot, S. *et al.*, Characterising the effect of raw and post-treated digestates on soil aggregate stability. *Waste Biomass Valor.*, 14, 2977–2995, 2023, https://doi.org/10.1007/s12649-023-02045-3.

7. Pavlů, L. *et al.*, Estimation of the stability of topsoil aggregates in areas affected by water erosion using selected soil and terrain properties. *Soil Tillage Res.*, 219, 105348, 2022, doi: 10.1016/j.still.2022.105348.

8. Xu, C. *et al.*, Forest conversion effects on soil organic carbon are regulated by soil aggregate stability and not by recalcitrance: Evidence from a reforestation experiment. *CATENA*, 219, 106613, 2022, doi: 10.1016/j.catena.2022.106613.

9. Shi, P. *et al.*, Vis-NIR spectroscopic assessment of soil aggregate stability and aggregate size distribution in the Belgian Loam Belt. *Geoderma*, 357, 113958, 2020, doi: 10.1016/j.geoderma.2019.113958.

10. Liu, J. *et al.*, Specific ion effects on soil aggregate stability and rainfall splash erosion. *Int. Soil Water Conserv. Res.*, 10, 4, 557–564, 2022, doi: 10.1016/j.iswcr.2022.02.001.

11. Zhou, W., Sun, X., Li, S. *et al.*, Effects of organic mulching on soil aggregate stability and aggregate binding agents in an urban forest in Beijing, China. *J. For. Res.*, 33, 1083–1094, 2022, https://doi.org/10.1007/s11676-021-01402-z.

12. Ma, R. *et al.*, Spatial distribution and scale-specific controls of soil water-stable aggregates in southeastern China. *J. Cleaner Prod.*, 369, 133305, 2022, doi: 10.1016/j.jclepro.2022.133305.

13. Xue, B. *et al.*, Straw residue incorporation and potassium fertilization enhance soil aggregate stability by altering the soil content of iron oxide and organic carbon in a rice-rape cropping system. *Land Degrad. Dev.*, 33, 14, 2567–2584, 2022, doi: 10.1002/ldr.4333.

14. Tang, X. *et al.*, Responses of soil aggregate stability to organic C and total N as controlled by land-use type in a region of south China affected by sheet erosion. *CATENA*, 218, 106543, 2022, doi: 10.1016/j.catena.2022.106543.

15. Luzio, W. *et al.*, *Soils of Chile*, University of Chile. Maval Press, Santiago, 2010.

16. Zeraatpisheh, M. *et al.*, Spatial prediction of soil aggregate stability and soil organic carbon in aggregate fractions using machine learning algorithms and environmental variables. *Geoderma Reg.*, 27, e00440, 2021, doi: 10.1016/j.geodrs.2021.e00440.

17. Mo, J., Feng, J., He, W., Liu, Y., Cao, N., Tang, Y., Gu, S., Effects of polycyclic aromatic hydrocarbons fluoranthene on the soil aggregate stability and the possible underlying mechanism. *Environ. Sci. Pollut. Res.*, 30, 4, 10245–10255, 2023.

# Index

# Also of Interest

## Check out these published and forthcoming titles in the "Artificial Intelligence and Soft Computing for Industrial Transformation" series from Scrivener Publishing

**Metaheuristics for Machine Learning**
**Algorithms and Applications**
Edited by Kanak Kalita, Narayanan Ganesh and S. Balamurugan
Published 2024. ISBN 978-1-394-23392-2

**Artificial Intelligence for Sustainable Applications**
Edited by K. Umamaheswari, B. Vinoth Kumar and S. K. Somasundaram
Published 2023. ISBN 978-1-394-17458-4

**Convergence of Deep Learning in Cyber-IoT Systems and Security**
Edited by Rajdeep Chakraborty, Anupam Ghosh, Jyotsna Kumar Mandal and S. Balamurugan
Published 2023. ISBN 978-1-119-85721-1

**Cognitive Intelligence and Big Data in Healthcare**
Edited by D. Sumathi, T. Poongodi, B. Balamurugan and Lakshmana Kumar Ramasamy
Published 2022. ISBN 978-1-119-76888-3

**The New Advanced Society**
**Artificial Intelligence and Industrial Internet of Things Paradigm**
Edited by Sandeep Kumar Panda, Ramesh Kumar Mohapatra, Subhrakanta Panda and S. Balamurugan
Published 2022. ISBN 978-1-119-82447-3

**Digitization of Healthcare Data using Blockchain**
Edited by T. Poongodi, D. Sumathi, B. Balamurugan and K. S. Savita
Published 2022. ISBN 978-1-119-79185-0

**Tele-Healthcare**
**Applications of Artificial Intelligence and Soft Computing Techniques**
Edited by R. Nidhya, Manish Kumar and S. Balamurugan
Published 2022. ISBN 978-1-119-84176-0

**Impact of Artificial Intelligence on Organizational Transformation**
Edited by S. Balamurugan, Sonal Pathak, Anupriya Jain, Sachin Gupta, and
Sachin Sharma and Sonia Duggal
Published 2022. ISBN 978-1-119-71017-2

**Artificial Intelligence for Renewable Energy Systems**
Edited by Ajay Kumar Vyas, S. Balamurugan, Kamal Kant Hiran Harsh S.
Dhiman
Published 2022. ISBN 978-1-119-76169-3

**Artificial Intelligence Techniques for Wireless Communication and**
**Networking**
Edited by Kanthavel R., K. Ananthajothi, S. Balamurugan and R. Karthik
Ganesh
Published 2022. ISBN 978-1-119-82127-4

**Advanced Healthcare Systems**
**Empowering Physicians with IoT-Enabled Technologies**
Edited by Rohit Tanwar, S. Balamurugan, R. K. Saini, Vishal Bharti and
Premkumar Chithaluru
Published 2022. ISBN 978-1-119-76886-9

**Smart Systems for Industrial Applications**
Edited by C. Venkatesh, N. Rengarajan, P. Ponmurugan and S. Balamurugan
Published 2022. ISBN 978-1-119-76200-3

**Intelligent Renewable Energy Systems**
Edited by Neeraj Priyadarshi, Akash Kumar Bhoi, Sanjeevikumar
Padmanabam, S.Balamurugan, and Jens Bo Holm-Nielson
Published 2022. ISBN 978-1-119-78627-6

**Human Technology Communication**
**Internet of Robotic Things and Ubiquitous Computing**
Edited by R. Anandan. G. Suseendran, S. Balamurugan, Ashish Mishra and
D. Balaganesh
Published 2021. ISBN 978-1-119-75059-8

**Nature-Inspired Algorithms Applications**
Edited by S. Balamurugan, Anupriya Jain, Sachin Sharma, Dinesh Goyal,
Sonia Duggal and Seema Sharma
Published 2021. ISBN 978-1-119-68174-8

**Computation in Bioinformatics**
**Multidisciplinary Applications**
Edited by S. Balamurugan, Anand Krishnan, Dinesh Goyal, Balakumar
Chandrasekaran and Boomi Pandi
Published 2021. ISBN 978-1-119-65471-1

**Fuzzy Intelligent Systems**
**Methodologies, Techniques, and Applications**
Edited by E. Chandrasekaran, R. Anandan, G. Suseendran, S. Balamurugan
and Hanaa Hachimi
Published 2021. ISBN 978-1-119-76045-0

**Biomedical Data Mining for Information Retrieval**
**Methodologies, Techniques and Applications**
Edited by Sujata Dash, Subhendu Kumar Pani, S. Balamurugan and Ajith
Abraham
Published 2021. ISBN 978-1-119-71124-7

**Design and Analysis of Security Protocols for Communication**
Edited by Dinesh Goyal, S. Balamurugan, Sheng-Lung Peng and O.P.
Verma
Published 2020. ISBN 978-1-119-55564-3

www.scrivenerpublishing.com

Printed in the USA/Agawam, MA
May 21, 2024

866493.008